Change and Decay?

Public Administration in the 1990s

Howard Elcock

Longman

LONGMAN GROUP LIMITED
Longman House, Burnt Mill, Harlow,
Essex CM20 2JE, England
and Associated Companies throughout the world.

*Published in the United States of America
by Longman Publishing, New York*

First published 1991
Second impression 1994

British Library Cataloguing in Publication Data

Elcock, Howard , 1942–
    Change and decay? public administration in the 1990s.
    1. Public administration. Theories
    I. Title
    350.0001

    OCR ISBN 0-582-03301-2   176553l

Library of Congress Cataloguing in Publication Data
Elcock, H. J. (Howard James)
    Change and decay? public administration in the 1990s/by Howards Elcock.
    p. cm.
    Includes bibliographical references.
    ISBN 0-582-03301-2
    1. Public administration – History.
    I. Title.
    JF1341.E43   1991
    350'.0009 – dc20

                                            90-30739
                                            CIP

Set in 10/12pt Bembo Roman
Printed in Malaysia by PA

Contents

Preface

This book looks back in order to look forward. It seeks to review the history of public administration, both as an academic discipline and as a field of practice, in order to suggest the future directions in which both its study and its practice may develop.

It takes as its starting point the Crichel Down affair of 1954, which revived long-standing concerns about accountability and the use of administrative discretion. Crichel Down also precipitated both a considerable academic debate about the accountability of Ministers to Parliament and a wide-ranging review of various administrative practices. The Home Secretary, Sir David Maxwell-Fyffe, redefined the accountability relationships between Ministers, civil servants and Parliament (Document 1). The Government appointed a committee under the chairmanship of Sir Oliver Franks to review the working of administrative tribunals and public inquiries (Document 20). Since then, there have been a wide range of developments but 1954 was somewhat of a watershed year and it seems sensible to start then.

The other watershed in the development of public administration was the election of the Conservative Party to office in 1979 and the consequent assumption by Mrs Margaret Thatcher of the office of Prime Minister. Since then, not only have major changes in the practice of government taken place; also a concerted attempt has been made to assimilate public administration to business administration. In its more extreme forms those advocating the merging of the two disciplines have sought to deny the existence of differences between administration - rather management – in the private and public sectors. It is a central purpose of this book to review that argument and reassert the contrary view, that public administration is different in important respects, most of which relate to the nature of accountability relationships in a parliamentary democracy.

This distinction is important for two reasons. The first is that the important issues, especially ethical issues, are neglected if the focus of public servants' managerial activities becomes exclusively that of the business manager. The second is that problems are confronting Britain and the world which cannot be dealt with by minimalist government and free market economics. Planning and regulation are therefore likely to become more necessary as we approach the year 2000. In any case, the present preoccupation with the 'Three Es' – Economy, Efficiency and Effectiveness – is likely to change further because different kinds of issues impose pressures on the Government which cannot be encompassed within that relatively narrow managerial focus, or because a Government holding different views wins office.

Acknowledgements

In a book which seeks to review over thirty years of recent developments in public administration and which has been influenced by over twenty years' teaching and research, a wide variety of debts have been accrued which must be acknowledged here. My colleagues in the Department of Politics at the University of Hull and the School of Government at Newcastle upon Tyne Polytechnic have contributed many ideas, comments, suggestions and information. My students in these two institutions have suffered my idiosyncrasies cheerfully (for the most part!) and helped me to think out and rethink my ideas. Of particular importance have been the members of the Public Administration Committee of the Joint University Council, who have helped me greatly over the years. In particular, presenters of papers and others attending the Committee's annual conferences and other events have supplied huge quantities of ideas and material. I am truly grateful to them all. During my years of service on Humberside County Council in the 1970s, I learnt much from both my fellow members and the Council's officers. Alex Clarke, David Gill and Alan Hunter are worthy of special mention in this context.

Much of the argument in this book is supported by my research work over the last twenty years. I must acknowledge my particular indebtedness to my collaborators in successive research projects. In particular these were:

Decentralised administration in the National Health Service.
This project was initiated by the late Dr R. G. S. Brown. After his untimely death it was completed by myself and Stuart Haywood, now at the Health Service Management Centre, University of Birmingham. Stuart has been a good colleague and friend, contributing much to my

knowledge of public management and the NHS. I am also indebted to our research staff on the project, including Rick Chandler, Stephen Jackson, Trevor James, Edwin Nelson and Philip Tether, as well as to the Social Science Research Council for its financial support for the project.

Learning from Local Authority Budgeting. Here the debts are manifold but the central actors were Grant Jordan of the University of Aberdeen and Arthur Midwinter of the University of Strathclyde. This project also involved seventeen teams of researchers who studied budgetary processes in local authorities up and down the land. They are too numerous to name here, although they have been so acknowledged in the two books which have resulted from that project (Elcock and Jordan (eds), 1987; Elcock, Jordan and Midwinter, 1989). None the less, they did the legwork from which I have profited here. We are grateful for financial support from the Leverhulme Trust for this research.

The Northern Network for Public Policy is run in collaboration with my colleagues in Newcastle, John Fenwick and Ken Harrop. They have both contributed much hard work and goodwill, as has the Network's Administrator, Judith Phillips, who has contributed many an unusual or provocative thought to the development of our work, which has kindly been supported by the Public Finance Foundation.

I am also indebted to Professor Leszek Garlicki, of the University of Warsaw, for arranging for me to visit his country and so gain a different perspective on public administration. The University together with the Centre for Public Administration in Warsaw, kindly provided me with hospitality while I was there. My stays in Warsaw, together with the railway journeys between Britain and Poland, also provided invaluable periods of tranquillity for reflection, reading and writing.

Sue Lingard and her family have provided me with a loving home environment where further thought has been possible and where I have been able to escape from immediate concerns to redress my jaded mind from time to time. Les Landon and Aidan Rose have ensured that I learnt word processing quickly enough to produce this book.

None the less, what I have written here is ultimately my responsibility and I accept entire responsibility for the blemishes and errors it contains.

Howard Elcock
Newcastle upon Tyne, Hull, Warsaw and Banbury,
1987-1989

NOTE: *Documentary Appendix*

At the back of the book is a Documentary Appendix which makes available some of the official documents and academic works which have particularly influenced this book. For this section I have selected in particular items which are perhaps not easy for students to find in their Libraries in the 1990s.

Publisher's Acknowledgements

We are grateful to the following for permission to reproduce copyright material;

American Political Science Association on behalf of the authors for the article 'Two Faces of Power' by P Bachrach & M S Baratz from *American Political Science Review* Vol 56 (1962); Basil Blackwell Ltd on behalf of Royal Institute of Public Aministration & the editors of *Public Administration* for an extract from the article 'The Individual Responsibility of Ministers' by S E Finer from *Public Administration* Vol 34 (1956); Elsevier Science Publishers, Physical Sciences & Engineering Division, for an extract from the article 'If Planning is Everything, Maybe It's Nothing' by Aaron Wildavsky from *Policy Sciences* Vol 4 (1973): the editors, R Greenwood & J D Stewart for an extract from *Corporate Planning in English Local Government* (pub Institute of Local Government Studies & Charles Knight & Co Ltd, 1974); the Controller of Her Majesty's Stationery Office for extracts from *The New Local Authorities: Management & Structure, The Bains Report* (pub HMSO, 1972) & extracts from *Management in Government: The Next Steps* (pub HMSO, 1988); Humberside County Council for an extract from *Humberside County Council: Structure Plan, Vol 2, Policies* (1979): School for Advanced Urban Studies, University of Bristol, for the article 'Is Comprehensive Planning Possible & Rational?' by P Self from *Policy & Politics* Vol 2, No 3.

We have been unable to trace the copyright holder in *Westminster & Beyond* by Anthony King & Anne Sloman (pub Macmillan Ltd, 1973) & would appreciate any information that would enable us to do so.

We are grateful to the following for permission to reproduce figures and tables:

Humberside County Council for figure 5.1 from Humberside County Structure Plan Policy Formulation Process; Oxfordshire County Council for figure 7.1 from the Oxfordshire County Council Budget of 1987–88 and to the Controller of Her Majesty's Stationery Office for table 7.2 which is reproduced and adapted from the Ministry of Agriculture Fisheries and Food *Consumption and Expenditure for 1976 and 1984*; for figure 4.3 from Management and Personnel Offices unpublished report, *Policy Evaluation*, May 1987; for figures 5.2 and 5.3 from a National Health Service document and for table 7.1 derived from data from the Office of Population, Censuses and Surveys.

PART ONE

The changing agenda: past certainties and new doubts

CHAPTER ONE

Public administration and public management

ACCOUNTABILITY AND THE DEMOCRATIC POLITY

Until the 1970's, modern public administration was relatively clearly defined, both as an activity and as a subject of academic study. As an activity it is concerned to secure the honest, economical provision of public services and the efficient administration of national and local government. Public servants are held accountable to elected representatives at the centre through the Constitutional conventions of individual and collective Ministerial responsibility to Parliament. In local government, public accountability is supposed to be assured by the requirement that all local authority officers and employees report to the elected members of the council. In consequence, public servants are expected to record their activities meticulously. Unconventional or unduly speedy actions tend to be frowned upon. Compliance with appropriate laws and regulations is of paramount importance, together with acceptance of the policies and decisions of elected representatives – whether Ministers or councillors on committees and the full council. These members must none the less be advised as to what decisions are or are not legal and practicable. Hence, it follows that the academic disciplines which have been regarded as appropriate for a public administrator to study are Law, History and increasingly Political Science.

Central to the processes of government in twentieth-century Britain has been the accountability of officials to elected representatives – in both central and local government. A sign of the importance attached to such accountability in Parliament was the storm which blew up in 1954 over the Crichel Down affair. This concerned a piece of land in Dorset – Crichel Down – which was compulsorily acquired in 1938 by the War Office for use as a bombing range. After the war, it was in the fulness of time declared surplus to Defence requirements and in the normal course of events the opportunity should have been offered to the previous owner (or his successors) to repurchase it. However, at this time civil servants at the Ministry of Agriculture were looking for a site for an experimental farming scheme and Crichel Down was transferred to their ownership for this reason, without being offered first to its previous owner. This infringed the rights and legitimate expectations of one Commander Marten, to whom in ordinary circumstances ownership of the land would have passed. His Member of Parliament challenged the civil servants' action. In consequence, the Minister of Agriculture, Sir Thomas Dugdale, took responsibility for his officials' actions and resigned: 'I have told this House of the action which has been taken and which will be taken ...to make a recurrence of the present case impossible ...Having now had the opportunity of rendering account to Parliament of the actions which I thought fit to take, I have as the Minister responsible during this period tendered my resignation to the Prime Minister.' (530 HC Debates, 5th Series, col. 1198) Dugdale's one moment of fame was that of his political passing.

Crichel Down is as good a point as any to begin an analysis of modern British public administration, because it stimulated a series of actions which set many of the major parameters for debate about how modern government works and should work. In particular, it raised − or perhaps revived − serious debate about how effectively civil servants could be controlled or held to account for their actions by Parliament or by other means.

Concern had been expressed since the late 1920's about two trends in particular. One was the increasing amount of delegated legislation being passed by Parliament which in effect gives civil servants regulatory powers whose nature and exercise are not effectively scrutinised by MPs. The second was the increasing number of fields in which disputes between citizens and public servants are adjudicated not by the courts but by administrative procedures − the machinery of administrative justice (Elcock, 1969a) whose capacity to render justice was in doubt. In 1929, the then Lord Chief Justice of England, Lord (Gordon) Hewart, published his *The New Despotism*, in which he proclaimed a clarion call to resist the increase of official discretion because officials were, in his view, acquiring excessive power whose exercise was not being effectively controlled. Hewart warned that:

> Much toil and not a little blood have been spent in bringing slowly into being a polity wherein the people make their laws and independent judges administer them. If that edifice is to be overthrown, let the overthrow be accomplished openly. Never let it be said that liberty and justice, having with difficulty been won, were suffered to be abstracted or impaired in a fit of absence of mind.
>
> (1929, pp. 16–17)

3

This and other expressions of concern, for example in William Robson's *Justice and Administrative Law*, which was first published in 1928, led to the appointment of a committee to review these matters. The Donoughmore Committee on Ministers' Powers reviewed both the extension of administrative discretion and the developing system (or non-system) of administrative justice. (On the latter point, see Elcock, 1969a, chapter 1.) This Committee reported in 1932 but the crises caused by the Great Depression and the increasing threat to peace posed by Mussolini and Hitler meant that little was done at that time to curb official discretion or improve administrative justice.

Crichel Down revived these concerns. A lively academic debate began about the effectiveness or otherwise of individual Ministerial responsibility to Parliament (see Chester, 1954; Finer, 1956; Marshall and Moodie, 1959). In a seminal article, S.E. Finer (1956: see Document 2) argued that – the Crichel Down case notwithstanding – resignation because of departmental errors had become a largely ineffective means for Parliament to hold Ministers to account for their own or their officials' misdeeds because they could be protected from the need to resign or the consequences of having to do so, in any one of four ways:

- The Minister concerned could be given another post after resigning;
- The Minister could be moved to another post, so that his successor could disclaim personal responsibility for misdeeds committed during the term of office of a previous incumbent;
- The Government could agree to accept collective responsibility for the mistake or misdeed, making it in effect an issue of confidence in the entire Government;
- The Prime Minister could indicate his (or her) support for the Minister.

After this, the convention that Ministers ought to resign over departmental failures fell into desuetude, until Lord Carrington and his Foreign Office colleagues demonstrated otherwise just after the outbreak of the Falklands War in 1982. Apart from this instance, the individual responsibility of Ministers is nowadays regarded as largely ineffective as a means whereby MPs can ensure the proper and efficient conduct of the government's business, or to enable them to scrutinise and control the Executive.

At around the same time, the government itself sought to reassure Parliament and the public that official discretion and misconduct were not getting and would not get out of hand. In 1954 the Home Secretary, Sir David Maxwell Fyfe, stated firmly that where a civil servant had been carrying out a Minister's instructions, or had acted properly within the policies established by Ministers, the Minister 'must protect and defend him'. Also, where officials make mistakes but they are not on 'an important issue of policy and not where a claim to individual rights is seriously involved', the Minister 'states that he will take corrective action in the Department'. However, 'where action has been taken by a civil servant of which the Minister disapproves and has no prior knowledge and the conduct of the official is reprehensible, then there is no obligation on the part of the Minister to endorse what he believes to be wrong, or to defend what are clearly shown to be errors of his officers.' (HC Debates, 5th Series, col. 1284 ff. Document 1) Since then, civil servants who have been found to be at fault have been named both in Parliament and in official reports, for example that into the collapse of the Vehicle and General Insurance Company. (Chapman, 1973) They also now appear before Select Committees to account for their actions – a practice which has become increasingly frequent since Departmental Select Committees were established in 1979.

So far, the focus of this discussion of the accountability of public servants has been on the relationship between Parliament and the central Executive. This relationship has long been regarded as one of the main problems faced by any democratic system of government and its development lies at the core of our constitutional history. A. H. Birch usefully distinguished two constitutional 'languages' which ought to be distinguished in discussing what he calls responsible government (1964, p. 165). One language is that of the 'liberal' view of the Constitution, which concentrates on the issues so far discussed here. According to Birch, however, a second, 'Whitehall' language also exists which 'talks of the responsibility of Her Majesty's Government for the administration of the country, of the importance of protecting civil servants from political interference, of Parliament's function as a debating chamber in which public opinion is aired.' (Ibid) On this view, Parliament is and should be a policy-influencing, not a policy-making legislature, a view also taken by Philip Norton (1987, p. 7).

ACCOUNTABILITY AND THE WHITEHALL ETHOS

One aspect of Parliament's policy influence role which has often been overlooked is that – however ineffective it may appear to be at Westminister itself – individual and collective Ministerial responsibility has been the major *definiens* of the civil servant's job, as a mass of writing by former civil servants has demonstrated. Responsibility to Parliament also lies at the heart of the problem entertainingly explored in the 'Yes, Minister' and 'Yes, Prime Minister' television series (Lynn and Jay, 1981 and following) concerning the balance of policy influence between Ministers and their senior civil servants. Constitutional theory presumes that Ministers make policy and civil servants execute it but the reality is much more fluid.

Many civil servants have indicated that they need to guide their Ministers in their decision-making, while recognising that the ultimate authority lies with Ministers, individually and collectively. In 1950 the then Head of the Civil Service, Sir Edward Bridges, declared that

> It is … precisely on broad issues (of policy) that it is the duty of a civil servant to give his Minister the fullest benefit of the storehouse of departmental experience; and to let the waves of the practical philosophy of the Department wash against ideas put forward by his Ministerial master.   (1950, p. 19)

Ministers must be advised as to what is possible or permissible but one has to ask at what point waves washing against Ministerial wishes begin to wash over them.

Richard Crossman cited many instances in his *Diaries of a Cabinet Minister* (1975–77) of the attempted or actual manipulation of Ministers by civil servants. Tony Benn wrote in 1980 of 'Civil service policy …an amalgam of views that have been developed over a long period of time and in the development of which the civil service itself has played a notable role.' (1980, p. 62) On the other hand, another ex-Minister, Lord Boyle, stated his belief that

> if a Minister arrives with some fairly definite opinions and in a mood to give fairly definite political directions on some points civil servants, far from resenting it, very greatly welcome it. In other words, civil servants like a Minister who knows his own mind; above all, they like a Minister whose reactions they feel they can gauge in advance.
>
>   (1965, pp. 253–4)

Benn's and Boyle's statements are two sides of the same coin, in that they both indicate a relationship of at least some tension between the influence of Ministers on public policies and that of their Civil Service advisers. However, this stems at least in part from civil servants' preoccupation with seeking to ensure that their Minister and Department avoid difficulties with the public, the Press, pressure groups and above all Parliament. One senior civil servant wrote in 1959 that near Ministers is 'a group of officials, now usually fairly numerous, who whatever the subject-matter of their particular work, may be said to specialise in the awareness of Ministerial responsibility.' (Sisson, 1959, p. 13) In consequence, civil servants must tailor their advice to what is likely to be acceptable not only to the Minister himself but also to his or her colleagues and the Party's backbenchers, among others. In consequences, these officials' opinions 'are a mediocrity arrived at not because they are likely to be true but because in a system of protests and objections a man may hold them and escape without too many rotten eggs plastering his head.' (Ibid., p. 8)

From this approach, many other aspects of civil servants' approach to policy-making and management follow, including two which have attracted a great deal of criticism. These are first that senior civil servants regard themselves as 'the confidential advisers of Ministers' (Kingdom, 1966), which produces a great deal of secrecy and means that senior civil servants do not act as managers ensuring that their subordinates work efficiently. The Management Consultancy Group which advised the Fulton Committee declared that:

> We regard it as a valid criticism that few Administrators saw themselves as managers, i.e. as concerned with organisation, directing staff, planning the progress of work, setting standards of attainment and measuring results, reviewing procedures and trying to quantify different courses of action. This in part was because they tend to think of themselves as advisers on policy to people above them, rather than as managers of the administrative machine below them.
>
> (Fulton Report, Volume 2, paragraph 52)

These views fell mainly on stony ground in 1968 but their substance has become a major part of the Thatcher Government's approach to administrative reform, under which demands for better management are bringing with them far-reaching, sometimes fundamental, changes in the structures and processes of the Civil Service (see Chapter 2).

The second main aspect of the Civil Service tradition which has its roots in Ministerial responsibility to Parliament is the essentially subordinate role it accords to specialist experts. The need above all to give acceptable advice means that expert recommendations may have to be modified or even rejected if trouble is to be avoided: 'The standard of odium is not a matter on which the expert is expert,' declared C. H. Sisson (1959, p. 16). Rather, he says that 'Senior administrative officials have to learn to extract from specialist flowers around them the honey their Minister needs, explaining as they do that the Minister does not live on honey.' (Ibid.) This failure to make effective use of expertise, coupled with the 'generalist' education and training of top civil servants, has been widely blamed for Britain's economic problems, as well as her loss of influence in world affairs.

Thus, in 1959 Thomas Balogh published his famous essay, 'The Apotheosis of the Dilettante', (see H. Thomas (ed.), 1968) in which he attacked the Civil Service's role in the development of both economic and foreign policy. Of the latter, he wrote that

> There has been a tragic monotony of failure to appreciate the meaning of changes, social and political, to measure the strength of nascent national feeling, to gauge the impact on Britain, to devise policies to strengthen the country's diplomatic, political and economic strength to cope with it. The result is the weakening of the links with the Commonwealth, the loss of allegiance of people in British colonies and spheres of influence which could easily have been secured by a less exclusive, less arrogantly (and unjustifiably) superior attitude by Britain's representatives.
>
> (Thomas (ed.), 1968, p. 27)

Balogh's attack has been echoed many times since, not least in the opening pages of the Fulton Report (1968) and by a succession of former Ministers who have written accounts of their periods in office. (For example, Bevins, 1965; Crossman, 1975–77; Castle, 1980) In 1977, the Expenditure Select Committee demonstrated that nearly 20 years after Balogh's essay appeared, little had changed. The reason is that civil servants are still generally of the opinion that their approach, dominated as it is by the need to build consensus on policy issues within Whitehall in order to present Ministers with policies that are acceptable outside it, is the only possible one given the convention of Ministerial responsibility to Parliament. Accountability, as defined (so far as it is) by the conventions of the Constitution, is therefore the major influence on how senior servants perceive their role. It has therefore also been one of the major preoccupations of students of politics and public administration.

ACCOUNTABILITY IN LOCAL GOVERNMENT

The nature of accountability in local authorities, together with its effect on their managerial structures and processes, stands in contrast to the effect of the individual accountability of Ministers to Parliament on central government administration. Local government officers are accountable to all members of the Council by which they are employed, not just to the members of the governing party, as is the case in Whitehall. Hence, local authority officers must answer to the front and back-benches of the ruling party alike, as well as to members of the opposition parties, even where one-party majority control prevails (Bulpitt, 1967; Leach, Game and Gyford, 1989; Widdicombe, 1986). One result of this more dispersed accountability structure is that there has been less pressure in local government to co-ordinate the advice given to politicians and the responses departments make to their instructions.

Local government officers therefore have come to regard themselves as specialist advisers to their authorities and they almost invariably offer that advice to councillors sitting on committees whom the Council has appointed to control specific functions and responsibilities. Indeed some such committees must be appointed by law including education, social services, housing and police committees by those authorities who have been given responsibilities for those services. Other committees are created at the discretion of the Council.

The authority's staff work in departments which report to these committees and only in the 1970s and 1980s have serious attempts been made to counter the consequent fragmentation of local authorities' policies and administrative arrangements. Policy and Resources Committees, Chief Executive Officers and Management Teams have only been generally created by local authorities since 1974. The committee system still provides a powerful pressure to maintain relative departmental isolation (see Elcock, 1986a, chapter 10 and Documents 8, 9 and 10). The departmentalism of local authorities is a direct consequence of the accountability of officers to councillors as a group, instead of to individual Ministers or a Cabinet made up of selected members of the ruling party. Although local authorities have tended to develop in the direction of the 'Westminster model' of control by a political executive consisting of the leading members of the ruling party, the tradition that officers must answer to all the members of the Council is highly valued and maintained (Widdicombe, 1986). It has also inhibited the development of general administrators or managers in local government because all councillors have direct access to expert advice. Local authority administrators enjoy a lower status than their specialist professional colleagues.

LIMITS ON ACCOUNTABILITY

The accountability of officials to politicians is a central value which must be preserved if a system of government is to be regarded as being democratic. However, there are a number of circumstances in which such accountability must be restricted, in order to secure other values. D. C. Hague (1971) offered five such reasons:

1. The first is that some activities ought to be protected from government intervention because free speech among their members should be specially protected. Thus the ability of the broadcasters to criticise the Government, or the freedom of university teachers to carry out and publish such research as they think fit, have long been deemed

worthy of special protection: a buffer is needed to protect these institutions and their members from attacks on their freedom of expression. In consequence, the founding statutes of the British Broadcasting Corporation, the Independent Broadcasting Authority and the University Grants Committee contained guarantees of the autonomy of these institutions from government control (see Document 4). The erosion of these guarantees has been a subject of widespread concern in recent years.

2.   Secondly, organisations which are required to operate commercially and take commercial risks must not be subjected to the detailed control which Parliamentary accountability requires in government departments. Hence, the nationalisation statutes of the 1940s all contain clauses which restrict Ministers to giving 'Directions of a general character' to the Boards of the Public Corporations which were given responsibility for running the national industries. Their day-to-day management was to be the responsibility of the Boards themselves, who were required originally to break even financially, taking one year with another (see Document 3). Since then, financial targets have been made more stringent. More worrying, however, is the extent to which Ministers have interfered with the corporations' activities behind closed doors or have summarily dismissed their chairmen and board members (Morrison, 1954; Coombes, 1967; Fiennes, 1967).

3.   Thirdly, some public organisations need to be freed from detailed accountability in order that their officials may be able to act creatively or be enterprising. Thus, in the Prime Minister's Efficiency Unit's proposals for the establishment of Executive Agencies (Efficiency Unit, 1988, see Document 7) one of the main purposes of creating Agencies is to give their managers more freedom to act in enterprising ways.

4.   Fourthly comes what W. J. M. McKenzie called the 'Back-Double theory.' Here, governments create autonomous organisations to carry out activities which cannot be carried out within the conventional administrative structure. The security services, MI5 and MI6 are in point here: even the existence of the latter and its Director, 'C', are not officially acknowledged.

5.   Lastly, an activity may be allocated to an autonomous agency in order to prevent those responsible for carrying it out from featuring in the official Civil Service numbers. Thus the government can claim to have increased the range of services it provides for the public without increasing the number of bureaucrats it must admit to employing. Examples include the National House-Builders' Registration Council

and the Irish Hospitals' Sweepstake.

In recent years, a number of these restrictions on accountability have become problematic. We shall see later that for various reasons, the ability of the nationalised industries to operate commercially has proved to be largely illusory. Partly because they therefore appear to be inefficient, most of them have been or are intended to be sold to the private sector, when they will, so the argument runs, be able to behave commercially. However, because many nationalised industries are natural monopolies, consumer protection offices have been imposed on most of those which have been privatised.

Another source of concern has been that the replacement of the University Grants Committee by the Universities Funding Council is widely regarded as reducing academic freedom. Equally, the deregulation of broadcasting seems likely also to render broadcasters more subservient to the government. In any case, pressure on the BBC licence fee and the establishment of the Broadcasting Standards Council, are widely held to have reduced broadcasters' autonomy – especially given the Thatcher Government's determination to fill posts within its gift with its supporters and sympathisers. We shall return to these problems in several different contexts later.

THE BUREAUCRATIC STRUCTURE

Another major feature of modern public administration, which has its roots partly in the demands of accountability to elected representatives, is the bureaucratic hierarchy. The principles of bureaucracy came into general use in the governments of the Western world for two main reasons. The first was to ensure that instructions of the elected representatives were transmitted to those responsible for their execution. The second was to replace the nepotism, jobbery and corruption which characterised eighteenth-century government with the more efficient systems required for the nineteenth century's industrialised societies. No longer was the kind of career progression personified by W. S. Gilbert in Admiral Sir Joseph Porter appropriate when industrial economies had to be regulated and increasingly complex weapons of war deployed.

The classic account of bureaucracy is contained in the writings of Max Weber (1947). His analysis has been set out many times, so here a brief summary will suffice. Weber's bureaucracy has five main features:

1. Decisions should be made in accordance with general, publicly known rules.
2. There should be an established hierarchy of offices.
3. The rights, duties and scope of authority of each of these offices should be clearly defined.
4. Appointments to each office should be made on the basis of merit and each officer's performance should be objectively assessed to determine whether he should be promoted or removed from the office.
5. Each officer should receive a fixed salary. (Summary taken from Haynes, 1980; Ham and Hill, 1983)

The Gladstone administration's Civil Service reforms of 1870, for example, which were themselves based on the Northcote Trevelyan Report of 1853, introduced competitive examinations for entry to the Service and regulated promotions. The old jobbery and corruption was removed and with it the appointment of incompetent, ignorant or otherwise unsuitable people to public offices because of their wealth or family connections. However, bureaucracy also imposed a rigid chain of organisational being in which each person's scope for taking the initiative is more or less strictly confined, as well as being subject to supervision and control from above.

Government by regulation is also inflexible. Rules cannot be adjusted to meet the needs of individual cases, which is the main cause of the pejorative use of the word 'bureaucracy', as well as of a great deal of satire on it, such as Esther Rantzen's 'Jobsworth Award' for the most ridiculous case of an official (or an employee of a private business) who says, 'It's more than my job's worth' to bend a regulation to suit an individual case where no harm would be caused by doing so. Adherence to rules is also a protection for officers who become the subjects of complaints by citizens to their elected representatives, the Courts of Law, or Ombudsmen. If you can say truthfully that you acted in accordance with the regulations, this must surely be accepted as a valid defence by your superiors and eventually by councillors or Members of Parliament.

The local government service is the best example to take of the bureaucratic hierarchy in operation. A local authority consists of a series of departments, each headed by a Chief Officer with beneath him or her a hierarchy of posts all, or nearly all of whose status and remuneration will be defined with reference to the national gradings established by the Local Authorities Conditions of Service Advisory Board (LACSAB). However, each local authority appoints its own staff and determines how many shall be employed and at which grades.

The frustrations of working at the lower levels of these hierarchies have been vividly described by C. P. Snow in *Time of Hope* (1949) and by John Braine in *Room at the Top* (1957). These frustrations are probably worst for service workers such as teachers, social workers, police constables and so on, who are usually the only members of their departments who come into frequent contact with members of the public. However, their ability to respond adequately, in their view, to citizens' needs or demands is constrained by regulations, lack of resources, as well as restrictions imposed by apparently unsympathetic supervisors.

Social workers, for example, appear to be particularly prone to this kind of frustration, which may cause them to rebel. Cynthia Cockburn has argued that:

> Social workers and teachers are quickly radicalised by their exposure to poverty and oppression. They find that the job they are supposed to do, alleviate deprivation, educate children and so on, would require many times the money they are given to do it. As a result, many of them come to recognise that their actual function in capitalism is quite different: social control and the management of reproduction.
>
> (1975 p. 176)

This Marxist analysis is, in its author's terms, over-optimistic; most social workers either swallow their frustrations and press on as best they can, or they become discouraged and leave.

Social workers tend to be caught in a series of frustrations. They receive an extensive training in psychotherapy which superior officers expect them to apply but their clients' needs are often different and more basic, such as assisted telephones, aids for the disabled or special teaching for disturbed children. Social workers may both be unable to obtain resources to meet these needs because of budget constraints or inflexible regulations and also be criticised by their superior officers for not responding to their clients' problems in the established social work ways. A client may ask for help to deal with the disturbed child, while the social worker's superiors expect him or her to enquire into the stability of the client's marriage, for example. The contradictions inherent in such a role have produced a dismal history of public criticism, major crises and a resultant lack of individual and collective confidence among social workers (Elcock, 1982). Not the least of their problems is the pressure imposed on them by the bureaucratic hierarchy, which inhibits their creativity and restricts their responses to their clients' needs and wishes. However, an alternative analysis (Lipsky, 1980) argues that social workers are among the 'street–level bureaucrats' who in practice set their employers' policy agendas and resources priorities because they transmit to their superiors the demands and needs of their clients. They also exercise professional discretion in circumstances in which their decisions cannot be directly controlled. There is no check on teachers when they are in the classroom, social workers visiting clients or policemen out on the beat. Control can be exercised only *ex post facto* when they return to the office and report on their actions. Hence, by the exercise of their discretion, such professional field-workers effectively determine aspects of the policies of their employing organisations.

Since politicians will be anxious to maintain the support of those clients and officials recognise that their professional duty is to try to meet their citizens' demands and needs, this will, according to Lipsky, become the main influence on policies and resources allocation.

PROFESSIONALISM AND ACCOUNTABILITY

The constraints imposed on the field-worker by bureaucratic regulation and supervision are reinforced by the demands of a profession. Again, local government provides clear examples, together with the National Health Service, since most of those who work in these sectors are members of professions – or at least 'semi-professions'. (Etzioni, 1969) The demands of professionalism often reinforce those frustrations and inappropriate responses to customers' needs and desires. They may even result in damage being done to those customers' interests. (Illich *et al.*, 1977)

We must begin by defining briefly what constitutes a profession and in particular the nature of professional accountability in the public sector organisations. Students of sociology of the professions are generally agreed that a profession possesses (to a greater or lesser extent) the following attributes:

- Specialist knowledge, acquired through a more or less lengthy period of education, training and supervised practice. Even in the United Kingdom, which has the shortest first degree courses in the Western world, the minimum time after leaving school in which you can become a qualified member of the profession is four years and in some cases it takes twice as long. As well as an extensive academic education, nowadays generally in the form of a more or less relevant degree course, the young would-be professional will undergo both training and periods of supervised practice. In consequence, the rest of us tend to assume that their long training gives professionals expertise and experience which entitle them to make judgements about us and give us advice which we ought to accept more or less uncritically: 'Doctor knows best.'

- Related to this is an assumption that professionals have a (more or less) exclusive right to advise their clients on matters which fall within the recognised ambit of the profession. Hence, lawyers have constantly resisted others' attempts to break their monopoly over property conveyancing and other routine legal procedures. Again, the medical profession is notoriously reluctant to admit the possible therapeutic benefits of alternative treatments like osteopathy or acupuncture. 'Generalist' civil servants likewise demand acceptance of their exclusive right to advise the Minister, although they lack specialist expertise. Thus Richard Crossman told in his diary that he was severely reprimanded by his Permanent Secretary, the redoubtable Dame Evelyn Sharpe, for seeking Lord Goodman's advice during the preparation of the Rent Act of 1965. The department, he was told, could provide all the advice he needed and he should have resort only to his civil servants when he needed it (Crossman, 1975, p. 45). This claim to the exclusive right to advise is often readily accepted by elected or appointed public representatives. Most councillors and health authority members obtain all or nearly all their advice and information from their authorities' officers and see no reason to look elsewhere for it (Newton, 1976; Elcock, 1978).

- Thirdly, the professions generally enjoy high public esteem. In all societies, doctors and their representative organisations are powerful because politicians and voters alike assume that they know how to save life and relieve pain. Not all other professions enjoy such high social standing but teachers, social workers, lawyers, accountants and the like all enjoy at least a measure of social esteem – which opinion polls demonstrate is often higher than some of their critics would have us believe. The corollary is that the profession will often exercise – formally or informally – control over its members' standards of professional conduct and possibly even their personal behaviour. 'Conduct Unbecoming' is accepted as a valid reason not only for dismissal from a specific post but also for temporary or permanent exclusion from the profession itself.

- Fourthly, professional workers usually possess a greater or lesser degree of autonomy in their working lives. Often this follows from the nature of their work. There can be no direct supervision of what teachers do while they are in their classrooms or what social workers say to their clients when visiting them. Control may be exercised by giving them instructions *ex ante* about what they should or should not do but these may or may not be heeded. Again, supervision may be

15

carried out *ex post facto*, when workers submit reports on their actions to their superiors but they may become adept at only reporting what their superiors want to hear. Autonomy may also be formally assured, as in the case of general medical practitioners, who are not employed by health authorities but are independent contractors to them. Autonomy may be asserted by demands to respect freedom of professional practice and judgement.

● Lastly, many professions transcend the boundary between the public and private sectors and this may further reinforce their autonomy. Some professionals, such as town and country planners, work mostly for local authorities or the central government, although a minority of planners are employed by large private companies or work as independent consultants. The majority of architects, by contrast, are in private practice but some are employed by public authorities. Accepted methods and standards, or professional ideologies (Gower Davies, 1972) may thus influence both private businesses and the business of government. Professional orthodoxies hence influence their customers as well as politicians, administrators and company directors alike.

We can further explore the influence of professionals on policy-making and management in the public services by considering the nature of their accountability. This may be summarised as being upwards, downwards and outwards. (Elcock and Haywood, 1980) Accountability upwards through the bureaucratic chain of command and ultimately to elected representatives is the most formalised accountability relationship and is a pillar of democratic government. Thus the Secretary of State for Health is formally responsible to Parliament for everything that happens in the National Health Service. Again, councillors are entitled to whatever information they require from their officers which is relevant to the performance of their duties. They are entitled to instruct their officers to follow the policies councillors determine. Accountability upwards is also commonly described as 'top-down' management (Barratt and Fudge (eds), 1982).

However, professionals – and public servants generally – are also accountable downwards to their customers – who are also citizens who possess rights and votes. Public service professionals may be sued for professional negligence in the courts or be called to account by an elected representative or an Ombudsman who is dealing with a citizen's complaints against them. Lastly, they are accountable outwards to their colleagues. A simple example of this is a group of manual workers digging a trench. If one of them does not dig as vigorously as the rest or makes frequent comfort stops, he will be pressed by his mates to work harder because otherwise the work is not distributed fairly. In a profession, not only will an equitable contribution to the organisation's work-load (teaching hours, case-load and so on) be expected and exacted by colleagues; also they will expect competence, devotion to duty and respectability – demands which are often enforced by a professional disciplinary body.

We shall explore the nature of accountability upwards, downwards and outwards more fully later. Here, however, we need to note three features of professionalism in the public services which have generated major debates. The first is that if accountability outwards (to professional colleagues) becomes too strong relative to accountability upwards (ultimately to politicians) and downwards (to customers), professionalism may become 'disabling.' (Illich *et al.*, 1977) Behaving in accordance with established professional norms, protecting professional interests and aspiring to conform to fellow professionals' expectations, may result in customers being given advice or treatment which is inappropriate or even harmful. It reduces the customer's autonomy as a citizen because it generates an unhealthy dependence of the client on the professional's wisdom and authority: 'The ultimate sign of a serviced society is a professional saying "I'm so pleased with what you've done." The demise of citizenship is to respond "Thank you."' (McKnight, 1977) A person so dependent is likely uncritically to accept the professional's instructions or treatment and is also unlikely to reinforce accountability upwards by appealing to a politician or downwards by complaining.

Secondly, the influence of a profession may distort the policies and priorities of public services, even where they have been expressly determined by the politicians who have a constitutional right to do so. Thus in the mid-1970s and early 1980s, three successive Secretaries of State for the Social Services (Barbara Castle, David Ennals and Patrick Jenkin) declared that priorities in National Health Service spending ought to be adjusted to reduce somewhat the amounts spent on acute high technology medicine and maternity services. Resources could then be transferred to other services, including geriatrics, primary care and the care of the mentally ill and handicapped, which have long been starved of resources and are hence known as the 'Cinderella' services (DHSS, 1976a; 1977; 1981). Although there is widespread agreement that this would improve the lot of many patients while damaging the interests of few if any, the policy of altering NHS priorities has been vigorously resisted by the medical profession and has not been implemented by many Health Authorities (Elcock and Haywood, 1980, chapter 4; Elcock and Haywood, 1981). To give one example, Barbara Castle's statement (DHSS, 1976) that priorities ought to be altered, was attacked in an editorial in the British Medical Journal (3 April 1976) as 'A Policy of Despair.' The Editor declared that 'by putting people before buildings and by giving practical expression to public sympathy for the old and handicapped, Mrs Castle has, perhaps, allowed sentiment to overrule intellect.' The proposed shift in priorities was resisted in Regional and Area Medical Committees (Elcock and Haywood, 1980, p. 65) and progress in changing priorities, despite repeated Ministerial pressure, was slight (see Table 5.1 below).

Thirdly, the specialisation of the professions renders their activities extremely difficult to co-ordinate. This has been a bugbear of British local government for many years. It has resulted in the pursuit of inconsistent or contradictory policies by different authorities or departments within the same authority. (Donnison, 1961; Butler–Sloss, 1988). Failures of the different professions concerned with the care of children to communicate with one another or to pool information about individual cases have been blamed in official reports for a series of disasters, such as deaths of a succession of children from parental abuse and the Cleveland crisis in 1987, when parents were wrongly suspected of sexually abusing their children, many of whom were needlessly taken into care. We shall see later that the improvement of such inter-professional co-ordination and communication has been a major concern for those who have sought to improve public sector – especially local government – management during the 1970s and 1980s.

PAST CERTAINTIES AND THEIR DECLINE: CONCLUSIONS

In conclusion, then, public administration in the post-war era was dominated by a series of traditional concerns and concepts, including accountability to elected representatives, the virtues and limitations of bureaucracy as a system of management and regulation, as well as the growth of professionalism in the public services. These preoccupations generated debates about a series of persisting problems, which included:

- The ineffectiveness of the accountability of officials to elected representatives: Max Weber argued that 'the dictatorship of the official' was inevitable where officials were permanent and expert, while politicians are temporary and amateur.
- The failure of the Civil Service to adjust its members' attitudes and the policy advice they have given to cope with Britain's economic decline and her diminishing world role.

- The inadequate or inappropriate use of expertise, especially in central government.
- The slow, uncertain and uneven development of management as a means of improving the efficiency of the public sector.
- The rigidity and insensitivity of the bureaucratic structure.
- The excessive power of some professions in determining responses to customers' needs and in setting service priorities.
- Failures of communication and co-ordination among individuals, departments and authorities which at best result in inefficiency and at worst have been part causes of major disasters.

These problems have evoked a variety of responses which in the last twenty years have changed public administration very greatly, both in terms of its practice and as an academic subject.

CHAPTER TWO

Problems and reforms: setting the agendas

APPROACHES TO CHANGE

By the late 1960s, then, a series of problems confronted those involved in or concerned about public administration. In addition, from the late 1950s on, politicians and academics alike were becoming concerned about Britain's increasingly poor industrial and economic performance, especially in comparison with its European neighbours. In particular, short-term responses to the repeated sterling crises of the 1950s and early 1960s produced the 'Stop-Go' economic cycle characteristic of that period, which was widely held to be damaging Britain's longer-term industrial and economical prospects. (Worswick and Ady, 1961) In consequence, a plethora of remedies were proposed, ranging from Britain joining the European Community (EC) to reforming the Civil Service (Balogh, 1959). In this chapter, we will be concerned only with those aspects of change which directly affected public service organisations, together with those who are involved in or study them. Change was demanded and came in many ways.

It can be explored in two ways. The first is to consider the different kinds of improved performance that were being sought, under a series of headings:

- *Reducing uncertainty.* Not only increasing the amount of information available to policy-makers, administrators and service professionals but also making them more aware of what colleagues in other organisations or other departments of the same organisation, are doing.
- *Developing Creativity.* Looking for new ideas about how to resolve long-standing problems or tackle new crises. In the early 1970s, for example, concern about the possibility that continuing economic

growth might be doing irreversible and ultimately catastrophic damage to the ecosphere has produced increasing demands for radical changes in economic, environmental and social policies (Club of Rome, 1970; Solesbury, 1976). Again, the growing realisation that Britain's economic performance was lagging behind those of her European neighbours produced pressure for new ideas and approaches to economic and industrial policies (Rothschild, 1977).

• *Developing processes of social learning.* Increasingly, both academics and practitioners who are involved in public policy-making have argued that incrementalism, the 'science of muddling through' (Lindblom, 1959), is no longer adequate and that policy-makers must seek to learn systematically, both from their own experience and from the pressures of their working environments. At the same time, or perhaps a little later, disillusion with linear, 'Comprehensive-rational' planning sets in, especially in economic and land-use planning.

In this chapter, we shall explore the changes generated by these three pressures before looking at the increasing impact of a fourth set of pressures which resulted from the revival of interest in economic liberalism (von Hayek, 1944; Friedman and Friedman, 1980; Brittan, 1988) in the late 1970s and 1980s, which has dramatically shifted the terms of the debate about improving the performance of the public sector, especially since the Conservative Party under Margaret Thatcher won office in May 1979.

Before doing this, however, we must also note that many of the problems and changes we will consider can also be addressed under a second (and perhaps more conventional) set of headings which constitute the subject-matter of Chapters 3–7. They may briefly be considered here:

• *Structures.* British politicians and public administrators, as well as many businessmen and academics, cling to a belief that the performance of an organisation can be improved by changing its internal structure. British governments went in for an orgy of reorganisation between 1965 and 1975 (Stacey, 1975). Local government, the National Health Service, the water industry and the personal social services have all undergone one or more radical reorganisations during this period and since. Apparent failure to secure improvement in performance has often provoked further reorganisations in response. Thus, both the NHS and the water industry were restructured again in the early 1980s and seven large local authorities were abolished in 1986. The alternative response has been to reject organisational change as ineffective or counter-productive. Some observers argue that restructuring is mere dramaturgy: policy-makers restructure their organisations because they can control their internal structures when they cannot improve the outside world. They therefore reorganise in order to convince themselves and others that they are addressing the organisation's problems but to no beneficial effect (Wildavsky, 1980).

- *Processes*. If structural change proves to be ineffective (as it often does), then it may be effective to try and change the ways in which public policy-makers take decisions and administer public services. The discussion of policy-making processes revolves around three rival approaches to policy-making: incrementalism, planning and social learning (see Chapter 4). The debate is concerned with attempting to increase our understanding of how policies are arrived at and executed, as well as with looking for ways to improve them. These twin objectives of description and prescription often get confused in the policy analysis literature and need careful teasing out. Increased understanding, however, is the essential prerequisite of improvement. These issues will be examined in Chapter 4.

- *Strategies*. These are allied to but distinct from processes. One way to encourage improvement is to plan in advance what you wish to do and identify the steps you need to take to achieve that goal. Hence, some policy analysts have advocated planning processes in which a government or subordinate organisation identifies the goals it wishes to achieve, identifies alternative means to reach them and chooses that which is most likely to result in the achievement of goals at the least cost (Simon, 1945, 1957). However, massive disillusionment with such 'rational' strategic planning processes in the 1980s has been supplemented with, or supplanted by approaches to strategic planning which have been developed in private industry. These developments will be explored in Chapter 5.

- *Resources*. In the 1940s and 1950s, there existed a demand for more resources for public services, both in order to restore war damage and so that citizens could escape from the rigours of wartime and post-war austerity. It was also more or less uncritically assumed that if more money was spent on a public service, its quality and effectiveness could not but be improved. Furthermore, low raw material prices and steady, if slow economic growth combined to ensure that with each succeeding year, the amount of resources available to the public sector increased, albeit sometimes only marginally. Then, the rapid rise in oil prices in the early 1970s was followed by a radical shift in the ideological climate which not only restricted the resources available for distribution to the public sector but also made it apparent that resource reductions would continue for the foreseeable future. This has in return produced changes in approaches to resource management which will be discussed later in this Chapter, as well as in Chapter 6.

- *Techniques.* The last twenty years have seen a massive increase in the number and range of techniques available to public policy-makers and administrators. The development of mainframe computers in the 1950s and 1960s was a centralising influence because their cost, accommodation requirements and data storage capacity were too great for their use to be restricted to individual departments. However, as information and communication technologies have developed, producing first the 'virtual machine concept' and then the cheap, small micro-computer, massive decentralisation has become possible, since access to information can easily be obtained at a local terminal or micro-computer. Some have argued that the arrival of the micro-computer has produced the 'Polo Effect' – the organisation with a hole in the middle. The periphery is powerful because it has access to both information and analytical capacity but central control is weak (Pitt and Smith, 1985). The effect of Information Technology has probably been most profound on routine operations but it is increasingly changing policy-making and resource allocation processes too.

Secondly, in the last 30 years a battery of new techniques in personnel management has been developed, which has introduced a range of new activities to management in both the public and the private sectors. Organisation and Methods (O and M), Work study and other similar techniques have combined with concern to improve staff recruitment procedures, training and career advancement considerably to increase the importance attached to personnel management in the public services, as well as the range of personnel managers' responsibilities. Their significance has also become greater as public sector trade unions have become more militant, requiring careful thought about how their demands should be met. More recently, legal requirements to observe gender and racial equality have strengthened the need to control personnel functions. The increasing importance of personnel management for local authorities was recognised in the Mallaby Report as long ago as 1966, which recommended that local authorities should appoint personnel officers at Chief Officer level, at a time when very few had contemplated such a move (Mallaby, 1966; Poole, 1978). Many have now done so.

Finally, the increasing financial pressure with which the public sector has had to cope in recent years has led to experiments with Zero-Base Budgeting (ZBB), which entails endeavouring to make systematic challenges to existing services and commitments, rather than concentrating policy-makers' attention on new schemes or services. However, its success has been limited because policy-makers cannot digest the mass of information ZBB generates and because challenges to the value of existing activities generate determined resistance from those who are employed in or are benefiting from them.

We shall explore these five sets of issues in greater detail later. The analyses based on our first three headings (Reducing Uncertainty, Developing Creativity and Social Learning) will be developed here, as well as later. After this, we shall seek to unite these analyses in an exploration of the relationships between organisations and individuals which determine policy outcomes. Two such sets of relationships need to be explored: accountability and power. Here, the conclusions drawn from discussing the issues raised in Chapters 2–7 will be used to identify cross-bearings which will both enable us to identify where public administration now stands, what is likely to happen in the 1990s and how we might seek to improve future policy outcomes.

ROADS TO IMPROVEMENT

Reducing Uncertainty and Improving Co-ordination

In the 1960s and 1970s, a number of initiatives were developed which were intended to produce improvements in the performance of public organisations by resolving what were perceived to be serious deficiencies in their established methods of working. The first was to improve the amount and quality of the information available to policy-makers and administrators, as well as encouraging them to communicate and collaborate more effectively with one another. The problems generated by departmentalism, often exacerbated by professional specialisation, were most apparent in local government. In consequence, major initiatives to improve co-ordination developed in local government, which have lessons to teach managers in other fields of public administration.

Local authorities consist of a series of departments, each of which reports to a committee of councillors. However, there have been few means of ensuring that these committees communicate with one another or co-ordinate their activities. A large urban authority (a County Borough Council) in the 1960s would have between 20 and 30 departments, each reporting to a corresponding committee of councillors. The authority's budget would be built up from the Estimates produced by the individual departments, which are then collected by the Treasurer's Department and then cut back, by more or less crude expedients, to match the resources available and avoid an excessive rise in the local rates (Hepworth, 1984; Connolly and McChesney, 1987). This traditional budgetary process is essentially 'bottom up' with the overall picture of the authority's likely financial position emerging only relatively late in the cycle. Generally, if policy co-ordination occurred at all it was carried out by politicians. Victor Wiseman (1963) argued that the only effective co-ordinating forum on Leeds City Council in the early 1960s was the Labour Group's Advisory Committee. On other authorities powerful – indeed dictatorial – Leaders controlled the authority's policies and single-handedly ensured departmental and committee co-ordination (Jones and Norton, 1979; Elcock, 1981).

In consequence, major problems could arise when departments acted in conflicting or contradictory ways. David Donnison gave a whole series of examples from the welfare services of citizens being given conflicting or contradictory advice by different departments of the local authority and still more by different public agencies:

> The National Assistance Board may encourage a mother to go out and work while a Health Visitor urges her to stay at home and mind her children; a hospital almoner may encourage a girl to have her baby adopted while the Children's Department (of the local authority) are trying to help her to look after the child herself; a boy may be sent home from a school for the maladjusted and run wild on the streets – soon landing in the juvenile court because none of the local headmasters will accept him as a pupil. ...Differences of opinion are inevitable and often legitimate but at least the workers concerned should be aware of their differences and endeavour to resolve them in the interests of their clients.   (1961, pp. 9–10)

Frequently, however, the different workers and agencies were not aware of the conflicting results of their efforts or the pressures and confusion they caused for their clients. However, complaints coupled with other developments in local authority management have produced movements for change. The first is that generally known as corporate management.

The major impetus towards more co-ordination and control over the activities of local authority departments and professionals came from two official documents: the Maud Committee's Report of 1967 (Document 8) and the Bains Committee's Report of 1972 (Document 9). They were accompanied by the work of an academic whose writings on local authority management have been unrivalled in their eloquence and influence for more than 20 years now: Professor J. D. Stewart of the University of Birmingham. His book, *Management in Local Government: A*

Viewpoint, which was published in 1971, presented a persuasive case for the development of corporate management by local authorities.

The corporate management movement encompassed a wide range of ideas and developments which have been extensively discussed elsewhere. Here let it suffice to summarise them under a few headings (see also Elcock, 1986a, chapter 10 for more extensive treatment of these issues). We shall treat each of the main proposals of corporate management's advocates by summarising them, together with the main developments concerning each of them since the Maud Committee's Report was published in 1967.

The first was the recommendation that a committee of council members should be established to develop overall policies for the authority, as well as co-ordinating the activities of its service departments and committees. The Maud Committee recommended that local authorities should create management boards of between five and nine members for this purpose (Document 8). However, this proposal found little or no favour among councillors because it would concentrate too much power in too few hands. Hence, when the Bains Committee considered the same issue in 1972, it recommended that local authorities should establish policies and resources committees with larger memberships (Document 9). It did not lay down what the size of these committees should be. This recommendation was almost universally adopted by the new local authorities established by the Local Government Act, 1972. In most cases, policy and resources committees consist of between a quarter and a third of the total membership of the council, often including all the committee chairmen. However, they are frequently not the main locations for the determination of policy, which is still done in practice by the party executive committees before the policies and resources committee meets.

Secondly, the number of committees appointed by a local authority has generally been reduced and the span of each committee's control has been increased. Thus for example, a leisure service committee covers the libraries, parks and recreation functions, as well as controlling municipal art galleries, theatres and cinemas. Before the advent of corporate management, each function would have been managed by a separate committee. Similarly, a single public protection committee commonly controls the fire brigade, consumer protection services and emergency planning, each of which would again have been governed by a separate committee under traditional structures. However, the Bains Committee's recommendation that committees' functions ought to be related to implementing the Council's programmes rather than performing their traditional functions of overseeing departments and services, has been largely ignored.

The number of departments has also generally been reduced, which renders more co-ordination among the service areas controlled by each department easier. It also increases the span of control allotted to each Chief Officer, as well as that of the committee responsible for overseeing the department's work. Thus the personal social services were unified within generic social services departments as a result of the recommendations of the Seebohm Committee (1968), although there are still organisational boundaries separating social services departments from education and housing departments, as well as inter-organisational barriers between them and health authorities, which can still create major difficulties for the co-ordination of social and health care policies. Such client groups as the elderly, the mentally ill or children at risk may suffer thereby (Butler-Sloss, 1988; Wistow and Brooks, 1985).

The most radical change on the officer side has been the appointment by most local authorities of a Chief Executive Officer. The creation of this post was recommended by the Bains Committee (1972) and the Widdicombe Committee (1986) recommended that it be made compulsory for all local authorities to appoint a Chief Executive. However, a few authorities never appointed one and a few more have subsequently eliminated the post, sometimes by summarily dismissing its incumbent (Haynes, 1980). One of the Chief Executive Officer's roles is to convene and chair a management team of Chief Officers. Lastly, the Bains Committee urged local authorities to establish performance review sub-committees (of the policy and resources committee), in order systematically to monitor the efficient achievement of the authority's objectives. Performance review languished in obscurity for a time but now seems to be becoming more significant as local authorities seek additional means to improve the value for money obtained from their staff (Elcock, Jordan and Midwinter, 1989, chapter 7).

The main theme underlying all these corporate management activities is the need to develop greater integration within local authorities, whose main characteristic has long been considerable differentiation, or departmentalism (Greenwood *et al.*, 1978). This has in turn produced an increasing, although possibly creative, tension between those local authorities' officers whose principal concern is with the provision of a service and those whose responsibility concerns the overall management of the authority's affairs. The numbers, status and significance of the latter group of officers have been significantly increased by the advent of corporate management. The tension between them and service officers may be described as being between 'technocrats' and 'topocrats'. In his work on budgetary processes, Wildavsky (1979) defines these roles as those of 'advocates', who press the service departments' case for increased spending and 'guardians' who try to control spending in order to preserve overall strategies designed to limit the calls to be made on taxpayers (see Chapter 6). Again John Stewart has described a tension between 'professional ideologies' and 'management values', (1983, pp. 102–5). On the one hand, '...a local authority as a collection of professionally organised services contains a collection of separate ideologies' (pp. 103–4). On the other hand, the manager '...sees the professional task as set within the constraints of the organisation, will focus on the limits of the budget and emphasise the needs of financial control. The manager is concerned with the uniform application of the policies of the authority, rather than with the requirements of individual cases' (p. 104). These tensions exist not only between individual officers who hold different perspectives on the work of the authority but also within an individual officer's own sphere of responsibility: he or she must perforce become a manager as well as continuing to be a service professional, as he or she rises up the departmental or organisational hierarchy.

A similiar tension between differentiation and integration can be found in the central government, where it has been heightened by the introduction and development of the Public Expenditure Survey (PES) and its associated Committee (PESC) since 1962. The survey was established after the Plowden Committee on the Control of Public Expenditure reported in 1961. It has two principal objectives. The first is to develop financial planning in the central government by preparing projections of expenditure over a five year period (reduced to three years in 1980) The financial implications of current service provision and present decisions could be projected forward, so establishing what room is left for new projects or increased expenditure on existing programmes in the years to come. The survey is 'rolled forward' each year for a further planning period.

The second objective of PES was to increase central control over the preparation of Estimates by government departments. This is done through a process of bilateral negotiation between the Treasury and each spending department in turn, the department being represented by its Principal Finance Officer. This bargaining process is supervised at Ministerial level by the Chief Secretary to the Treasury. Those disputes which are not resolved are referred to the Cabinet for final decision, although the Cabinet now usually appoints a small group of senior Ministers, which has inevitably been dubbed the 'Star Chamber', to resolve these final disputes (Heclo and Wildavsky, 1974; Gray and Jenkins, 1985). One consequence of this bilateral bargaining is that the Treasury alone has an overall picture of the extent of the demands which the spending departments are making on the Exchequer. Furthermore, the Treasury alone knows what resources are available. Treasury officials can therefore play the departments' representatives off against one another, as well as advising them all solemnly that resources are limited. The process therefore becomes disjointed and incremental, rather than producing a rational, coherent resource allocation policy. Reviewing the Heclo and Wildavsky book, Jack Hayward remarked that this process of bargaining among the members of the Whitehall 'village' rather than developing coherent policies constituted a transformation of PESC's 'five-year public expenditure planning into an even more formidable bulwark of inert incrementalism (which) is breathtaking' (1975, p. 291). In this case, innovation served to preserve the traditional way of developing policies rather than, as was the case with corporate management in local government, acting as a force for change, however marginal its effects may have been on individual councils.

Increasing Creativity

Corporate management and the PES are both concerned, among other things, with reducing uncertainty – in the first case by trying to improve the flow of information and consultation across departments; in the second by extending the time-scale of public expenditure decisions further to the future. A second thrust of reform has been to attempt to increase creativity in government organisations, principally through the establishment within them of policy units, popularly known as 'Think Tanks'. A prototype was the American RAND Corporation.

The establishment of 'Think Tanks' or policy units has been advocated in particular by Yehezkel Dror (1973). He has advocated the adoption of a cyclical process of policy-making that includes a strong feedback mechanism, as do cybernetic models of the governmental process (Dunsire, 1989). As a means of stimulating ideas for injection into the policy cycle, he proposes the establishment of policy advice units whose members will be able to explore possibilities without being distracted by day-to-day problems, demands or administration – hence the need for a 'Think Tank'.

In British government, the best known such experiment was the establishment in 1971 of the Central Policy Review Staff (CPRS), which was charged with the task of 'producing a strategic definition of objectives'. (Cmnd 4506, 1970, para. 46) The staff was a part of the Cabinet Office and its role was defined as follows:

Under the supervision of the Prime Minister, it will work for Ministers collectively; and its task will be to enable them to take better policy decisions by assisting them to work out the implications of their basic strategy in terms of policies in specific areas, to establish the relative priorities to be given to the different sections of their programme as a whole, to identify those areas of policy in which new choices can be exercised and to ensure that the underlying implications of alternative courses of action are fully analysed and considered.

(Ibid., Para. 47, see Document 14)

According to an early student of the Staff's work, Christopher Pollitt (1974), the CPRS's advice was chiefly of one of two kinds:

1. Programme Advice: offering a view on the overall balance of the Government's programme. This kind of strategic advice was most in demand during the term of office of the CPRS's founder, Edward Heath. Every six months Ministers would gather at Chequers (the Prime Minister's country seat) for a strategy review meeting which included presentations by members of the staff. Mr Heath's successors did not continue this practice, however (Blackstone and Plowden, 1988).

2. Process advice on specific issues, such as the future of the British motor industry, the construction of the Drax B coal-fired power station and the Joint Approach to Social Policy. Especially controversial was the CPRS report on Britain's overseas representation, which argued for reductions in the size and cost of the Diplomatic Service, as well as for a change in its role. Diplomats should, the CPRS argued, become more concerned with promoting Britain's commercial interests and less with the traditional preoccupation of Great Power diplomacy.

One device which was available to the Staff was the 'collective briefing', by which its members could offer the Cabinet its own views on the papers being submitted to it by Departments. Such collective briefings were not offered frequently but when they were, they offered Ministers an alternative analysis of the chosen subject to that presented by the originating department, together with additional policy options. The Staff could thus stimulate debate in the Cabinet by increasing the amount of information and ideas available to its members.

The availability of alternative advice to Ministers was, of course, an irritant to established civil servants. However the small size of the Staff (never more than 18), coupled with the appointment of around half its members from within the Civil Service, seems to have prevented major opposition to its existence and activities developing within the Whitehall machine (Heclo and Wildavsky, 1974). However, the Staff's survival depended on Prime Ministerial support and this dependency was eventually to be its undoing. A 'Think Tank' is bound to find itself sooner or later in the position of King Lear's bitter Fool, proffering advice or information which his master does not wish to hear. The first Head of the CPRS, Lord (Victor) Rothschild, was rebuked by Edward Heath for revealing in a public lecture that Britain's economic performance was declining relative to those of its European neighbours, so that fairly soon she would be among the poorest members of the European Community. However, Rothschild and the Staff survived, although Harold Wilson (in his second term of office between 1974 and 1976), James Callaghan and Margaret Thatcher all created partisan Policy Units at No. 10, Downing Street, whose advice was likely to be more supportive of the ruling party's ideology and programme than that of the CPRS. Then, shortly before the 1983 general election, the bitter fool overstepped the mark. The CPRS produced a report which argued that the government would soon have to make a choice between increasing taxes and radically reducing the scope of the social services. The first was ideological anathema; the second was electorally embarrassing and shortly after the 1983 general election, the CPRS was disbanded (Blackstone and Plowden, 1988). Hence, the devices by which creative advice has been made available to Prime Ministers have altered quite rapidly over a fairly short period. This constitutes a continuation of the long-term trend identified by G. W. Jones (1987) for successive Prime Ministers to make their own arrangements to obtain information, support and advice other than that made available by Ministers and their departments – a need which most Prime Ministers since Asquith have felt more or less acutely. However, the CPRS and the No. 10 Policy Unit are distinctive in that their purpose was essentially to generate creative or dissident ideas for the Prime Minister and his or her senior colleagues to consider (Willetts, 1987).

The history of the CPRS makes it clear that units dedicated to creativity, as well as creative individuals do not fit easily into bureaucratic structures which are dominated by the demands of political accountability. Several of the Staff's reports were embarrassing to the government of the day. Thus, had the recommendations to reduce the size of the car industry by a third and not to construct Drax B been accepted, regional unemployment in areas which strongly supported the Labour Party would have increased sharply at a time when a Labour government was struggling to survive on a very precarious or non-existent Parliamentary majority. Again the report on overseas representation constituted a direct and much resented challenge to powerful vested interest in the Diplomatic Service. The report on the choice which needed to be made between raising taxes and reducing the social services was ill-timed, as well as being leaked in embarrassing circumstances (Blackstone and Plowden, 1988). However the Staff was required by its terms of reference to challenge established orthodoxies.

Further evidence of the ambiguities that surround policy units which are supposed to increase the creativity available within government organisations, emerged from the Northern Network for Public Policy's study of management in public service organisations in the North-East of England (Elcock, Fenwick and Harrop, 1988). A number of the organisations studied had established Policy Units but there was a good deal of uncertainty about what was expected from them. Some units were expected to help prepare formal strategic plans but others were required to play 'fire brigade' roles, proposing solutions to immediate problems. One senior manager said that 'Central Policy Unit mainly has a "fire brigade" role...is issue-related...*ad hoc*...rather than the policy role'. (Ibid., p. 46) This restriction of creativity because of the need to deal with pressing crises may relate to a more general sense of inability among public managers to plan at all far ahead (Ibid, p. 20 ff).

Developing Collective Learning

Reducing uncertainty and increasing creativity were often components of the third thrust of administrative reform which characterised development of social learning (Dror, 1973; Schon, 1975). We shall explore the issues raised by social learning more fully in Chapters 4 and 5. Here, we can note the increasing acceptance among policy-makers of cyclical, reiterative learning processes, such as Yehezkel Dror's model discussed earlier, to develop major planning documents (Elcock, 1979a). One example was the preparation by County Councils of Structure Plans, following the 1968 and 1971 Town and Country Planning Acts (see Stephenson and Elcock, (eds), 1985, p. 218 ff). In the early 1970s, the Department of the Environment advised councils who were preparing Structure Plans that

> Planning, in short, is a continuous process which is not completed when a plan is produced. The plan is necessary as a statement of the authority's intentions at a particular time for the initiation, encouragement and control of development but the assumptions on which these intentions are based must be regularly monitored and the plan must be amended if and when necessary. ...Plans should thus be regarded as part of a rolling programme of planning, to be updated (in the light of monitoring) if and when necessary and in any case, regularly extended to cover a further period.   (DoE, 1974, paras 27 and 29)

The process of developing the plan must therefore be continuous and reiterative; indeed some people have argued that the process of planning is more important than the final product: Tony Eddison declared bluntly that 'Planning is more important than plans.' (1973, p. 177; see also document 13)

THE SHIFT TOWARDS 'GOOD HOUSEKEEPING'

The Conservative victory in the general election of May 1979 has brought about a fundamental shift in the main thrust of attempts to improve the performance of government organisations. Reducing uncertainty, increasing creativity and developing learning processes all tend to be predicated on an assumption that government activity is at the very least necessary and often desirable. If the performance of government agencies can be improved, their activities can be made both more cost effective and more beneficial to citizens. In any case, the post war political consensus was based on the general acceptance that a massive increase in the role of the State was necessary. This had first been necessitated by the requirements of the war effort and post-war reconstruction. It was extended by the post-war Labour government and largely maintained by the Conservative Governments which held office during the 1950s. Apart from a few right-wing individuals who shared Friedrich von Hayek's fear that the extension of State intervention in the economy must sooner or later result in reducing political freedom to the point at which the regime became a tyranny, politicians of all parties accepted the value of Keynesian economic demand management and provision of extensive welfare services (Elcock (ed.), 1982). The resignation from the Macmillan government of Peter Thorneycroft as Chancellor of the Exchequer in 1958, together with Enoch Powell and Nigel Birch because they believed that the level of public spending was excessive, was an isolated disruption of the general consensus in favour of economic intervention and the Welfare State: in the Prime Minister's words, 'A little local difficulty.'

In 1970, however, Edward Heath and a group of Conservative colleagues produced a blueprint for free enterprise, market-orientated economic and industrial policies but although Heath gained office in June 1970 and his government attempted to implement these policies in their first two years or so in office, they largely reverted to the established policies of the post-war consensus after the 'U-turn' of 1972. In any case, the Heath Government's approach to policy-making and public administration was characterised by attempts to improve its management, rather than to reduce its scope. This approach was set out in the White Paper, *The Reorganisation of Central Government* (Cmnd 4506, 1970), which among other things announced the establishment of the CPRS, together with the structural reorganisation of several departments to create two 'Super-Ministries' (the Department of the Environment (DoE) and the Department of Trade and Industry (DTI)) as well as other managerial changes. Later the Heath government reorganised the NHS (Brown, 1975, 1978; Elcock and Haywood, 1980), local government and the water industry in attempts to improve their managerial performance (see Stacey, 1975 and Chapter 3).

Margaret Thatcher's election as Leader of the Conservative Party in 1975, however, presaged a fundamental change of focus. Classical economic liberalism now reasserted itself as Conservative policies were radically changed under the new Leader. The role of the State must be reduced and public spending cut, in order to increase individual freedom and encourage enterprise. In consequence, the watchwords of the new public management are the 'Three E's: Economy, Efficiency and Effectiveness'. Their impact has been seen in all the public services. Although important innovations have resulted from the Thatcher Governments' policies, both their scope and intellectual content are curiously stunted. Furthermore, major issues of accountability and the need to ensure the proper conduct of public business have been neglected (Chapman and Hunt (eds.), 1986; Chapman 1988b and c; Hugo Young, 1989).

In the Civil Service, change began with the introduction of the Rayner Scrutinies, combined with the determination to reduce the size of the Civil Service by 100, 000 by 1984. Mrs Thatcher established an Efficiency Unit at No. 10, Downing Street, whose first head was Sir Derek (now Lord) Rayner, the managing director of Marks and Spencer. He created a series of Scrutiny Teams to look at departmental operations with a view to detecting waste and proposing savings. In this, the government was following the advice of a former Ministry of Defence civil servant, Leslie Chapman, who had written a book which exposed large areas of waste where significant savings could easily be made – for example in the year-round heating of aircraft hangars in 'which aircraft parts were stored but which were rarely entered by staff' (Chapman, 1978). In June 1984, the Treasury claimed that the Civil Service had been reduced in size by 14.8 per cent, more than half of which had been achieved through efficiency savings (HM Treasury, 1984). In the same year, the Efficiency Strategy was claimed to have produced about £50 million in once-for-all savings and £450 million in recurrent savings.

The second thrust towards change was the development of the Management Information System for Ministers (MINIS) by Michael Heseltine, first at the Department of the Environment and then at the Ministry of Defence. The system was extended to the whole of Whitehall after 1982 as the Financial Management Initiative (FMI) (Gray and Jenkins, 1985). A major principle which MINIS and the FMI have in common is the division of departments into cost-centres, each of which is made responsible for the efficient and effective use of the resources allocated to it (Document 6). The adoption of such a principle had been recommended by the Fulton Committee in 1968 in the form of Accountable Management; its hour had now come. The purposes of the FMI have been so defined as to concentrate civil servants' minds on achieving greater efficiency and assessing their performance systematically, by obliging them to act as managers of cost-centres within departments.

One civil servant who is in charge of a large government office – the Department of Social Security Central Office at Longbenton, Newcastle upon Tyne – has described the operation of the FMI's cost-centre system in some detail (Thorpe-Tracey, 1987). He describes the increased discretion available to cost-centre managers, who 'have ...budgets which include basic staff costs, overtime, travelling time, substitution, staff travel/subsistence, telephone call charges, typing and also some miscellaneous items' (p. 333) There is therefore an incentive to use such services as frugally as possible in order to maximise the value obtained from the restricted resources available to the cost-centre. He concludes that 'Managers at all levels are much more cost conscious and on the lookout for more cost-effective ways of carrying out their tasks.' (p. 335) It seems likely, therefore, that savings or more service for each pound spent are likely to result from the implementation of the FMI.

Since the general adoption of the FMI in 1982, two further developments have occurred. The first was the development by the Joint Management Unit (JMU) in the Cabinet Office of means to evaluate the effects of government policies, including the production of a guide to evaluation for Civil Service managers (HM Treasury, 1985). This emphasis on evaluation was strengthened by the introduction of a rule that new proposals submitted by ministers to the Cabinet must include a statement as to how their effects are to be evaluated. The JMU declared that: 'Evaluation helps policy managers to achieve their objectives. It can be seen as part of a policy-making cycle which begins with appraisal, followed by implementation, monitoring and evaluation, back to reappraisal.' (HM Treasury, 1985, Para. 2, p. 1) The learning cycle therefore lives in central government but its purposes are now directed towards the achievement of the 'Three E's' rather than to the exploration of wider policy issues (see Chapter 4).

A much more radical initiative based on the principles of accountable management contained in the FMI was launched in February 1988, with the publication of a report by the Prime Minister's Efficiency Unit entitled, somewhat innocuously, *Improving Management in Government: The Next Steps* (Efficiency Unit, 1988; see Document 7). This document, commonly known as the Ibbs Report, although the Head of the Efficiency

Unit was never mentioned in it, proposed that most routine Civil Service work should be devolved or 'hived off' (Fulton, 1968) to a series of autonomous departmental agencies, each to be headed by a Chief Executive responsible to the Minister. The authors of the Ibbs Report declared that '...the management and staff concerned with the delivery of government services (some 95 per cent of the Civil Service) are generally convinced that the developments towards more clearly defined and budgeted management are positive and helpful'. (Para. 3, p. 1) Furthermore, 'senior management is dominated by people whose skills are in policy formulation and who have relatively little experience of managing and working where services are actually being delivered'. (Para. 4, p. 1) Shades of the Fulton Report! However, some observers have expressed fears that the development of such agencies may reduce still further the already limited effectiveness of Ministerial accountability to Parliament (Chapman, 1988 b and c; Fry *et al.*, 1988). Democratic accountability may be sacrificed at the altar of the 'Three E's'. In addition safeguards against corruption may be weakened.

Economy, efficiency and effectiveness have also been vigorously promoted in local authorities, in particular by the Audit Commission, since the early 1980s. Generally the search for value for money in local government has produced four main trends (Elcock, Jordan and Midwinter, 1989, chapter 7). These are:

1.   The extension of the scope of the auditor's role to include the assessment of a local authority's efficiency and effectiveness as well as the auditor's traditional concern with ensuring that the ratepayers' money has been spent honestly and for lawful purposes. Even this traditional preoccupation has become politically controversial in recent years. The scope of audit has therefore been extended from fiscal to cover programme and process accountability (Robinson, 1969).

2.   The dissemination of information about good management practices identified in individual local authorities so the others can follow suit, coupled with more general comparisons of local authorities' management processes and practices.

3.   The development of performance indicators and of performance review by local authorities in order better to assess their efficiency and effectiveness in achieving their objectives. Here, developments in local government have to some extent paralleled the work of the Joint Management Unit in the Civil Service and the development of performance indicators for health authorities by the Department of Health (Pollitt, 1985)

4. The introduction of compulsory competitive tendering for an increasing number of local authority activities, which acts as a spur to greater efficiency and the dismantling of restrictive practices within local authority departments.

CONCLUSION: IS PUBLIC MANAGEMENT THEN BUSINESS MANAGEMENT?

All these developments demonstrate the increasing influence, indeed dominance of business management, its methods and tools, in the management of government agencies which has developed since 1979. The assumption seems to be that if economy, efficiency and effectiveness are improved, taxes can be reduced and that what public services are not privatised or contracted out will be improved in quality. In consequence, it has been argued in a number of quarters that public management and business management are now so closely aligned that the distinctions between them have largely disappeared. Thus Perry and Kraemer (1983) argue that in management education, 'The central organising principle of generic (business) schools is that the knowledge, techniques and skills necessary for effective administration or management are similiar for organisation in a variety of sectors of society.' Lewis Gunn has argued, less simplistically, that

> Public management is an attempt to combine much that is still relevant in the classical view that public administration is different, with the insights of the generic management approach which holds that managers in the public and private sectors face many common problems which are as much similiar as they are different. (1988, p. 24)

The crucial issue is the debate about the extent to which public administration is different, as well as whether the 'Thatcherite' approach to management is adequate. The distinctive features of public administration are usually argued to be:

- The requirement of accountability to elected or appointed citizens' representatives and ultimately, therefore, to the electorate. This results in the development of hierarchical structures in public services which may be seen as clumsy and unresponsive but which are supposed to ensure accountability upwards to elected representatives.
- Accountability upwards to politicians has also resulted in the development and maintenance of accounting, auditing and record-

keeping systems which ensure that all actions and transactions are recorded so that they may be explained fully if they are subsequently challenged. Likewise, personnel (or Establishment) practice tends in the public services to be concerned with the propriety of appointments and promotions, rather than with career management and development (Chapman, 1988a).

- Ethical problems arising from relationships with clients which are concerned at the same time with both dependency and citizenship. The unemployed or sick person or the impoverished single parent needs State help but is also a citizen with rights to privacy and personal dignity, as well as possessing a vote and access to his or her MP and councillors. Public servants cannot therefore treat those with whom they deal merely as customers; they are also in a real sense their masters.

- The need to try to achieve the multiple, conflicting and changing goals which are set by politicians, as opposed to the relatively simple goal of profit maximisation that prevails in the private sector. In any case, even the 'Three E's' are value-laden terms. For instance, efficiency may mean either gaining more benefit for the same input or reducing the resources required to achieve the existing level of benefit. The choice of improving services at the same cost or providing the same service more cheaply is a value choice which must be made by politicians (Kingdom, 1986; Elcock, 1986b). In any case, goals change if an election produces a change in the party holding office – which may happen at least once in four years in most liberal democracies.

- Just as goals may be multiple, conflicting and changing, so is the organisation's role. Many government organisations must play 'reticulist' roles in which they co-ordinate the activities of their own departments, other government agencies, private firms, interest groups and others (Friend, Power and Yewlett, 1977).

In consequence, many people have argued that the education and training of public servants must remain distinct from that offered to private managers, despite attempts by some business schools and the Business and Technician Education Council (BTEC) to assimilate private and public sector management courses so that students from both sectors are taught together most of the time (Bellamy and Franklin, 1985; Kingdom, 1986; Chapman, 1988b). Lewis Gunn (1988) argues that the 'Three E's' ought properly to be five, with Excellence and Enterprise added to Economy, Efficiency and Effectiveness. In this he leads us to a recognition that although the business management approach may unduly impoverish both the practice and the teaching of public administration, the traditional approach has also to some extent been discredited and that there are common lessons to be taught to private and public managers alike. Overlap, however, does not imply an identity between management in the two sectors.

The popular appeal of the 'New Right', reflected in three successive Conservative election victories, coupled with the apparent inability during most of the Thatcher years of Opposition parties to develop convincing or attractive alternative policy agendas, indicates that the business management approach is likely to prevail over much of the public sector. This will come about through further privatisation, as well as the introduction of compulsory competitive tendering for more public services, unless a convincing alternative is found. In consequence, the practice of public administration must change. Thus Roger Prentice (1987, p. 11) told Labour-controlled local authorities that 'The consumers of local government services test the claim of Labour authorities against their own direct experience of council services. And too often these services are found wanting'. Paul Hoggett and Robin Hambleton (1987) have argued that the public is no longer willing to accept 'bureaucratic paternalism' and the massive, alienating organisations that so often provide these services must be found. They postulate three possible routes for change. These are:

1. Market-based approaches, associated with the 'New Right', which 'seek to challenge the very notion of collective and non-market provision for public need.' (Hoggett and Hambleton, 1987, p. 14) Privatisation and contracting out are the main methods adopted here.

2. Consumerist solutions, where attempts are made to render public services more attractive to their citizens and more responsive to their needs.

3. Collectivist solutions, where methods of service provision are changed in order to relate them more closely to citizens' needs and wishes. The establishment of decentralised neighbourhood offices by local authorities is an example of such an approach (see Hoggett and Hambleton, 1987; Elcock, 1988).

Consumerist and collectivist solutions entail an acceptance that if the public services are once more to command the legitimacy they enjoyed before the 1970s; they must become both less inward-looking and more concerned with giving satisfaction to their customers. For Hoggett and Hambleton, then there is a need

> ...to develop a new kind of organisational culture which is capable of being more open, democratic and self-critical – an organisational culture which is anxious to learn and eager to appraise its own performance. Such an organisational culture is very different from the form of service provision we have labelled bureaucratic paternalism.

(1987, pp. 24–5)

This shift has become evident in a range of changes all of which have as one of their main objectives, making public organisations more responsive to public views and needs and hence winning back citizens' support for the concept of public service.

All these developments will be discussed in more detail in later chapters; here we need only comment briefly upon them. Many such initiatives have been concerned to encourage the application of the 'Principles of Excellence' (Peters and Waterman, 1982) to the public services, as part of the development of a 'Public Service Orientation' (Stewart, 1986; Clarke and Stewart, 1988). The 'Principles of Excellence' were established after a study of America's most successful companies. They are:

- Bias for Action: act rather than analyse and debate indefinitely.
- Stay Close to the Customer: establish the customer's preferences and respond to them. Quick responses, rather than most careful administration, are needed. There is an obvious conflict between this tenet and the demand for meticulous record keeping imposed on public servants by their accountability to Parliament or to councils.
- Autonomy and Entrepreneurship: break the organisation into small components whose members are encouraged to think independently and creatively. F. E. Schumacher's (1973) proposal that large organisations should be divided into 'Quasi-Firms' was a similar proposal to increase the organisation's members' creativity. Arguably the FMI and the creation of departmental agencies could have the same effect.
- Achieve Productivity through People, or as Sir John Harvey Jones (1988) has put it: 'switching people on'. His own definition of management cannot be bettered as an expression of this principle: 'Management is ...about energy, about courage and determination as well as foresight. ...It requires the most delicate balance of sensitivity to the feelings and reactions of others. ...Management is essentially about people, about the organisation of people, about obtaining their commitment to worthwhile commonly shared values and objectives.' This approach is a far cry from the stultifying bureaucracy that has characterised many traditional public organisations.
- Hands On, Value-Driven: executives must stay in touch with the activities of the organisation and promote a strong corporate culture. In public administration, such concern with the organisation's internal management has tended to take second place among senior officers to the preparation of policy advice for politicians (Sisson, 1959; Fulton, 1968).
- Stick to the Knitting: confine the organisation's activities to what it

does best. Its strengths and weaknesses should be clearly identified, the strengths developed and the weaknesses remedied if possible. However, this principle may have limited application in government because the organisation's task is largely prescribed for it by legislation and its political masters.

- Simultaneous Loose-Tight Properties: foster a climate in which the organisation's central values are clear and its members are dedicated to their achievement but in which there is tolerance of debate and discretion within these broad central values. This may be difficult to achieve in hierarchical organisations dedicated to achieving effective accountability to politicians but it is by no means impossible (Stewart, 1986; Clarke and Stewart, 1988: Elcock, 1988).

These Principles of Excellence constitute a very general manifesto for organisational change. To be more specific, two trends in the development of public sector management have developed in recent years as public organisations have come to recognise the need to change their methods of working in order to win back their lost public legitimacy. In local government, they are the major parts of the 'Public Service Orientation' recommended by John Stewart and Michael Clarke (Stewart, 1986; Clarke and Stewart, 1988). These trends are:

- Consumer Responsiveness: make an attempt to discover what consumers want and need, as well as exploring their perceptions of the services the local authority provides, as a preliminary to changing delivery systems and processes in order to make the service more attractive to citizens. An increasing amount of consumer research is now being carried out by or on behalf of local authorities (Fenwick and Harrop, 1988) and health authorities (Pollitt, 1985).
- Decentralisation, or 'Going Local', the creation of neighbourhood units or offices to provide services and offer easy access to staff and services. They may be given some control over some resources to meet neighbourhood needs and demands. An increasing number of local authorities have developed a bewildering variety of such decentralisation schemes (Hoggett and Hambleton, 1987; see Chapter 3).

Thus the crisis that practitioners and students of public administration have had to face in the 1980s has both stimulated a wide-ranging debate and a range of experiments with new structures and approaches to public management. In Part Two, we explore the nature of the modern public sector and the major recent developments within it.

PART TWO
Issues

CHAPTER THREE

Can we improve government through structural change?

RESTRUCTURING: A LONG-STANDING CURE-ALL?

In Part Two, we shall discuss the major issues which have concerned both practitioners and students of public administration in recent times. The first such issue is concerned with the structures of government, because changing the structures of government agencies has been a long-standing preoccupation of British public administrators. Structural change has been undertaken in the hope and belief that it would solve some of the major problems confronting those agencies and improve their performance, although bringing about structural change can be a long, difficult process. Although it was generally agreed after the Second World War that local government ought to be reorganised so that its areas and functions conformed more nearly with the changes in economic, social and political realities which had occurred since local government as we know it was established at the end of the nineteenth century, reorganisation none the less took 27 years and five attempts to achieve. Again, in the late 1960s it was widely accepted that the National Health Service (NHS) needed to be reorganised because the pattern of disease and disability had changed fundamentally since the Service was established in 1948 but it took six years and three attempts to accomplish reorganisation. None the less, between 1965 and 1975 much of the public sector was reorganised in what might well have been termed an orgy of reorganisation (see Stacey, 1975). During this period, major reorganisations were carried out of local government, the NHS, the water industry and other public sector agencies.

Government organisations themselves resort to changing their internal structures in the hope of solving, or at least ameliorating, the major problems which beset them. Thus, the corporate management movement in local government (Elcock, 1986a, chapter 10 and see Documents 8, 9

44

and 10) has been an attempt both to improve interdepartmental co-ordination within local authorities, which is the besetting problem of local authorities whose management processes are dominated by specialist professionals, as well as to improve their efficiency.

In universities and polytechnics, organisational restructuring has repeatedly been used to try and save money, although its only actual achievement may, so senior managers hope, be to convince outside observers, such as the Department of Education and Science, local authorities or the Universities Funding Council, that an institution is attempting to come to grips with its financial and managerial problems. Restructuring thus becomes an exercise in dramaturgy which will not produce any real economies or improve the institution's performance (Barker, 1986).

Some observers are totally cynical about both the motives of those who advocate structural reorganisation and the lack of benefit which accrues from reorganisations once they have been carried out. Notable among them is Aaron Wildavsky, who has written that:

> Organisations may change in order to influence people in the manner desired by some specific public policy. If this doesn't work, the difficulties may be traceable to defects in the organisation's structure or to achieve desired external effects, organisations may exert influence in the one place where their powers are most nearly adequate to their preferences – their own internal affairs. Agencies may be reorganised because they are a lot easier to change than social structure. It reminds me of the old joke about looking for a missing button not where it was lost but in the kitchen because the light is better there.
>
> (1980, p. 79)

For Wildavsky, then, structural reorganisations are intended to alter people's behaviour and may therefore be justified if they succeed in doing so. However, reorganisation may also be (but not admittedly) an exercise in dramaturgy. It satisfies the need of senior managers to justify their existence to themselves and others by seeming to be doing something to resolve their organisation's problems.

Wildavsky's view is perhaps overdone, for there are good reasons to carry out structural reorganisations, as well as outside pressures that may render it inevitable sooner or later. A look at some reorganisations will demonstrate that organisational restructuring is sometimes an appropriate response to internal or external difficulties but that much thought should be given before it is accepted as the appropriate course of action. In the next section we shall consider some major nationwide reorganisations, such as those of local government and the NHS. We go on to discuss some reorganisations whose main focus is an individual organisation, such as a local authority.

REORGANISATION IN PRACTICE

National Reorganisations

Local Government. By the mid-1970s, it was clear that social and economic changes had rendered the local government structure which was established by the Municipal Corporations Act, 1835, the County Councils Act, 1888 and the District Councils Act, 1894 inappropriate, to such an extent that it was damaging both the effectiveness and the credibility of local government itself. Three main problems had developed. They were:

First, population movements had produced huge anomalies in the local government structure. For instance, Rutland County Council, which had a population of 23,000, had the same powers and functions as Lancashire County Council, with a population of over 1 million. Again, the little town of Bishop's Castle in Shropshire had a Municipal Borough Council, complete with mace, aldermen and fairly extensive powers – but a population of 800.

Secondly, the arrival first of the railways (see H. G. Wells, 1908; Perkin, 1970) and then the mass-produced motor car, fundamentally changed the relationship between towns and countryside. When this was coupled with the rapid decline in agricultural employment, which has more than halved since the Second World War, the implication was the destruction of the self-sufficient rural community. Today, less than 3 per cent of Britain's workforce is engaged in agricultural production. Because of these changes, most rural dwellers now depend on towns and cities for their jobs, education, shopping, leisure services and a great deal else besides. It was therefore no longer sensible that they should neither have a say in the management of those urban services nor contribute to them through local taxation. The independence of town and country in the nineteenth century has given way to interaction and interdependence in the twentieth century.

One aspect of this interdependence caused increasing friction after the Second World War. Many town and city councils, especially the county boroughs (i.e. the larger cities) needed to build large numbers of houses on their outskirts in order to be able to move residents out of slums or bomb-damaged housing while those areas were redeveloped. However, their applications for planning permission to build on sites on their peripheries, which were located in the areas of adjacent counties, were frequently rejected. Former slum-dwellers were not wanted in rural or suburban areas and in any case their presence might increase the Labour Party's vote in safe Conservative wards. Slum clearance was therefore inhibited by the inability of towns and cities to expand into adjacent areas (Jones, 1966).

All these were good reasons to reorganise local government but successive proposals to do so were fiercely resisted by a wide range of interests. The existing local authorities and the Associations that represented them at national level (Rhodes, 1987a; Isaac-Henry, 1980) did not want to lose their existence and be merged with neighbouring authorities. Often, sentiment combined with councillors' self-interest to produce popular agitation against reorganisation proposals. One example was that when Shropshire County Council sought to merge its small borough councils with their neighbouring rural district councils, knives and pitchforks were sharpened in Bishop's Castle and elsewhere for the march on the Shire Hall in Shrewsbury. Public resistance was so great that in the end, in order to placate it the government created a new type of local authority: the rural borough. Rural boroughs were to have most of the panoply of a municipal borough council, including a mayor and a mace but the powers of a parish council. According to Peter Richards, the rural borough 'has no *raison d'être* other than tradition'. (1966, p. 89) More substantially, several suburban authorities resisted incorporation into the nearby city, quite often successfully. They did so both because they did not want more townspeople to come and live in their areas and because they would be subjected to political regimes which they regarded with hostility.

The political parties – especially the Labour Party – also resisted reorganisations because they feared that it would produce disadvantageous consequences for them. Thus the London Labour Party opposed the creation of the Greater London Council (GLC) by a Labour Government because its members believed that the Party would not be able to gain control of the new authority – which is ironical when one considers the GLC's subsequent history! Again, when Richard Crossman became Minister of Housing and Local Government in 1964, he found that reorganisation schemes proposed by the 1958 Local Government Boundary Commissioners were being resisted by Labour MPs as well as Labour-controlled local authorities because they feared that if the boundaries were redrawn to incorporate Tory-voting suburbs, the Labour Party would lose both control of the Council and (later) some Parliamentary seats. After facing a particularly determined resistance to the Commission's proposed new boundaries for Leicester, Crossman decided that local government would have to suffer radical surgery. After a meeting with that city's Labour MPs, he decided that the piecemeal approach to reorganisation required by the 1958 Local Government Act had run into the sand (Crossman, 1975, p. 65). He therefore appointed a Royal

Commission, under the Chairmanship of Lord Redcliffe-Maud, to prepare comprehensive local government reorganisation proposals. When the Commission reported in 1969, its proposals were accepted by the Labour Government but considerably altered by the Conservatives after they won office in June 1970. A new local government system was fully established in England and Wales on 1 April 1974, with Scotland following a year later. However, this was achieved only after 27 years and several attempts to reorganise local government. The major episodes in this process were:

- The 1947 Boundary Commission, whose proposals were rejected by Clement Attlee's Government because they were likely to be disadvantageous to the Labour Party. In any case, the Commissioners themselves protested that their remit to consider only the geographical structure of local government was too narrow: they needed to be able to review the distribution of functions among local authorities as well.

- None the less, the next attempt at reorganisation was also confined to the adjustment of geographical boundaries. The Boundary Commission established by the Local Government Act, 1958 was required to review the boundaries of county and county borough councils, after which the former were to review the boundaries of the districts within their counties. Some changes were achieved by the Commissioners, among them the creation of the County of Teesside, which was the first estuarine local authority in the country but resistance to many of their proposals was fierce – including the Rutland, Bishop's Castle and Leicester instances discussed earlier.

- The slowness of reform by Boundary Commissioners persuaded Richard Crossman to pursue comprehensive reform by the appointment of the Redcliffe-Maud Royal Commission in 1969. This followed the earlier example of the Herbert Commission on the Government of London, whose recommendations resulted in the establishment of the GLC and the 32 London borough councils in 1968, replacing the old London County Council and smaller metropolitan borough councils (Chandler, 1987). These recommendations were implemented only after a battle royal against the old authorities, the London Labour Party and many others who had a real or perceived interest in preserving the old structure (Rhodes and Ruck, 1970).

- The Redcliffe-Maud Commission reported in 1969 and recommended the creation of single-tier unitary authorities over most of England and Wales, with three sets of two-tier metropolitan authorities in the largest provincial cities (Birmingham, Liverpool and Manchester). These recommendations were accepted with some modifications by the Labour Government but were rejected by Edward Heath's Conservative Government, which opted for a two-tier system throughout the country (Elcock, 1986a, chapter 2).

The costs involved in overcoming resistance to local government reorganisation were very great and the political costs in particular were hard for successive Ministers to accept. On the other hand, once reorganisation had taken place it became addictive. By the late 1970s, dissatisfaction among the largest cities which had been included in 'Shire' (non-metropolitan) counties in 1974 was considerable because the city councils had lost many of their major functions to the county councils. These cities – the 'Big Nine'[1] – led an agitation for control over education, social services and libraries to be given to the larger 'Shire' district councils and thus bring them more into line with the metropolitan borough councils which still controlled all these services. It would also restore the former county boroughs to something approaching their old status. This agitation persuaded Labour's Secretary of State for the Environment, Peter Shore, to develop proposals for 'organic change' (Department of the Environment, 1979) under which powers could be gradually transferred to the larger 'Shire' districts from the county councils where this was desired. However, these proposals were rejected by Mrs Thatcher after her election victory. A few years later, her government embarked on its own programme of change in the form of the abolition of the GLC and the metropolitan county councils in 1986 – which was achieved only after a major propaganda battle. These events demonstrate that local government reorganisation has been both costly and addictive.

The National Health Service. The NHS provides a slightly different example of the 'policy stress' which gives rise to structural change. When the Service was established in 1948, the medical profession resisted Aneurin Bevan's initial proposal that it should be controlled by local authorities (Willcocks, 1967). In consequence, the Service was organised along lines which largely separated hospital medicine from general practice and community health services, the last of which was controlled by local authorities through the Medical Officers of Health.

At that time, the main focus of health care was still on containing the 'great infections', such as tuberculosis, diptheria, poliomyelitis and whooping cough. More generally, the major concern of the NHS was with curative medicine, with public health being left mainly to local authorities and the Medical Officers of Health. The NHS's tripartite organisation separated the hospital, general practice and public health sectors from one another. Thus hospitals were managed by Regional

Hospital Boards (RHBs) and Hospital Management Committees (HMCs). General practitioners, dentists, opticians and pharmacists reported to Service Committees, which had a majority of fellow practitioners serving on them (Elcock, 1969a) and public health was the province of Local Health Authorities.

By the late 1960s, however, the pattern of disease had changed. The 'great infections' had largely been conquered and the major health care concerns were becoming increasingly conditions which cannot be cured but can be alleviated by the provision of care (Brown, 1975; Elcock and Haywood, 1980). Thanks to improved sanitation, better housing and healthier diets, as well as major inoculation programmes, the main focus of health care had shifted from curing acute infections to caring for the disabled and the chronically or incurably sick. The provision of such care for the increasing number of elderly people, the physically and mentally handicapped and the mentally ill, together with the chronically sick, demands co-ordination of health and social services provision which cuts across both inter-departmental and inter-organisational boundaries.

In consequence, by the mid-1960s the need for structural reorganisation to create an integrated health care system more suited to changing problems and priorities, was increasingly evident but – as with local government – resistance, not least from the medical establishment, made the task of preparing reorganisation blueprints both difficult and politically unrewarding. Failed attempts at reorganisation by Kenneth Robinson in 1968, who wanted to vest responsibility for the NHS mainly in local authorities and Richard Crossman in 1969 were followed by Sir Keith Joseph's success in reorganising the NHS between 1972 and 1974. This established a unified NHS structure with three tiers of management:

- The fourteen Regional Health Authorities (RHAs), which were based on the old Regional Hospital Board areas but which were given responsibility for the overall planning and resource allocation functions in the regions.
- 90 Area Health Authorities (AHAs), in whom the major responsibility for service provision was vested.
- District Management Teams (DMT): between one and four in each AHA.

RHAs and AHAs were controlled by boards of members, all formally appointed by the Secretary of State but drawn from three 'constituencies':

1. The Health Care Professions. Each Health Authority must include among its members a hospital doctor, a general practitioner and a nurse.

2. The local authorities in the region or area. From 1973 to 1976 four councillors had to be appointed to membership of each Health Authority. Between 1976 and 1980 they constituted a third of the total membership but in 1980 the number of councillors reverted to four. The 1989 NHS White Paper proposes that local authority representation should be eliminated entirely. However, it should be noted that council representatives have been drawn mainly from the local authorities which are responsible for the provision of the personal social services. Hence, when local authority representation is abolished, a useful co-ordination link will be lost.
3. Other persons who, in the Secretary of State's opinion, can contribute to the management of the NHS. These members include local business people, trade unionists, professional people and those involved in voluntary organisations in the health care sector, locally or regionally (Elcock, 1978).

These Health Authorities usually had between 15 and 20 members and – like the teams of officers who reported to them – were expected to reach their decisions by consensus.

As in the case of local government, this reorganisation had bred further instability. The Labour government of 1974-9 increased local authority representation, as noted above, only for it to be cut back again after 1979. By the end of the 1970s, the Merrison Royal Commission (1979) had recommended that one tier of management ought to be removed and in 1982, AHAs and DMTs were replaced by 192 District Health Authorities (DHAs), controlling areas usually intermediate between the old areas and districts. Again, the example of the NHS demonstrates that restructuring is addictive. The problems created or left unresolved by reorganisation generate pressure for further structural change which tends to be acceded to sooner or later.

Internal Reorganisations

Having discussed some major restructurings of national scope in which the administrative geography of the country as a whole has been radically changed, we can further explore the lessons to be learned about organisational change by looking at some examples of organisations which have changed their internal structures with a view to improving their performance or resolving problems originating in their environments. The first two sets of examples are drawn from local government, the third from the NHS.

Corporate Management in Local Authorities. Corporate management in local government, as advocated by the Bains Report (DoE, 1972) for English and Welsh local authorities and the Paterson Report (1973) in Scotland, was an attempt to alleviate one of modern local government's most serious and long-standing weaknesses: departmental and professional isolation, together with concomitant poor co-ordination. Corporate management attempted to do this mainly by altering the formal structures of local authorities, as outlined in Chapter 2, by establishing policy and resources committees, chief executive officers and other formal devices which would in turn encourage more cross-departmental working and better co-ordination (Stewart, 1971). The advice of corporate management's advocates was widely accepted by the new local authorities which were created by the 1972 Local Government Act and its 1973 Scottish equivalent. However, within a few years some corporate structures and offices were abandoned, sometimes in dramatic circumstances. For instance, Birmingham City Council dismissed its Chief Executive Officer and dismantled much of its corporate structure after the Conservative Party gained control of the council in 1978 (Haynes, 1980). Equally, some Labour-controlled authorities have dismissed their Chief Executives: dissatisfaction with this post has not been confined to one party. However, the Widdicombe Committee (1986) recommended that the appointment of a chief executive officer should be made a legal requirement for all councils. Other chief executives have acquired departmental responsibilities, contrary to the recommendations of the Bains Committee, because doing so gives them a more substantial job description, as well as enabling them to keep more closely in touch with the rest of the authority through the staff they control. Chief executives are likely to acquire 'topocratic' rather than service responsibilities. Some have taken control over their authorities' administration departments, which gives them control over the committee administrators, who are particularly well-placed to advise the chief executive of what the other departments and committees are doing. Others have combined the post of chief executive with that of treasurer, as in Oldham (Barberis and Skelton, 1987).

A similar comment can be made about policy and resources committees. Most local authorities now possess such a committee, albeit with a variety of titles but some have found its usefulness to be limited. In particular, where no one party has overall control of the council, it may be difficult or even impossible to use a policy and resources committee to develop coherent policies which are certain of adoption by other committees and the full council (Haywood, 1977; Barlow, 1987; Clements, 1987). A more common experience has been that recounted by a senior local authority officer who declared bluntly that 'The Policy and

Resources Committee is not "Policy and Resources" except at budget time – otherwise, it deals with trivia.' (Elcock, Fenwick and Harrop, 1988, p. 46) He went on to point out that in his authority, the main focus of co-ordination was the ruling Labour Group and its executive committee – thus echoing Victor Wiseman's conclusions about Leeds City Council in the early 1960s (Wiseman, 1963). Royston Greenwood and colleagues (1976) found in a survey of local authorities soon after reorganisation that policy and resources committees generally played one of three roles:

1. Co-ordination of the service committees' activities, in particular the provision of resources to them.
2. Commenting on the other committees' minutes, especially on their new proposals or activities.
3. Generating policies for implementation by service committees.

Only the third role gives the policy and resources committee the significance that the Bains and Paterson Committees said it should have, in that it should determine overall policies for implementation by service departments and committees. However, it was found only in a minority of local authorities, mainly those which had one-party policy and resources committees which could function as a local equivalent of the Cabinet. If the Opposition is present, the committee can quickly become little more than a dress rehearsal for the party debates at the full council meeting a few days later (Greenwood *et al.,* 1976, pp. 188-9; Elcock, 1986a, chapter 10).

One more example of how corporate management structures intended for one set of purposes end up serving different and more traditional ones is the role of Central Policy Units. Their advocates, notably Yehezkel Dror (1973) and Aaron Wildavsky (1969), proposed their establishment as a means of injecting detached, creative thought into government organisations. Thus Dror has argued that what is required is 'systematic thinking that is based on knowledge and oriented towards innovation on medium and long range policy issues.' (1973, p. 260) More vividly, Wildavsky wrote that new policies needed to be generated away from the day-to-day administrative pressures: 'By getting out of the fire-house environment of day-to-day administration, policy analysis seeks knowledge and opportunities for dealing with an uncertain future.' (1969, p. 190) In 1970, Edward Heath took such advice by establishing the Central Policy Review Staff to increase the policy-making capacity in central government (see Chapter 5). However, two of its former members have reported that its original strategic thinking role receded into the background within a few years of the Staff's foundation, to be replaced by preparing studies of specific issues (Blackstone and Plowden, 1988).

In general, corporate management has not succeeded in eliminating the problems caused by inter-departmental and inter-organisational co-ordination that have bedeviled British local government for most of its recent history. The Butler-Sloss Report on the child abuse scandal in Cleveland (1988) recorded numerous failures of co-ordination. Recent studies of the budgetary processes of local authorities have revealed that budgets are still mostly prepared by processes of incremental bargaining between the service departments and the treasurer, with other 'topocrats', especially the chief executive, assisting the treasurer to try and secure greater coherence in financial allocations, as well as more careful scrutiny of departmental estimates. However, 'managing the margins' still seems to be a fair summary of the nature of most budget-making processes (Elcock and Jordan (eds), 1987; Elcock, Jordan and Midwinter, 1989). Similarly, in 1978 Royston Greenwood and colleagues found that local authority budgeting is 'largely dominated by a weakly articulated theory of incremental decision-making', in which 'organisational budgetary complexity overwhelms the ability of decision-makers to examine anything more than the margins (increments) of expenditure and...this inevitably produces a budget close to that settled the previous year' (1978, p. 45), a finding amply confirmed by more recent studies.

However, although the impact of the formal structures introduced by corporate management has been limited, increased centralisation of control within local authorities has developed, partly under the pressure of the central government's insistent demands for spending cuts in the last decade or so. This centralisation of control has tended to occur outside most of the formal corporate structures of local authorities, however.

Two examples will suffice. The first has been the developing role of the leader of the council – an office now formally recognised in many local authorities, for example by its inclusion in their standing orders but whose development preceded such recognition. Leaders have become increasingly important in two ways. The first is that the leader, probably working closely with the chief executive, tends to arbitrate among the chief officers over policy disputes and resource allocation, to such an extent that he or she may become a 'Local Prime Minister' (Cousins, 1984). More generally, as Cynthia Cockburn (1975) and John Dearlove (1979) have noted, corporate management has tended to widen the gap between leading and back-bench councillors because the former become heavily involved in arbitrating inter-departmental disputes and making policy decisions, increasingly often as virtually full-time politicians.

Secondly, as more local authorities have developed 'governmental' approaches to their roles and functions (Greenwood and Stewart, 1974, see Document 10), in which they expect and are expected to exercise an 'all-round responsibility for the safety, health and well-being, both material and cultural, of people in different localities' (Redcliffe-Maud, 1969) council leaders have emerged as focal points for the co-ordination of inter-organisational as well as intra-organisational activities. For example, Humberside County Council's first leader, Councillor Harry Lewis, co-ordinated a major effort in 1975 by all those involved in the deep-sea fishing industry to bring to the attention of both Whitehall and the European Commission the dangers to the local economies of Hull, Grimsby and Fleetwood posed by the exclusion of British trawlers from their Icelandic fishing grounds. This involved co-ordinating the activities and campaigns not only of several local authorities but also those of the employers' organisations, unions and others in Humberside and Lancashire whose members' livelihoods depended on the deep-sea fishing industry.

Significantly, such initiatives are conducted largely outside the formal structures of committee and council meetings. This is especially the case with a second major development which has become evident as local authorities have altered their budgetary processes to cope with fiscal stress. A common response has been to establish informal central groups of leading councillors and senior offices to negotiate budget reductions with committee chairmen and service departments' chief officers (Elcock and Jordan (eds), 1987). These groups, which inevitably get dubbed 'The Star Chamber', 'The Gang of Four', 'The Magnificent Seven' and so forth, commonly play either or both of Greenwood's (1983) 'Spanish Inquisition' and 'Sweat Shop' roles. The first entails holding private meetings relatively early in the budget cycle to influence the preparation of the departments' estimates; the second is used to prune them towards the end of the process in order to reduce the impact of spending plans on rate or Community Charge levies (1983, p. 163). Financial pressure has therefore increased integration within local authorities through informal mechanisms, whose effect has been greater than that of more formal corporate structures.

Corporate management caused much excitement and not a little disruption of established working methods in local government when it was introduced but its formal devices are now often regarded sceptically, if not cynically. However, events have forced local authorities to increase central control of their activities by more informal teams made up of those councillors and officers who, individually and collectively, need to be able to influence, if not control, the work of their colleagues in the service departments and committees. The most important changes have therefore been those in actors' behaviour, not those in local authorities' formal structures.

'Going Local'. The second major form of structural change which has developed in local government has very different policy objectives in view, although one of its effects has also been to increase integration. 'Going Local', or (more formally) Decentralisation and Area Management, embraces a very wide variety of schemes which local authorities have developed to make their services more accessible to citizens and more responsive to their needs and wishes, as well as to encourage better collaboration among those responsible for delivering services. This last feature could be described (*pace* Lenin) as introducing corporate management 'from below' by encouraging cross-departmental working by relatively junior staff: 'street-level bureaucrats' (Lipsky, 1980), as opposed to corporate management 'from above' through the appointment of chief executive officers, management teams and policy and resources committees.

Decentralisation initiatives in local government can be explored in two main ways. We first discuss their historical development, then offer a simple classification of the wide range of initiatives that have been developed. To commence with the history, decentralisation has developed in three main phases:

1. The first was the development of 'urban parish councils' in the 1960s and 1970s. Thus Lambeth London Borough Council established Neighbourhood Councils throughout its area (Cockburn, 1975). However, the energy with which some of them pursued their local or sectional interests tended to alienate leading councillors. One politician declared of one neighbourhood council: 'Angell: I'd shoot the lot!' More seriously, they responded to such pressure by excluding the neighbourhood councils from access to the borough council's leading figures.

2. The second phase was the introduction, with the Department of the Environment's encouragement, of a series of area management initiatives in the mid-1970s. Their progress was monitored by a team of researchers from INLOGOV supported by the Department of the Environment (Harrop *et al.*, 1978). Most of these initiatives enjoyed at least some success although one, in Liverpool, was short-lived. However, few of the area management teams or committees succeeded in significantly influencing the policies of the local authority itself or obtaining a formal status in its structures. Exceptions were in Middlesbrough and Newcastle upon Tyne. However, in the latter city the priority area teams consistently complain about being unable to obtain sufficient attention or resources from the central decision-makers at the Civic Centre (Elcock, 1983).

3.   The recent development has been decentralisation as part of the 'New Urban Left' approach to local government which developed in the early 1980s among many Labour-controlled local authorities (Gyford, 1984). The 'New Urban Left' sought to develop alternatives in local government to Margaret Thatcher's free market policies, including alternative local economic strategies and decentralisation initiatives. The latter were intended to replace the remote bureaucratic paternalism of the traditional local government service with more accessible, responsive and therefore more popular service provision (Hoggett and Hambleton, 1987). These initiatives often involved the establishment of neighbourhood or community committees, consisting of ward councillors, community leaders and representatives of ethnic or other minority groups, to control or at least influence the activities of neighbourhood offices. Walsall Metropolitan Borough Council and Islington London Borough Council have been leaders in this line development (see Elcock, 1988; Islington, 1987; Hoggett and Hambleton, 1987).

Conceptually it may be easier to explain what is being attempted by comparing 'going local' in its various forms with F E Schumacher's proposals for the restructuring of large organisations (1973, chapter 16). Schumacher's book, *Small is Beautiful*, is justly famous for its advocacy of small co-operative firms and of the development of intermediate technology in Third World countries. However, he recognised that large organisations are an inevitable feature of developed societies, so he argued that they should be broken down into a series of 'quasi-firms', each of which should have a degree of autonomy, including control over its budget, subject only to general guidance from the organisation's centre. Schumacher drew an analogy with a balloon seller who holds the strings of all the balloons but each of which floats with its own positive buoyancy, whereas the traditional bureaucratic hierarchy is like a Christmas tree with the centre of attraction being the fairy at the top.

Organisational structures akin to 'quasi-firms' have emerged in three main forms in local authorities. They are:

●   Departmental Decentralisation, where a single department establishes teams of workers responsible for providing services to relatively small localities. This approach has gained increasing currency in social services departments, where it is often called 'patch' working (Payne, 1978). The size of the basic areas for which units are responsible for service provision is reduced and their number increased; thus Humberside County Council replaced its 17 area offices with 48

57

neighbourhood teams (Elcock, 1986b). In addition, the neighbourhood teams include workers from the fieldwork, residential and domiciliary case sectors of the social services which traditionally operate largely in isolation from one another. This improved co-ordination and reduced status conflicts within the department. Housing departments have become involved in a similar movement, establishing local housing offices where tenants can go to pay their rents, request repairs and seek housing advice. Often, repair teams are attached to these offices (see Hoggett and Hambleton, 1987). Tenants do not therefore have to travel to the Town Hall or Civic Centre to pay their rents, request repairs or seek help. Equally, the staff of the local offices are more in contact with the problems of the neighbourhood.

- Corporate Decentralisation entails the establishment of local offices staffed by members of several departments who work together to meet local needs. They will also develop liaison with other local service providers, such as local schools or police stations. They will often also advise callers on their welfare and other rights and again may have repair teams attached to them who can meet demands for repairs quickly.

- Political Decentralisation means that the neighbourhood offices are advised and supervised − even if not totally controlled and formally responsible to − committees composed of ward councillors, community leaders and minority group representatives. An element of public participation and representation is thus superimposed on the service provision structure. Many political decentralisation schemes are intended in particular to encourage increased participation in decision-making by racial and other minority groups.

This classification of approaches to decentralisation leaves much to be desired, although it does make the point that different structural forms are and ought to be related to the objectives sought from 'going local.' Thus departmental decentralisation should result in more sympathetic, appropriate service provision. Corporate decentralisation will also improve co-ordination and political decentralisation adds popular participation to the benefits sought. However, the classification ignores the question of what are the appropriate geographical areas for decentralisation schemes. It seems that coterminosity with ward boundaries makes success more likely, in part because the scheme is more likely to attract the support of ward councillors (Harrop *et al.*, 1978; Elcock, 1986b). It also does not deal with the extent to which powers should be devolved to the neighbourhood teams or offices. However, the classification does enable us to tease out the objectives being sought by 'going local': improved service delivery, better co-ordination or public participation. A last problem is that inevitably, the demands generated by the local offices or committees may conflict with authority-wide policies, such as racial or gender equality policies, as well as with the need to secure equity between localities. Thus equity may be the main concern of political leaders at the Civic Centre, while neighbour-hood committees press the claims of their localities.

Like other forms of organisational restructuring, 'going local' can impose significant costs on the local authority that carries it out and a decision to embark on a decentralisation scheme should be taken only after preparing a careful balance sheet of its likely costs and benefits, albeit that they may not be quantifiable (Elcock, 1988). Costs are likely to include the need to overcome internal resistance from staff and their trade unions, who may oppose changes in established working practices. Thus staff may object to being sent to work in neighbourhood offices where their contact with the public will be more frequent: they may see the new offices as places where people will be 'noisy and nosey'. (Quoted in Elcock, 1988, p. 43; see also Islington, 1987, p. 7.) An even more significant cost may be the need to secure radical changes in the attitudes and approaches of middle and senior managers to their supervision of local teams, which will require a significant investment in training to ensure that supervision is not so close that it stifles the neighbourhood workers' initiative and responsiveness. They must be left free to learn from their own mistakes (Elcock, 1986b, 1988; Islington, 1987; Hoggett and Hambleton, 1987).

The fundamental dilemma, however, is between allowing local discretion and thus giving scope for service providers to be more accessible, responsive and creative and maintaining sufficient central control to ensure efficiency and protect equity. Coherent resource allocation, effective internal audit and ensuring equity all demand a degree of central control. Hence each authority needs to make a managerial judgement – or more likely a series of such judgements – about what functions to decentralise and how far to go. F. L. E. Brech has written that

> Delegation through an organisational structure created by the determination and definition of responsibilities means that the firm's managers, supervisors and specialists have had mandated to them accountability for specific activities, operations or services. The basis of that mandate lies, on the one hand, in the firm's requirements for maintaining effective direction and management and on the other, in the skills, knowledge and experience that the nominated managers and others can offer. (1975, p. 49)

The balance between the benefits and disadvantages of centralisation and decentralisation respectively needs to be prepared carefully but in the

end, politicians must make a value judgement about whether decentralisation's benefits are worth the problems and costs it will cause. Two
decentralisation initiatives: the Newcastle Priority Area Teams (Elcock,
1984) and the decentralisation of Humberside County Council's Social
Services Department (Elcock, 1986b) succeeded at least partially because
leading politicians were firmly committed to them. In any case, some
activities are more suited to decentralisation than others: the provision of
services can beneficially be decentralised but resource allocation must be to
a large extent centralised.

A final problem about decentralisation arises in the public sector from
the requirement that public servants should be accountable to elected
representatives because decentralisation weakens the chain of
accountability that ends with the Minister or the committee chairman.
Thus, Richard Chapman has warned that the development of accountable
management in the Civil Service through the Financial Management
Initiative, followed by the establishment of departmental executive
agencies, may weaken the responsibility of Ministers to Parliament for
their department's activities (1988b and c). Equally, local authorities which
have developed decentralisation schemes have had to persuade councillors
that they should take up their constituents' complaints directly with
neighbourhood teams or offices, rather than using the traditional
hierarchical route of contacting the chief officer. This may be easier when
political decentralisation has been developed, with ward councillors sitting
on local committees, or where the neighbourhoods have been made
coterminous with ward boundaries. Overall, however, the benefits of
'going local' can be seen to be significant but the costs involved must be
borne in mind too.

Consensus Management in the NHS. A further aspect of the 1974 NHS
reorganisation, apart from the changes in its geographical structure, was an
attempt to change the balance of professional power within the Service by
introducing consensus management. Each RHA, AHA and DMT was
required to establish a Team of Officers, including the Administrator, the
Treasurer, the Medical and Nursing Officers, together with the Community Physician where appropriate. At the District and Area levels these
Teams were joined by two clinical representatives, one a hospital doctor
and the other a general practitioner. Decisions were to be made by consensus, each member of the team having a veto. The team of officers
reported to the Regional or Area Health Authority, as appropriate (DHSS,
1973).

The intention was to improve the status and influence of the
paramedical and administrative officers in the service relative to that of the

medical profession, as well as increasing the influence of general practitioners relative to that of the traditional power-holders in the Service – the consultants (Brown, 1979; Elcock and Haywood, 1980). This attempt to alter the traditional pattern of influence in the health care system by changing the formal management structures of the NHS was bound to encounter resistance. Criticism of the cumbersome decision-making and administrative processes which consensus management entailed soon developed. One Regional Medical Officer declared in 1978 that 'the consultative process inevitably blurs the crispness of decisions' (Elcock and Haywood, 1980, p. 90). An area administrator said that 'I'm not sold on consensus management but we make it work'. (Ibid.) In later years, criticism of unwieldy decision-making processes became more and more widespread and in 1982, Sir Roy Griffiths recommended that consensus management should be replaced by the appointment of general managers who would have overall responsibility for running the service at unit, district or regional level. This reform was quickly introduced and was coupled with the development of stronger accountability links between the Secretary of State and Health Authorities through annual review meetings. However, neither consensus management nor general management seem yet to have succeeded in more than marginally altering the behaviour of the professionals within the NHS or significantly reducing the primacy traditionally accorded to the consultants.

CONCLUSIONS

To accept Wildavsky's view that reorganisation is almost always an attempt to convince oneself and others that managers are tackling an organisation's problems and that they seek to do so by changing its internal structures because they can control them, whereas they have no control over its external environment, would be too cynical and too simplistic. However, the examples discussed here suggest that structural change is an approach to dealing with an organisation's problems which is fraught with major difficulties and dangers. Several main ones can be identified.

The first is that reorganisation is difficult to accomplish. It will be widely seen as a threat and will therefore be resisted by vested interests within the existing structure. If these interests are not placated or accommodated, overcoming their resistance may be difficult or even impossible. Thus the political benefits likely to accrue to a Minister who reorganised local government were insufficient to persuade successive Ministers to override the determined opposition of politicians and others who did not want the changes to take place. Again, both Aneurin Bevan and Kenneth Robinson gave way before the medical profession's opposition to vesting control over the NHS in local authorities. The alternative to overriding such resistance is to buy off the opposition with concessions or inducements but the concessions may have to be large and the cost of the inducements great. We can note also in this context the resistance of unions to local authority decentralisation initiatives because they entail changes in their members' locations and conditions of work. At least one such initiative has been blocked by union opposition and others have been achieved only after considerable efforts to persuade or induce union branches and their members to accept them.

Secondly, reorganisation is addictive; because those individuals or interests who are left dissatisfied by a reorganisation begin more or less at once to press for further reorganisation to meet their demands. Thus reorganising local government in 1974 led before the end of the decade to the proposals for 'organic change' and then to the abolition of the GLC and the metropolitan county councils in 1986. The abolition of the Scottish regional councils is being actively debated at the end of the 1980s and even the abolition of the remaining English county councils has been mentioned. Again, the NHS underwent further major structural surgery in 1982, together with changes in its management arrangements through the appointment of general managers and the introduction of annual review meetings. Corporate management structures in local authorities tend to be changed quite frequently.

Reorganisation invariably involves making a judgement which will not satisfy all those involved. Local authority decentralisation initiatives require senior officers and councillors to make judgements about the balance to be struck between maintaining central control and devolving powers to the neighbourhood offices and committees which give rise to tensions. Some councillors will persist in wanting to deal with their ward cases through the chief officer. Administrators will demand control over resource allocation and the retention of such administrative procedures as the writing of detailed reports on casework and the maintenance of hierarchical reporting relationships. In consequence, the judgements made at the time of decentralisation are likely to be challenged and changed in the future, leading to repeated, disruptive reorganisations.

One polytechnic in the north of England radically revises its structure once every five or six years and the institution has barely recovered from one reorganisation before the next begins. Furthermore, reorganisations seem to coincide with the arrival of new members in the Polytechnic's Directorate. A case of dramaturgy indeed!

Thirdly, reorganisation will be ineffective if it does not produce changes in the organisation's members' attitudes and behaviour. In the NHS, reorganisation did not produce policy change because it left established professional power-structures and their concomitant attitudes unchanged – in particular the power of the consultants was not diminished in 1974 (Brown, 1979; Elcock and Haywood, 1980; Haywood and Alaszewski, 1980). Again, local authority decentralisations must include, if they are to succeed, extensive retraining for middle and senior managers so that their behaviour alters, in that they allow the decentralised units discretion and freedom from detailed, critical supervision.

Lastly, reorganisation is costly, not only in money but also in terms of the disruption it causes. Financial costs include the appointment or promotion of managers to new, senior posts in the new structure as well as compensating or making redundant those who lose office through it. It was widely alleged in the mid-1970s that local government reorganisation had been formidably expensive because many senior officers won promotion to new jobs at higher salaries. The salaries of most of the top jobs in local government are in part determined by the population size of the local authority. Since most of the local authorities created in 1974 were much larger than their predecessors, many senior officers won very considerable salary increases, while those who did not get such promotion were kept on protected salaries when they had lost their former status and responsibilities. Certainly NALGO drove a hard bargain as its price for accepting reorganisation, in the form of tight rules controlling appointments to the new authorities and protection for those officers who did not get their equivalent posts in the new structure.

Again, NHS reorganisation was followed by frequent complaints about excessive bureaucracy and delay. The disruption caused by reorganisation can have a serious effect on the organisation's performance. In the late 1960s a senior railway manager claimed that frequent managerial restructurings of British Rail were damaging both the punctuality and the safety of the railway system: 'For many months the few top people who keep the momentum up are distracted from their proper job. Punctuality goes to Hell. Safety starts to slip. Don't reorganise! Don't! Don't! Don't!' (Fiennes, 1967, p. 113).

Structural change is therefore expensive, disruptive, addictive and its effectiveness is uncertain. None the less, there are valid reasons for restructuring, as demonstrated by some of our examples. They are:

● When restructuring is clearly the appropriate response to major anomalies or 'policy stress' in the existing structure. Thus, while local government reorganisation was hard to achieve, it was undeniably made necessary by economic, social and demographic changes. Similarly, changes in the predominant nature and incidence of disease and patterns of care rendered NHS reorganisation necessary.

- Where clear, realisable improvements in performance will be achieved or persistent problems solved by reorganisation. The local authority decentralisation initiatives do appear to have improved both staff morale and consumers' images of local authority services by making those services more accessible and responsive to citizens' needs, wishes and views.
- To achieve clearly defined goals, such as better co-ordination or more coherent resource allocation.

However, in all these cases, politicians and their advisers, as well as the managers of large organisations, must first satisfy themselves not only that reorganisation is an appropriate means of tackling the problems they have identified or of moving towards achievement of their goals but also that there is no cheaper, less disruptive means to these ends available to them. Incremental changes in structures are less expensive, less disruptive but as Richard Crossman found, easier for determined opponents to resist. Radical structural change is expensive and disruptive but may be steamrollered through over the heads of its opponents. Then, however, it may be rendered ineffective if behavioural changes do not follow the structural changes. If all these dangers are not recognised, reorganisation becomes a means for politicians and managers to deceive themselves but probably no-one else that they are taking effective action to solve the organisation's problems, as successive waves of ill-considered reorganisations have repeatedly demonstrated in modern British government. In consequence, we may seek more productive means to improve the performance of government. One way is to examine the processes by which public policies are made, implemented and reviewed, as well as the ways public services are administered.

NOTES

1. The 'Big Nine' were: Bristol, Derby, Kingston-upon-Hull, Leicester, Nottingham, Plymouth, Portsmouth, Southampton and Stoke-on-Trent.

CHAPTER FOUR
Processes

THEORIES AND PRACTICE OF POLICY ANALYSIS

At least since the end of the Second World War, students of politics and government, as well as some of its practitioners, have become increasingly concerned both to understand more fully the processes by which public policies are determined and executed and with seeking means to improve both the processes and the decisions that result from them. In consequence, by the end of the 1960s an increasing number of academics turned their attention to the development of policy analysis and postgraduate centres concerned with this activity were created in a number of universities. Among the most notable is the one established at the University of California's Berkeley campus, which is headed by Aaron Wildavsky. Another eminent policy analyst with a world–wide reputation is Yehezkel Dror, of the Hebrew University of Jerusalem.

Wildavsky has tended to debunk many of the pretensions of those who have advocated new methods or techniques to improve public policies (1969; 1973; 1980, for example) while Dror has urged policy-makers to think systematically about how policies are made and how those processes of policy formulation could be rendered more systematic (1973). Fundamental to the work of these and other scholars, however, is an assumption that policy analysis is both a descriptive and a prescriptive activity. It is concerned both with the extension of knowledge about how public policies are made and with their improvement. In doing this, policy analysis seeks to develop multi-disciplinary contributions to the improvement of public policies from the social sciences and to encourage the use of information technology, social statistics and analytical techniques.

At some risk of over-simplification, we can begin by arguing that the modern approach to policy analysis has developed from the recognition that two longer-established approaches to the making of public policies have proved to be in important respects inadequate. These approaches are commonly known as Incrementalism and Planning. In order that we may better understand the reasons for the development of policy analysis, we need first to explore the nature, advantages and disadvantages of these two approaches. In doing so, a major conflict emerges between politics and 'rationality'. This conflict has been encapsulated by Wildavsky in his phrase, 'Speaking Truth to Power.' (1980) On the one hand, the advice of experts and the deployment of statistical and other techniques produce policy proposals which their proponents will argue – more or less honestly and with greater or lesser justification – are well grounded in knowledge and analysis. These proposed policies may well not be acceptable to those who wield power and hence must approve them. In their turn they may force modifications to the policies in return for accepting them, which may destroy part, if not the whole, of their rational basis. Hence, experts may cease to support them. It follows, therefore, that a successful policy analyst must possess both a command of the means available to develop better policies and an accurate perception of the power-structures and power-holders whose co-operation must be assured before the policies can be adopted and implemented. This dilemma is reflected in the two other approaches we have mentioned, incrementalism and planning, but in each it is resolved in very different ways.

Incrementalism has been aptly described as 'The Science of Muddling Through' (Lindblom, 1959). In the article which has become one of the classics of the policy analysis literature, Charles Lindblom argued that incrementalism both accurately described how public policies are made and offers the best – because it is the only practicable – approach to making public policies. He advocates preparing policies by 'successive limited comparisons'. New policies are developed by making marginal changes from existing ones.

It is helpful to disentangle two slightly different forms of incrementalism. The first is admirably exemplified by Samuel Pepys' summary of a day in his work as a seventeenth–century civil servant: 'Reckoning myself to have come off with victory, because not overcome in anything or much foiled.' (Diary, 3 October 1666) This view still commands wide tacit support among civil servants – and probably many other public administrators as well. Senior civil servants regard their role as the confidential advisers of Ministers as being that of trying to ensure that their Ministerial master and therefore themselves, avoid trouble in Parliament or elsewhere. On such a view, survival is all. The task of civil servants and their Ministers is to keep the ship of state afloat without worrying about where she is heading. It is a view redolent of Michael Oakeshott's dictum that

> In politics men sail a boundless and bottomless sea. There is neither harbor for refuge nor floor for anchorage, neither starting point nor appointed destination. The enterprise is to keep afloat on an even keel; the sea is both friend and enemy; and the seamanship consists in using the resources of a traditional manner of behaviour in order to make a friend of every hostile occasion.
>
> (1962, p. 127)

Such an approach can be characterised indeed as 'muddling through'; simply coping with each demand, crisis or incident as it arises. Those public services, such as the police, the fire and the ambulance services, which must respond to emergencies as they are reported, would certainly recognise 'muddling through' as much of what their jobs consist of.

Somewhat more systematic is the making and development of public policies by incremental escalation. If flying a hundred bombing missions a day fails to subdue the Vietcong or the Sandinistas, then fly two hundred tomorrow and so on until you succeed. A common consequence of such approaches is an assumption that the application of more resources to an economic or social problem cannot but render a solution – or at least an improvement – more likely. Local authority service departments, for example, will seek extra funds and personnel each year because employing more teachers, social workers, policemen and so on must improve the quality of the service being provided to the public or to specific client groups – or must it ? Hence the characteristic tussle in preparing public sector budgets between 'advocates' who assume that extra spending will improve their services, while the 'guardians' must persuade them to have a care for the limits of the public purse.

Incrementalism is often regarded with suspicion by politicians and others – especially idealistic party activists – because it offers no hope for the fulfilment of the party manifesto, let alone the millennium (Benn, 1980). However, it does offer several advantages to policy-makers. Among the most important are:

- Realism: policy-makers will not set themselves impossible tasks or goals; indeed, if any goals are set at all, they are likely to be more or less marginal changes from the status quo.
- The level of resources available is easily taken into account and adjustments can be made if the resources available are increased or reduced, unless the change is so great that radical measures must be taken to make use of an opportunity or make severe spending cuts.

- Incremental policy-makers will value extra-rational processes highly, such as tradition, experience and 'hunches' based on either or both of these. As long as policies and environment remain relatively stable, the accumulated wisdom of experience is valuable.
- Since change is likely to be marginal, the level of consent to policies prepared incrementally is likely to be relatively high, since marginal changes are unlikely to generate extensive protests or opposition – unless, of course, existing policies are already unpopular.

These advantages are considerable and constitute the main reasons why many policy-makers are reluctant to cease making their policy decisions incrementally. However, there are major disadvantages to incrementalism as well, some of which become more severe as uncertainty increases, as well as new demands being made, for example about conserving or improving the environment or bringing about more equal treatment of minorities. The major disadvantages of incrementalism are:

- Radical change is impossible, even when it is needed to meet new demands or tackle new problems. Without their fund of accumulated 'wisdom', incremental policy-makers are lost.
- Creativity will tend to be discounted. New ideas or approaches will be rejected as 'unrealistic' or 'not in accordance with present policies.' Creative people working in such organisations will become frustrated because they are not used and cannot use their own abilities to the best advantage.
- Rational factors, including expertise, will be undervalued: 'Experts should be on tap but not on top.' One particular problem may be that responses to crises or demands from outside may be inadequate because the solution falls outside the established parameters of incremental decision-making. High rates of teenage illiteracy, for example, may be met with the incremental responses of employing more teachers when the real reasons for pupils' under-performance at school are poor housing and diet rather than the lack of sufficient teachers.
- Few if any goals are set for policy-makers and implementers to work towards. Policy-makers may become excessively preoccupied with their day-to-day survival. Political ideologies are not easily accommodated by incrementalism, unless they demand few changes from the status quo. However, some traditional Conservatives might regard this as an advantage. It can also produce much frustration:

...The central theme of consensus, or Whitehall policies which have been pursued by Governments of all parties for the last twenty years or more have been accompanied by a steady decline in Britain's fortunes, which has now accelerated into a near-catastrophic collapse of our industrial base. The Governments which followed these policies...have paid a heavy price in electoral terms, whilst those who furnished the briefing for the Ministers concerned have continued in power, subject only to the normal wastage occasioned by retirement at 60.   (Benn, 1980, pp. 64–5)

Tony Benn's bitterness has been echoed by other former Ministers who felt that their attempts to achieve their ideological goals were frustrated by a Civil Service which is wedded to incrementalism.

- Problems which are not soluble within the existing incremental parameters will be ignored or rejected, for example as being 'Not the Government's business.' Groups with non-conforming life-styles, such as tramps or gipsies, may find themselves disadvantaged because there is no policy basis for dealing with their problems upon which incremental decisions can be built. Positive discrimination in favour of such disadvantaged groups is likely to be resisted on the grounds (among others) that it would breach established views about equality and equity: equality is not regarded as a justification for giving extra resources to the disadvantaged.

- Feedback will be limited, unsystematic and probably weak. It will occur only in the form of complaints, protests or questions which simply become the next set of problems to be dealt with incrementally.

- Lastly, incrementalism cannot cope with policies which are radically unsatisfactory or inadequate, for example energy and industrial policies whose continuance will do unacceptable damage to the environment. A switch from energy consumption to energy conservation which is made incrementally will be slow, hesitant and uncertain. More environmental damage will result than if radical changes are brought quickly and this damage may be unacceptable – as it certainly will be if one accepts the gloomy prognostications of the Club of Rome that continued resources use and pollution will destroy life on the Planet Earth (1970, see also Solesbury, 1976).

Comprehensive rational planning lies at the opposite extreme from incrementalism. It was the approach advocated by H.A. Simon (1945, 1957; see also Self, 1974 (Document 12)). Policy planning is here to be considered essentially as a linear process of moving towards a defined objective by a series of progressive steps, rather like travelling by train from Newcastle to London, while passing through a series of intermediate stations. The steps are:

- First, the decision-maker is confronted with a given problem that can be separated from other problems or at least may be considered meaningfully in some degree of isolation from them. Problems are assumed, therefore, to be to some extent discrete entities.

- Secondly, the goals, the values or objectives to guide the decision-maker in tackling the problem must be defined and ranked according to their importance. Goals are thus assumed to be, at least in principle, clearly identifiable and susceptible of being ranked in a hierarchy of importance. Many organisations, indeed, try to prepare such hierarchies of long-term objectives, medium-term policies and short-term actions. Thus a public transport plan might contain a statement like the following:

Primary Aim: To secure a co-ordinated transport system which meets the needs of the community and ensure a choice between all modes of transport.
a). Public Transport:
i.   To secure within available resources an efficient public transport system which meets the needs of all members of the community.
ii   To achieve a balanced system of fares and finance which takes into account costs falling to the individual.
(Humberside County Council, 1975, para. 3:3:3, pp. 14–15.)

Within these general objectives and policies, specific actions to be taken in the immediate future included improving or creating road-rail interchanges, as well as producing, with the support of a county council subsidy, an integrated timetable showing all the road, rail and ferry services operating within the county.

- The various means available for dealing with the problem and achieving the objective must be examined, their costs and benefits must be established and compared. This may entail the making of more or less risky assumptions about likely consequences which cannot be certainly predicted (Keynes, 1923). Then,
- The decision-maker chooses the option that maximises achievement of the selected goals at the least probable cost. This option will then be implemented. However, there may be more than one optimal option – just as a Paretian welfare analysis may generate more than one optimum (Account based on Anderson, 1975).

Such a rational process of decision-making is ideal in theory but has been widely attacked as being impossible to carry out in practice. It has a number of clear advantages if it can be executed but its disadvantages indicate that success is unlikely, if not impossible.

The advantages of rational-comprehensive planning include the following:

1. It encourages the collection and analysis of comprehensive information before decisions are taken, which may also be useful for other purposes. Thus population projections prepared for a county structure plan also indicate concentrations of particular client groups in particular locations for whom resources and services ought to be provided – for example old people or children of school age.
2. Extensive use of expertise in data collection and preparation of the plan.
3. Apparent certainty: prospects for the future, such as the 3.8 per cent annual growth target set for the British economy in the National Plan (DEA, 1965), are set out. In consequence, other actors may behave in accordance with such declared intentions, thus both assisting the implementation of the plan and improving their own prospect of success – provided that others also comply with the plan.
4. It sets clear objectives and goals towards whose achievement all actors in and outside the planning organisation are expected to work. Again, if they all do so, the plan should produce benefits for most of them, especially if objectives and goals have been fully defined.
5. The process of preparing the plan should involve extensive communication and consultation with other organisations, which will also tend to secure their commitment to its execution.

However, there are so many difficulties with planning as thus conceived that today one of its main functions has become to serve as a 'straw man' which can easily be demolished. The problems include the following:

1. Plans once prepared are vulnerable to disruption or destruction by unexpected outside events or 'exogenous shocks': as Harold Wilson put it, plans are apt to get 'blown off course'.
2. Little or no scope is left for extra-rational processes which may produce better results than implementing the plan. This problem is closely related to:
3. The impossibility of measuring the effectiveness or otherwise of the plan because we cannot compare its results with what would have happened without it. At best we can try and make some informed guesses as to what difference the plan has made to policy outcomes.
4. Plans tend to be rigid, with the result that alternative policies which might be needed or desired are likely to be ignored or rejected while the plan is in force.
5. There is also a danger that a new 'high priesthood' of planners may be created: power becomes concentrated in the hands of a small expert elite whose decisions may subsequently become unacceptable to the

citizens affected by them, as happened to the Greater London Development Plan in the early 1970s. Aaron Wildavsky has warned that:

> Planners may …be everything. They may become the government and exert
> most of the public force in their nation. The vision they have of themselves is
> of a small but dedicated band that somehow enables the nation to meet goals by
> bringing it to its senses when necessary.
>
> (1973, p. 173)

6. The collection and analysis of data, followed by the preparation of the
   plan, is expensive in terms of money, time and manpower. The
   process may absorb the organisation's members to the exclusion of all
   else.
7. The goals set in the plan may become unattainable because of
   resource constraints.

Both in economic and environment policy, comprehensive-rational
planning of the kind discussed here is now largely discredited. Town and
country planners have largely lost their belief that they could create a new
and better environment – Le Corbusier's 'machine for living' – by
comprehensive redevelopment. Such beliefs inspired many of the city
centre redevelopments which took place in the 1950s and 1960s under the
combined pressures of the need to repair war damage and clear slums,
which have been widely denounced since for creating soulless urban
environments. It also underlay the Buchanan Report, *Traffic in Towns*,
which advocated altering town and city centres in order to separate
pedestrians from vehicle. Today, such approaches have few friends. The
Thatcher government announced in 1983 that it proposed to abolish the
Greater London Council and the metropolitan county councils in part
because they had been created in 'the heyday of a certain fashion for
strategic planning, the confidence in which now appears exaggerated.'
(DoE, 1983, para. 1:3, p. 2) Structure plans were threatened with abolition
because '…the preparation and approval or adoption of development plans
takes far too long, some of the policies they contain may be out of date
and their overall effectiveness can be greatly diminished.' (DoE, 1986,
para. 34, p.11) Certainly, public service managers do not seem commonly
to believe in the value of long-term planning: of seventeen public service
organisations in the north-east of England studied in 1988, only four were
attempting to develop strategic plans more than three years ahead; five had
abandoned planning beyond the coming budgetary year altogether.
(Elcock, Fenwick and Harrop, 1988, p. 21)

However, planning still has some defenders, although they all propose
its modification. Thus Amitai Etzioni (1968) proposed a 'mixed scanning'

approach in which only a few key or 'contextuating' issues would be dealt with by carrying out a full analysis, after which routine 'bit' decisions could be taken incrementally within the bounds of the key decisions. The key policies could be revised when dissent or difficulties indicate 'policy stress'. Again, Peter Self has urged that more attention should be given to 'problems and feasibility of planning on different scales and at different levels and the relation between planning and organisation.' (1974, p. 203) Planners can survive but only if they lower their sights.

Social learning

So far, we have considered policy processes in terms of a rather stark choice between rationality and incrementalism but increasingly, policy analysts have urged the adoption of approaches which attempt to combine the advantages of each, while avoiding at least some of the problems associated with planning and incrementalism. More specifically, such authors argue that both the opportunities becoming available to policy-makers, such as advances in information technology, as well as the problems they face, such as pollution and fossil fuel depletion, are increasing too fast to be dealt with incrementally (Dror, 1973). Planning, however, has become too discredited to offer an acceptable alternative to incrementalism. In consequence, a variety of different but related approaches have been advocated which may be described under the generic title, 'collective learning.'

One of the foremost advocates of such approaches is Yehezkel Dror, who proposed a highly sophisticated model of the policy process, which consists of four main stages. These in turn contain 18 detailed phases (1973, Appendix B). The model is needed, according to Dror, both because the problems facing policy-makers are increasing rapidly in number, range and severity and because the opportunities available to them to tackle those problems are also rapidly increasing. Neither the problems nor the opportunities can be coped with incrementally.

Dror's four stages of policy-making are:

1. Meta Policy-Making, including assessments of the values which should govern policies, the resources available, preparing strategies and designing or redesigning the policy-making system itself.
2. Policy-Making: establish goals, priorities and alternative means to achieve them. Predict the likely costs and benefits of the alternative policies determined in the first stage and evaluate them. Choose a policy from among the options identified in accordance with the

evaluation policy-makers have made of the costs and benefits of each.
3. Post-Policy-Making (Implementation): carry out and evaluate the results of the selected policy.
4. Feedback: assess the effects of the policy and prepare new options on the basis of that assessment. Return to Meta-Policy-Making or Policy-Making phase depending on whether the defects in the policy that have been revealed in the Implementation Phase are marginal or radical.

From this brief account of Dror's model, two other features in particular should be noted, in addition to its concern with improving the quality of the policy process as well as that of its outcomes. The first is that it contains many of the elements of the planning model we discussed earlier. It demands extensive data collection and analysis, as well as the systematic comparison of the costs and benefits of policy options. The second is that it is essentially cyclical, requiring as it does systematic evaluation from which a further round of the process commences. In considering the policy–making process as a cycle, Dror's approach draws upon structural–functional and cybernetic models of the political system, which postulate a system which converts inputs to outputs and include feedback loops by which policy–makers learn from the mistakes they made in the past or alter policies which have undesirable or unacceptable consequences (Easton, 1965; Deutsch, 1966; Dunsire, 1973; 1989).

This cyclical approach has been adopted by other writers. Donald Schon asked,

> How can we, as a society or a nation, learn to identify, analyse and solve our problems? …Government as a learning system carries with it the idea of public learning, a special way of acquiring new capacity for behaviour in which government learns from the society as a whole. In public learning, government undertakes a continuing, directed enquiry into the nature, causes and resolutions of our problems.   (1975, p. 109)

Like Dror, Schon urges that this must entail changes in processes as well as decisions and this entails systematic thinking about a number of issues. These include:

1. The emergence of 'ideas in good currency': understanding how issues arrive on policy-makers' agendas, recede from them or fail to reach them.
2. Overcoming 'dynamic conservatism' by getting new ideas taken up by people who possess power.
3. Dealing with crises without reinforcing 'dynamic conservatism.'
4. Identifying 'vanguard roles': people who generate new ideas, like

inventors, artists, prophets, 'muckrackers'. (Schon, 1975, pp. 123–4)

5. Diffusing ideas and struggling to gain their acceptance.
6. Responding to pathologies of 'ideas in good currency': seeking to overcome obstructions to their acceptance and implementation, leading to further development of policies to secure better implementation of the ideas.

Schon concludes that this public learning process 'demands a shift in the social system of government, which now serves and reinforces stable, compartmentalized policy. The concept of a government project system made up of task forces and competence pools, serves only to illustrate what government as a self-transforming system might become.' (Schon, 1975, p. 166) Such a preoccupation with process leads to such declarations as Tony Eddison's 'Planning is more important than plans' (1973). Public policies can best be improved by changing the processes by which they are developed, implemented and reviewed.

Most students of policy analysis would now accept as axiomatic a cyclical account of the policy process, which disaggregates its stages and enables us to develop means to improve each of them. Each author produces his or her own cycle but they all contain the components shown in Figure 4.1, which describes a system which can learn systematically both from its environment and its own experience. The stages of the cycle can be addressed in turn and the implementation stage in particular has generated a large literature which discusses the difficulties that frequently result in incomplete or even non-implementation of declared policies – the phenomenon frequently dubbed the 'Implementation Deficit' or 'Implementation Gap.' (See, for example, Barrett and Fudge (eds), 1982.) It raises a central issue of how far policies emerge from the decision-makers at the top of an organisation or are generated by the actions of 'street-level bureaucrats' who are trying to meet citizens' needs and demands (Lipsky, 1980). Equally, policies generated at the top may fail to be implemented if 'street–level bureaucrats' regard them as impracticable or unacceptable.

Another area of increasing concern is the review or evaluation phase – a concern reflected in the development in many countries of lists of performance indicators and other evaluative techniques.

First, we need briefly to assess the strengths and weaknesses of the public or collective learning approach and in particular to see how far it succeeds in combining the advantages of both planning and incrementalism, while avoiding the problems associated with each of them. We can begin by setting out the advantages and problems of collective learning in the same format as that adopted when we discussed the two earlier approaches.

AGENDA-SETTING
(Party manifestoes,
crises, pressures
group demands)

POLICY FORMULATION
(Identify options,
carry out research,
compare options)

REVIEW
(Monitor and assess
effects of policy

POLICY SPECIFICATION
(Select option, Pass
Legislation, Regulations)

IMPLEMENTATION
(Issue instructions to
execute policy, secure
its execution)

Figure 4.1   The Learning System

There are eight main advantages of the public learning model, which
may be summarised as follows:

1. It can take account of both rational and extra-rational processes.
    Traditions, 'hunches' and experience can be fed into the policy cycle,
    as can statistical projections or sample survey results.
2. It can allow radical changes in parameters to be made, especially since
    the policy preparation phase ought to include reassessments of the
    process as well as of existing policies. The possibility of major
    environmental changes or exogenous shocks is explicitly recognised in
    the model. Both Etzioni (1968) and Dror (1973) recognise the need
    for major, 'contextuating' decisions to be taken from time to time.
    We shall explore ways of doing this in Chapter 5.

3. It encourages strong and systematic feedback.
4. It will establish realistic, relevant objectives both by encouraging thorough research and investigation in the policy preparation and policy specification phases and because the impact of existing policies will have been systematically evaluated.
5. During the cycle, resource limitations or opportunities can be taken into account and policies adjusted accordingly.
6. It encourages the extensive use of expertise, which can be consciously applied in the successive stages of the process.
7. It allows continuous adjustment to meet changing needs or circumstances.
8. Lastly, it ensures effective collection and analysis of information.

Alas! Since Adam and Eve were ejected from the Garden of Eden, nothing has been perfect and this approach also has several disadvantages, which are:

1. It is unlikely to set policy-makers, implementers or citizens inspiring goals or objectives to aim at, since the objectives that are set will tend to be tied closely to assessments – albeit thorough ones – of what is fairly immediately achievable.
2. Similarly, the collective learning process may not easily accommodate political ideologies, especially where they involve making commitments to the ultimate achievement of ideal states of society, since the results of learning processes which conflict with progress towards the ideal are likely to be rejected by believers in the ideology. The treatment of science and scientists in the Soviet Union during Joseph Stalin's rule is in point here: Lysenko's biological theories were accepted not because they were true but because they were ideologically sound.
3. Like planning, the collective learning approach may strengthen the power of the executive relative to that of the legislature and the citizenry because its size and developing expertise will make it hard for legislators or citizens to challenge it (see Document 11). On the other hand, collective learning encourages sensitivity to the government's environment, which includes citizens and their elected representatives.
4. The learning system may easily revert to 'dynamic conservatism' and incrementalism, unless its systematic learning processes are consciously maintained and supported.

None the less, public learning cycles do represent what public policy-makers do, although they may not be aware that they are doing it – just as

M. Jourdain was not aware until his tutor told him that he had been speaking prose since early childhood. It also provides pointers towards means whereby policy-making, implementation and evaluation alike can be improved.

THE POLICY PROCESS: SOME KEY ISSUES

Means of improving public policies by developing the processes by which they are made and carried out may conveniently be considered in the light of the three pervasive problems that confront all students of the policy-making cycle, to which we gave some consideration in Chapter 2 (Elcock and Stephenson, 1985, p. 5). They are: reducing uncertainty, increasing creativity, and promoting collective learning.

Reducing Uncertainty

In the first two stages of the learning cycle as illustrated in Figure 4.1, one of the main needs is to acquire as much information as possible in order that policy decisions may be as soundly based as possible on reliable data. However, the achievement of complete certainty will rarely if ever be possible. In any case, limitations on time, money and manpower will prohibit its achievement in practice. Furthermore, there comes a point at which maximising certainty ceases to be cost-effective. Thus, the difference in cost between a sample survey which, if properly conducted, offers up to a 98 per cent probability of the sample being representative of the population to be studied and carrying out a census of the entire population, is usually huge. Hence, policy-makers will almost invariably be prepared to accept a high probability of accuracy at far less cost.

In the late 1960s, the Institute of Operational Research developed a simple model of the uncertainty reduction process, which is helpful in identifying the different sources of uncertainty and proposing means of reducing it (Friend and Jessop, 1969). The model is illustrated in Figure 4.2. It suggests that there are three principal sources of uncertainty, which should each evoke an appropriate response. Thus, uncertainty about information indicates a need for more research in order that policymakers may move nearer to the 'bullseye' of maximum certainty. Again, uncertainty about the values which policy-makers are seeking to realise entails requesting guidance from them, probably by asking politicians such as Ministers, committee chairmen and members, or the chairman of the health authority, what values they wish to pursue. Uncertainty about the intentions or actions of other organisations leads to a request for increased communication and co-ordination.

In their later writings, the Institute of Operational Research (later COOR) team proposed that inter-organisational co-ordination could be promoted through the development of 'reticulist' roles by some individuals, groups or organisations. Reticulists facilitate communication and co-ordination through the deployment of negotiation and communication skills (Friend, Power and Yewlett, 1977). They sit at the crossroads, as it were, of inter-departmental and inter-organisational communication and their role is to improve both. Units and departments concerned with strategic planning and management will commonly assume the reticulist role.

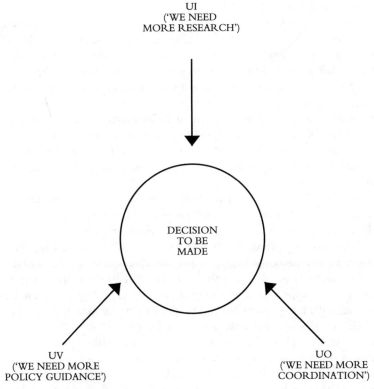

Figure 4.2   Decision Model

Creativity

A second way to improve public policies is to inject into the policy preparation and policy specification phases of the process more sources from which novel or unconventional ideas can be generated or additional information can be obtained. In sum, the object here is to inject more creativity into the process. In the traditional, incremental policy process, creativity is at a discount. New ideas or information will tend to be frozen out as irrelevant, subversive or even insane by policy-makers and (even more) administrators who do not wish their own or their masters' dynamic conservatism to be disturbed. One is reminded of the Cardinal-Archbishop of Milan's response to Galileo's request that he should look through his telescope: 'It might disturb my faith.' Again, in the comprehensive-rational planning model, creativity is more acceptable when the plan is being prepared but will probably be rejected if it comes in the form of a challenge to established, agreed plans which have already been written and are being implemented.

One device which is frequented advocated as a means of increasing policy-makers' creativity is the establishment of a 'think tank': a small unit within the organisation which is at least to some extent insulated from its day-to-day administrative and managerial preoccupations so that it can consider in a detached manner the issues the organisation faces. Also, it should contain at least some members who are drawn from outside the organisation and hence are not bound by its existing ideas and interests. Nowadays, many public and private sector organisations have created 'think tanks' – albeit with a bewildering variety of titles and roles. There is considerable lack of agreement and clarity as to what their roles ought to be.

Yehezkel Dror has provided a detailed blueprint for the establishment of 'think tanks'. Following the example of the RAND Corporation in the United States, which '...emerged as an independent, non–profit research institute, working mainly for the US Air Force but enjoying a significant degree of autonomy' (1973, p. 261), Dror advocates the establishment of '...organisations for policy analysis (which) can be institutionalised and located with respect to other organisations' (Ibid., p. 263). They must be professionally independent but also be able to win the trust of their clients, while maintaining their links with outside research institutes and other 'think tanks.' There is, also a need to create within policy-making organisations '...units for overall system management, meta–policy-making and comprehensive policy-making.' (Ibid., p. 264) They may have one or more of three roles: serving as professional staffs offering policy advice; providing surveys and knowledge, as well as policy-oriented research.

For local authorities, Dror has advocated the establishment of central policy units. However, the introduction of policy analysis has much wider implications for local authorities or other agencies which develop it:

> Usually, new units are necessary. But the connection of such units with actual policy–making is a very complex political and bureaucractic operation, the success of which cannot be taken for granted. Changes in the training of senior officials, new advisory services for the Council, formalisation of deliberation patterns by the Chairman and even courses for the senior politicians – these are among the possibly–needed innovations in the broad policy–making system if one wants actually to use policy analysis broadly and deeply.
>
> (Dror, 1975, p. 45)

Thus a 'think tank' can only succeed if its establishment forms part of a wider set of changes in attitudes and working methods among the councillors and senior officers who have the main responsibility for developing a local authority's policies.

The need for such a wider view, as well as the problems to which the creation of a 'think tank' gives rise, have been explored in our discussion of the establishment and work of the Central Policy Review Staff. We saw that the Staff's role became in the main to provide the two kinds of advice which Christopher Pollitt (1974) defined as programme advice on the overall balance of the government's programmes and process advice: analyses of particular problems or policies, which were intended to propose the most cost-effective means to achieve the government's policy objectives. Only about 5 per cent of the Staff's work was published but these reports and others generated considerable debate and publicity. In the context of increasing creativity in government, the CPRS's right to deliver a collective brief to the Cabinet when it felt that a department's proposals to the Cabinet as set out in the Cabinet Papers were inadequate or mistaken, or where the Staff felt that an alternative view should be put to Ministers, was important. The range of policy options available to Ministers would therefore be increased – one might think this form of creativity would be especially valuable in a Civil Service which tends to be dominated by 'the pressure to agree' (Jay, 1968) in which departments present reports whose conclusions have the support of a Whitehall consensus, whether or not they offer the best proposals or even a good solution to the problem.

On coming to office for the second time, Harold Wilson felt a need for more politically sympathetic sources of advice than that available from the politically detached CPRS. He recognised, however, the value of having access to independent, creative advice, so he established a No. 10 Policy Unit, initially led by Professor Bernard Donoughue of the London School of Economics and Political Science, which consisted of Labour Party supporters who possessed relevant expertise and talents (Jones, 1987).

At around the same time, Margaret Thatcher and Sir Keith (now Lord) Joseph established the Centre for Policy Studies to provide the Conservative Party, which was then in Opposition, with policy advice based on free market economic liberal principles. In this it joined with the Adam Smith Institute and the Institute of Economic Affairs in being able to offer policy advice to the new Leader of the Opposition. This advice was used initially to construct the 1979 Conservative election manifesto and these private 'think tanks' have since played crucial roles in developing such policies as the Community Charge and the proposal to establish privately run remand centres. At the end of the 1980s a former CPRS member, Baroness Blackstone and others established a left-wing 'think tank', the Institute for Public Policy Studies, along similar lines.

On her accession to office, Margaret Thatcher retained the No. 10 Policy Unit but obviously she replaced the Labour incumbents with her own supporters. Its role has also become more diversified, with the result that some observers have argued that Mrs Thatcher has effectively established a Prime Minister's Department (Weller and Jones, 1983). Hence, the number of 'think tanks' which are now involved in providing analyses and ideas to British Governments has increased quite markedly over the last twenty years. Several lessons for the role of creativity in modern government can be gleaned from their activities, which include the following:

- The need for independent advisers to be given firm support by political leaders if they are not to be rejected or ignored by established administrators. Edward Heath's firm support for the CPRS ensured that it was accepted as a necessary part of the Whitehall policy-making system, unlike Harold Wilson's 'Irregulars' in the 1960s, who were largely excluded from the policy-making process by the established civil servants (Brittan, 1969).

- The dilemma policy advisers in 'think tanks' face between providing objective advice and having to take account of the government's ideological stance. The civil servants who served in the CPRS wanted to maintain their traditional political neutrality, although its outside members were not so bound. They would tend to offer advice based on research and expert knowledge whether or not it was acceptable to a Government of a particular political complexion. Harold Wilson, James Callaghan and Margaret Thatcher all felt a need to have access also to politically sympathetic policy advice and therefore maintained their own policy units at 10 Downing Street for this purpose. The existence of the Prime Minister's Policy unit inevitably weakened the position of the CPRS (Jones, 1987).

• A policy unit like the CPRS must inevitably put itself at risk by telling rulers the things they do not wish to hear.

None the less, the 'think tank' concept continues to flourish. First, a number of policy advice organisations exist which offer advice based on a variety of ideological assumptions. Some organisations which play the 'think tank' role are of relatively long standing, such as the Fabian Society and (in varying forms) the Policy Studies Institute on the moderate left and the Institute of Economic Affairs on the right. Others have developed more recently, most notably the Centre for Policy Studies and the Institute for the Study of Public Policy – the left-wing 'think tank'. Many other public service organisations have also maintained 'think tanks', although there seems to be some confusion about what role they should play. Furthermore, their role may have changed as those organisations have had to cope with unremitting demands to reduce their spending since 1979. A recent study (Elcock, Fenwick and Harrop, 1988) has revealed that policy units might be expected to play one or more of three roles:

1. Policy Initiation: the preparation of strategic plans and policy proposals. However, as with the CPRS, other pressures have tended to squeeze out this function. Spending restrictions have reduced opportunities for policy innovation and frequently cuts have resulted in the members of policy units being diverted to more routine tasks, especially when they have been affiliated both to the policy unit and a department.
2. Co-ordination of departments' activities, which is often hard to achieve because of departmental and professional insularity; thus one manager declared that 'We have the trappings of corporate management but not the reality. ...There are no common objectives and there is conflict – departments safeguard their own interests.'
3. Fire-fighting, where the policy unit becomes preoccupied with developing responses to particular demands or crises. The CPRS's increasing preoccupation with process advice rather than programme advice indicates a similar shift in role under pressure.

Hence, there is considerable uncertainty about what 'think tanks' should or should not be used for, as well as difficulty for them in winning acceptance by both politicians and administrators. Creativity is still a difficult value to insert into public sector bureaucracies which are preoccupied with the demands of accountability and the need to cope with immediate pressures.

The Promotion of Learning

This third keystone of policy analysis will be discussed only briefly here, because many of the issues to which it gives rise will be explored in the next chapter. The need here is mainly to develop the feedback or evaluation aspect of the policy-making cycle and we can note two examples of attempts to develop systematic learning through evaluation.

The first was the introduction of Programme Analysis and Review (PAR) at the same time as the CPRS was created. The intention of PAR was to secure the detailed review of departmental policy programmes by teams consisting of civil servants and external businessmen advisers. The beginning of the process was intended to be 'explicit statements of the objectives of expenditure in a way that would enable a Minister's plans to be tested against general Government strategy.' (Cmnd 4506, para. 50, p. 14) Hence,

> The teams of businessmen based in the Civil Service Department are well advanced in developing a system for regular reviews which would provide more and better information. These reviews …would be designed to provide Ministers with an opportunity to identify and discuss alternative policy options which can be explored in greater depth before final decisions are taken on the expenditure programmes.
>
> (Ibid., para. 51, p.14)

One problem becomes apparent immediately: that reviewing policy options 'in depth' entails a considerable commitment of time and resources if it is to be carried out properly. If the Government's entire programme were to be thus reviewed, either large numbers of PAR teams would have been required – including the appointment of a large number of outside members – or the process of reviewing all the government's programmes would be very protracted.

However, this was not the rock on which PAR foundered. There were two other major obstacles to it which were never overcome. The first was how the PAR teams were to gain access to discharge their role in an administrative system which has had long experience of neutralising or excluding outside advisers and scrutineers. The second was the opposition of the Treasury, which believed that the responsibility for ensuring the financial probity and efficiency of the government's business belonged to it alone. In order to assuage the Treasury's opposition, it was given control over PAR, with the result that it never developed beyond a small-scale review of departmental programmes (Heclo and Wildavsky, 1974). It was abolished in 1979 and replaced by first the Rayner Scrutinies, which were more closely focused on the need to increase efficiency and later by MINIS and the Financial Management Initiative (FMI) (see Gray and Jenkins, 1985).

In recent years, however, the systematic review of the achievements of government programmes has come back into fashion, especially after the establishment of the Financial Management Initiative in 1982. Subsequently, evaluation studies were developed by the Joint Management Unit in the Cabinet Office. This was originally the Financial Management Unit which directed the FMI. It is now part of the Office of the Minister of the Civil Service (OMCS). These evaluation studies grew from the FMI, hence we need first to state the FMI's main objectives, which are that all managers in the Civil Service ought to have:

1. A clear view of objectives and the means to measure performance in relation to these;
2. A well-defined responsibility for making the best use of resources (including value for money);
3. The information (particularly about costs) needed to exercise this responsibility effectively (Cmnd 8616, para.13, see Document 6 and Gray and Jenkins, 1985).

Arguably, these propositions constituted a resurrection of the Fulton Committee's (1968) recommendation that the Civil Service should adopt accountable management as one of its organising principles. A manager should have responsibility for the proper and effective discharge of a set of administrative tasks and in doing so, should also be responsible for the most efficient possible use of the resources entrusted to him or her for meeting the objectives. In consequence, the manager acquires a degree of autonomy, so long as his or her superiors remain satisfied with the way the tasks are being carried out and the resources used.

This concept has now been carried further by the establishment of departmental executive agencies, which it is intended will eventually be responsible for most Civil Service work – perhaps eventually for 95 per cent of it (Efficiency Unit, 1988, Document 7). This proposal revives another Fulton recommendation, that government functions should be 'hived off' to formally separate organisations which are responsible for defined blocks of work or the provision of public services (1968, paras 188–191).

However, this is to anticipate other subjects. Meanwhile, in the context of social learning we need to note that the Joint Management Unit has emphasised the need to develop systematic methods of evaluating government services. The Unit has introduced a rule that all new proposals put to the Cabinet must include a statement of how they are to be evaluated. The approach to evaluation has itself been developed by the JMU to a high level of sophistication. Figure 4.3, which was taken from a

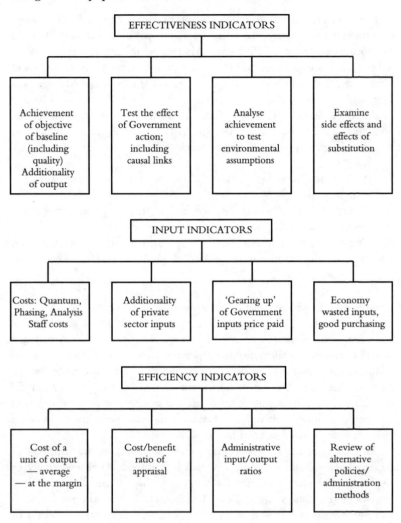

Figure 4.3   Some Topics for Evaluation

JMU report, shows that a range of indicators are being developed to measure a programme's effectiveness and efficiency, as well as the resources being put into it. The Unit has also published an Evaluation Handbook for managers. This development is related to the increasingly widespread use in public administration of performance indicators, which we discuss in Chapter 7.

CONCLUSIONS

The policy cycle, then, raises three key issues of uncertainty, creativity and learning which have been addressed in a number of innovations adopted in various parts of the British governmental system over the last twenty years. The move away from policy planning and towards a preoccupation with the 'Three E's may not only restrict and diminish the scope of public policy-making, as well as threatening public accountability by causing politicians to neglect the wider policy and ethical issues with which they ought to be concerned. It may also cause politicians and senior public managers to neglect the need to determine where they and their organisations are heading. Hence we discuss the role and nature of strategies for public organisations in the next chapter.

CHAPTER FIVE
Strategies

PROCESSES AND THE IMPORTANCE OF STRATEGY

Many of the proposals for the improvement of public policy-making processes we discussed in the last chapter were developed in the hope of improving the strategic plans of government organisations. Although as we shall see later, the necessity for planning in government is now a matter of political controversy, it used to be widely accepted that it is both necessary and desirable. However, the processes by which plans are prepared, as well as their contents, have aroused a great deal of dispute.

The problems can be illustrated by a brief account of the recent history of town and country planning (Cullingworth, 1967, Allison, 1975; Elcock, 1979a and 1986a, chapter 10). From its beginning in the Garden City movement of the late nineteenth century, planning has always involved attempting to relate individual decisions about buildings and environments to wider policies about what kind of environment people want to create. Under the 1947 Town and Country Planning Act, local planning authorities (then county and county borough councils) were required to prepare development plans for their areas. They were intended to cover land use in each county or county borough comprehensively but delays in their preparation occurred within the local planning authorities because of the magnitude of the task of collecting information about existing and prospective land-use throughout the area. After collecting this mass of information, of course, planning authorities needed to decide what they wished the future of each area to be. Furthermore, these development plans had to be approved by the appropriate government department, a process which itself took several more years. In consequence, development plans were frequently out of date before they came into force. In the late

1960s, therefore, the planning system was revised as a result of the work of the Planning Advisory Group, which Richard Crossman had established in 1965.

The Planning Advisory Group was charged to review the planning system and recommend ways of producing development plans which would both command public support and could be produced more quickly. The system which emerged and was enacted in the Town and Country Planning Acts of 1968 and 1971, established two main types of plan: Structure Plans and Local Plans. Structure Plans were to be general statements of land-use and transportation policies prepared by local authorities and approved by the appropriate Minister. They cover a 20-year period but they are supposed to be revised every five years. They set out general policies rather than specific proposals. The five-year review cycle would encourage the continuous revision of Structure Plans to meet changing circumstances, political values and public opinion. In the 1970s, the Department of the Environment encouraged the adoption of selective, 'Key Issue' approaches by county councils preparing Structure Plans (DoE, 1974). This allows their efforts to be concentrated on dealing with a limited number of the most important matters before them, rather than the energies of council members and officers being dissipated over a wide range of issues many of which do not need immediate attention. Structure Plans are subject to approval by the Secretary of State for the Environment. Within their context, are prepared local plans of various kinds (Local Plans and Subject Plans, for example) which set out detailed policies for the development or conservation of specific areas, such as a town, a village or a housing estate, or for the regulation of a particular activity like intensive livestock farming. Such plans may include the development of particular villages, the desired approach to conservation in a medieval town or the control of intensive livestock units which generate traffic and pollution problems. Local Plans are required to be consistent with the Structure Plan and must be certified as such by the Structure Planning Authority: the county council. Local Plans do not, however, have to be approved by the Secretary of State, so that detailed local planning is no longer subject to Ministerial approval. However disagreements among local planning authorities may be referred to the Secretary of State for resolution. Equally, applicants whose planning applications are rejected because they are not in accordance with Structure and Local Plans may appeal against that refusal to the Secretary of State, who may overturn the policies laid down in such plans if he grants a series of planning appeals which breach them (see Stephenson and Elcock, 1985, chapter 5 for an example).

The example of Structure Planning, to which we will return later, illustrates the three main features of strategic policy planning. Strategic plans need to be:

- *General.* They set out the rules which the responsible public authority intends to apply when it makes specific decisions within its sphere of competence, as well as expecting subordinate authorities to do likewise. However, the purpose of strategic plans is not the resolution of specific issues or cases. In Britain, the law requires that each individual case must be tested against the policy on its merits to see whether it constitutes a case for exemption from the general rules (see Elcock, 1969a, pp. 7–10) but it is none the less often desirable to make general statements of policy against which particular cases can be tested. To do this will bring at least two sets of benefits.

  For politicians and officials, the existence of general policies speeds up the decision-making processes on individual cases, since all they need to do is to test the specific case against the established policies, instead of having to consider each proposition as requiring a new decision. Equally, for citizens and organisations who are considering actions in the planning area, declared planning policies create an area of certainty within which they can make their own decisions. If an entrepreneur knows that the local planning authority is unlikely to approve a planning application in one location but will approve it nearby, he or she will choose the path of least resistance, unless there is a major reason to challenge the policy – which is likely to entail a lengthy, costly appeal procedure of whose outcome he or she cannot be certain.

  Furthermore, the promulgation of such general policies relating to, for instance, the preferred location for industrial development, will probably in turn lead public or private utilities to provide services to the preferred location, such as roads, sewers and energy supplies. In consequence, our entrepreneur will find when he accepts the policy that the appropriate services are easily available at the sites which have been designated for the proposed use. Hence, strategic planning makes action easier as well as inhibiting development in those areas where the council deems it to be inappropriate.

- *Long Term.* Strategic plans will seek to extend policy statements beyond the immediate preoccupations of public servants and others, in order to indicate to administrators and the public alike how policies and events are likely to develop in coming years. Thus, many industrial and commercial developments have lives of ten, twenty or more years and it will be helpful to those proposing such developments to know how the area is expected to change over a fairly long time. Equally, public investment decisions to build new schools, roads, hospitals or refuse disposal plants take years to complete and will be used long after they have been completed. They are more likely to be built where they will be most useful if policy-makers have first acquired knowledge about likely future population and economic trends, as well as making decisions about what they think ought to happen over a period of up to twenty years. These are the two main attributes of strategic planning: the projection of trends into the future and setting policies for future development. Strategic planning hence involves both the extension of knowledge and the taking of decisions which have long-term implications.

Although forecasting is always subject to uncertainty, long-term trends can be predicted in ways which are useful for policy- and decision-makers. Demographic change is one example. Declining birth-rates and increasing longevity in developed countries indicate that in future an increasing number of elderly people will make progressively heavier demands on health and social services. Furthermore, they will have to be supported by a smaller proportion of economically active people. Again, old people or families with young children may be concentrated in particular localities, where services need to be provided for them. Identifying such likely stress points through population projections will help determine where new schools and hospitals, for example, need to be built.

Financial planning, similarly, can reduce uncertainty about the longer-term future. Decisions taken in the current budgetary year commit resources for future years. These commitments can be identified and aggregated to indicate the resources likely to be needed in the future, as well as indicating what resources will be available for new developments in the next few budgetary years. Hence, projecting the financial consequences of current service provision and decisions into the future may show that in the next year or two only marginal resources will be available to support new developments but in later years, the prospects for new ventures will be better. This approach to financial planning was central to the development of the Public Expenditure Survey in central government after 1961 (Plowden, 1961; Heclo and Wildavsky, 1974; Gray and Jenkins, 1985), as well as to the financial planning systems developed in local government in the early 1970s (Elcock, 1986a, pp. 183–9).

- *Contextuating*. This feature is closely related to the first proposition about strategic plans we have discussed in this section; the general nature of strategic plans. However, regarding strategic plans as contextuating enables us to make the specific point that the policy statements contained in strategic plans provide a context within which smaller, short-term or routine decisions like whether or not to approve a particular planning application, to build a new building or accede to an individual's case, can be taken quickly and in a manner consistent with the organisation's values and objectives as they are set out in its plans. Thus, Amitai Etzioni (1968) advocated an approach to policy-making which he termed 'Mixed Scanning'. Decisions can be divided into two classes. Fundamental, or contextuating decisions should be taken after careful research, analysis and consultation in order to reduce uncertainty as far as possible (see Chapter 4). Routine, 'bit' decisions can then be taken within the context of the major 'contextuating' policies but difficulties arising from routine decisions may indicate 'policy stress' and the need therefore to revise the 'contextuating' policy. The organisation's major research, analytical and consultation effort is therefore concentrated on the key issues facing it, while less important or controversial matters are dealt with quickly and economically by incremental decision-making within the context of the main policy framework.

STRATEGY AS A CYCLICAL PROCESS.

The preparation of a strategic plan is – even using 'mixed scanning' or 'key issue' approaches – protracted and expensive. Although it proved to be possible to prepare the Humberside Structure Plan for submission to the Secretary of State for the Environment in less than three years if an 'issue-oriented' approach was adopted and excessive detail avoided (Stephenson and Elcock (eds), 1985, chapter 5; see also Document 13), many county councils took at least twice as long to prepare their Structure Plans. Each of the major stages of the process involves substantial data collection, analysis, decision-taking and consultation. The process usually begins with the setting of objectives and at least provisional policy guidelines, including selection of the 'key issues' to be addressed in the plan. At this stage, the collection and analysis of such material as information about the present and likely future location of people – especially groups like young children or pensioners who make heavy demands on public services – as well as the nature and location of economic activities, are likely to indicate at least some of the major pressures which need to be addressed during the planning period. In addition, political leaders must identify and declare the values whose achievement they wish to promote through the plan.

The planners may then decide to prepare hierarchies of long-term objectives, medium-term policies designed to move the organisation towards the achievement of its objectives and short-term actions. However, this is not always necessary and if it is commenced too early, it may unduly prolong the objective-setting stage of the process. The preparation of a public transport plan, for instance, might entail setting such a hierarchy of objectives, policies and actions:

- Objectives (Long-term): To establish an integrated public transport system which will provide the most convenient possible transport system at the lowest cost to the travellers;
- Policy (medium-term): To establish interchanges between car, bus and rail services to encourage changes in use of transport modes;
- Action (short-term): Subsidise the preparation of a common timetable for regional rail, bus, Metro and ferry services.

In this example, the action of preparing a common timetable should encourage the closer matching or connections between the different services. Over three or four years, bus and railway stations can be turned into interchanges and perhaps ten years hence, the system will become fully integrated with good connections, convenient interchanges and through-ticketing arrangements.

However, although such a plan may appear – or be made to appear – value-neutral, it is not. The creation of an integrated public transport system will not be accepted as a desirable objective by those who believe that efficiency and meeting public demand are best promoted by encouraging competition among service providers.

Having established objectives and provisional policies, processes of consultation and implementation can begin. Consultation serves several functions. It may elicit further information which may in turn cause plan policies to be modified. It should also increase the range of support for the planners' policies and hence render their implementation easier: people are more likely willingly to comply with policies about which they have previously been consulted and which they may (although not necessarily will) accept as being reasonable, even if from their point of view they are not ideal. Such consultation cycles may be repeated at successive stages of plan preparation, as illustrated in Figure 5.1, which is taken from the Humberside Structure Plan. Here, two stages of consultation were involved. The first led to the preparation of draft policies on the 'key issues' identified at the beginning of the process, which had themselves been identified in part through a consultation exercise. This could itself have been presented as a further loop on the left hand side of Figure 5.1.

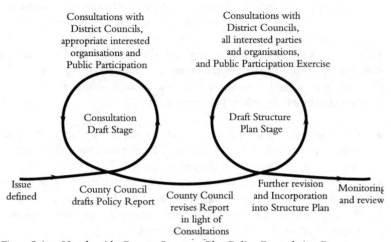

Figure 5.1 Humberside County Structure Plan Policy Formulation Process
Source: Humberside County Council

Secondly, consultees were asked to comment further on the policies proposed, including making preliminary assessments of their likely impact. In consequence, all concerned could learn about one another's opinions and needs, as well as from the information made available by the county council. The planning authority and those affected by its decisions alike were therefore able to develop better informed policies, which were more likely to win consent and hence be implemented relatively easily. However, such planning processes now seem to be discredited as a consequence of (sometimes spectacular) failures. Not all County Councils prepared their Structure Plans quickly and in any case, after 1979 the ideological climate became increasingly hostile to strategic planning of the kind discussed here.

THE NATIONAL HEALTH SERVICE PLANNING SYSTEM

An example of the ways in which strategic planning can fail to produce the results expected of it is the history of the National Health Service Planning System. One of the intentions of those who reorganised the National Health Service in the early 1970s was to introduce a planning system which would combine sensitivity to local circumstances with better implementation of Ministerial policies: the slogan of NHS reorganisation was 'Maximum devolution downwards, coupled with maximum accountability upwards.' On the other hand, the (then) Regional and Area Health Authorities and District Management Teams were expected to implement Government policies and the Secretary of State for Social Services was responsible for the entire Service. On the other hand, local needs, demands and resources varied widely and the planning process must therefore take account of such regional and local differences.

In consequence, the Department of Health and Social Security developed a cyclical planning system (see Figure 5.2), which had two main phases, which are illustrated in Figure 5.3. The first phase is 'top-down', with planning guidelines being prepared by the Department for transmission to the 14 Regional Health Authorities (RHAs). They in turn were to amplify the Department's guidelines in the light of their own judgements about regional health care priorities and in turn transmit guidelines to the 90 Area Health Authorities (AHAs), who would further amplify them and pass their Area Guidelines to the District Management Teams (DMTs). Having received their guidelines, the DMTs would then prepare their District Plans. These were aggregated and expanded by the AHAs into Area Plans, after which the same exercise was repeated by the RHAs. These Regional Plans would then provide a major input into the next stages of the DHSS's planning process. The intention was that AHAs and RHAs would prepare two sets of plans: Strategic Plans for the coming ten years and Operational Plans for three years ahead (DHSS, 1976b; Elcock and Haywood, 1980, chapter 4).

This brief account indicates that the NHS Planning System was designed in accordance with the models of policy-making process and strategic planning discussed in the last chapter and here. Thus, there were to be the two levels of plan: strategic plans and operational plans. Arguably, therefore, the system included a form of 'mixed scanning'. The NHS Planning System was intended to develop a cyclical process, with the centre and the localities alike learning from one another's experiences. Above all, the system's designers hoped that it would produce more coherent health care policies at the national, regional and local levels.

In particular, however, the Planning System was intended to bring about a shift in Health Service priorities. Traditionally, acute hospital and obstetric services had enjoyed high priority despite increasing concern, heightened by a series of scandals about the under-resourcing of geriatric care and the care of the mentally ill and handicapped: the 'Cinderella' services. Successive Secretaries of State for Social Services (in turn Barbara Castle, David Ennals and Patrick Jenkin) declared that a shift in priorities in favour of the 'Cinderellas' ought to take place (DHSS, 1976a; 1977; 1979). The Planning System was intended to be a major engine of such change. However, Table 5:1 shows that change was at best marginal and at

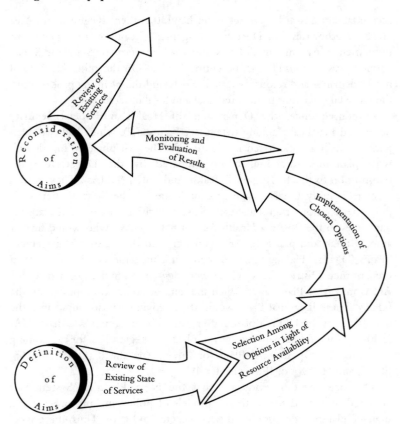

Figure 5.2 NHS Planning is a Learning Process
Source: DHSS, 1972

Note: This model representing the NHS's cyclical planning system was developed in 1972 and is not relevant to current practice

Table 5.1 National Health Service Expenditure on Selected Services, 1975–6 and 1979–8

	Obstetric Services	Elderly	Community Services	Mental Handicap	Mentally Ill	Acute Hospital Services
1975–6	6.6	6.4	4.0	8.7	35.1	4.1
1979–8	6.8	6.3	3.9	8.4	34.5	3.8

Source: Elcock and Haywood, 1981

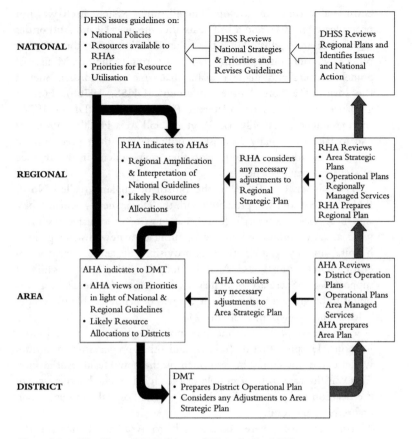

Figure 5.3   The Flow of Guidelines and Plans for the NHS

Source: DHSS, 1972

Note: This model representing the two main phases of the NHS's cyclical planning system was developed in 1972 and is not relevant to current practice

worst non-existent. The reasons for this failure indicate the problems that existed at both the national and the devolved levels of the Service. The problems which prevented the implementation of the Ministerial demands for a shift in resource priorities had been insufficiently considered by the authors of the 'Blue Book' (the Planning Manual: DHSS 1976a) and the subsequent policy statements, with the result that at best marginal priority shifts had been achieved. These problems fell into three categories.

1.   First, that both the planning process and the policy guidelines took a

considerable time to develop. The Planning System itself was not promulgated for two and a half years after the new Health Authorities assumed their responsibilities: the 'Blue Book' defining the planning process was only published in 1976. Furthermore, the first Ministerial guidelines were only made available that same year and then only in the form of a consultative document (DHSS, 1976b). Further guidance came a year or so later in *The Way Forward* (DHSS, 1977). In consequence, not only had Regional and Area Health Authorities had to take over many established policies from their predecessors; they had already begun to develop their own policies in the absence of Departmental guidance.

Thus, when one RHA in the North of England (called North RHA in the study) was presented with the Department's demand for a shift in service priorities, it found that most of its available resources were already committed to the opening of a new district general hospital mainly geared to the provision of acute services. In consequence, North RHA informed the DHSS that while it supported the Secretary of State's view that the 'Cinderella' services ought to be given a higher priority, it was presently unable to comply (Elcock and Haywood, 1980, pp. 74–5).

2.   A second set of problems concerned policies developed by the former Regional Hospital Boards (RHBs) and other predecessor authorities which could not simply be jettisoned by the new Health Authorities. This was the case in the example of North RHA cited above, where the decision to build the new district general hospital had been taken before reorganisation.

3.   Thirdly, decisions were taken locally to avoid implementing the Secretary of State's policies where they challenged established professional interests and local priorities. This problem occurred in a case which was involved with another major NHS policy initiative of the 1970s: the introduction of the RAWP exercise. Ever since the NHS was founded in 1948, considerable differences had existed in the availability of health care resources between regions and localities. Hence in the mid-1970s, the DHSS appointed a working party to devise statistical formulae on the basis of which resources could be reallocated in order to enable worse-off regions or localities to 'catch up' with the better-off ones, whose growth would have to be to some extent restrained. At that time, it still seemed likely that sufficient growth money would be available to ensure that each Region and Area would receive some extra funds each year, even if the better-off

ones got only marginally more. Hence, discontent would be minimal because every Region and Area would be becoming better off each year.

This Resource Allocation Working Party (RAWP) soon identified enduring inequalities among the fourteen English NHS Regions. Oxford was best-off and Trent the worst-off. The Working Party therefore developed two formulae for the allocation of resources which could be used to reduce regional inequalities. In turn, RHAs were expected to apply the formulae in distributing funds to AHAs, who would then do the same when making their allocations to their Districts. However, where the results of RAWP allocations challenged established policies and entrenched professional interests, they were often resisted or evaded.

For example, 'North Sea AHA' had four Districts which were also given pseudonyms and according to the RAWP formulae were ranked as follows: Wealthiest, 'Harrier', 'Buzzard', 'Sparrowhawk'; Poorest, 'Goshawk'. However, by applying its own (admittedly quite sensible) criteria, North Sea AHA ranked Goshawk as in reality the wealthiest District and Harrier the poorest! Hence, '...the target allocations for Harrier were increased, thus legitimising the allocation of RAWP deficit monies to that District.' The effect of the centre's policy decision was hence radically altered by the exercise of local discretion, which was justified by reinterpretation of the centre's own formula (Elcock and Haywood, 1980, pp. 46–7).

The late preparation of the Planning System and of central policy guidelines, coupled with local resistance, quite rapidly discredited the NHS Planning System. After 1979 it was first 'simplified', not least by the removal of one tier of management in the 1982 reorganisation. It has since been largely displaced by a system of annual review meetings which strengthen 'Top-down' accountability, albeit at the expense of attempts to develop policy frameworks which can embrace both central policies and local interests. Now, each RHA chairman meets the Secretary of State for Health annually and is expected to account for the implementation (or otherwise) of the government's policies in each Region. Afterwards, the RHA chairmen are expected to hold a similar round of meetings with their DHA colleagues to ensure that Ministerial policies are being implemented at District level. The cycle of national and local interaction developed through the 1976 Planning System has been replaced by what purports to be a 'Top-down' process of instruction. Time will tell whether Ministerial policies are more extensively implemented as a result.

DEATH AND RESURRECTION: STRATEGIC PLANNING IN THE 1980S

The arrival in office of Mrs Thatcher's Government in May 1979 led to major decline in the credibility accorded to strategic plans as a means to develop better public policies. In part, this is because Mrs Thatcher believes that if short-term decisions are sound, the longer term will look after itself (Blackstone and Plowden, 1988). Again, the town and country planning system has been repeatedly criticised for the length of time it takes to produce decisions, as well as for the apparent arrogance of 'the planners', who claim to know what we want better than we do ourselves (Gower Davies, 1972). Also, there are frequent complaints about planners' apparent unwillingness to take account of popular opinions (Gower Davies, 1972; Norris, 1982). In consequence, we need to ask some fundamental questions about both the practicability and the desirability of strategic planning.

First, we need to enquire whether strategic planning is possible – in current circumstances or at all. Two features of modern government render this question particularly crucial:

1. The first is the increase in uncertainty produced by such exogenous shocks as the quadrupling of oil prices in 1973–4, the threat posed to the climate by the 'Greenhouse Effect' or – more parochially but perhaps having a greater impact on many politicians and officials – frequent changes of mind by the central government. Although the overall thrust of the Thatcher Administrations' policies has been extremely consistent: reducing the role of the State and cutting the proportion of GNP devoted to public spending - the effect of the government's successive attempts to enforce its policies has been that the government has made repeated changes in the rules under which politicians and administrators must operate, especially at the regional and local levels.

    Thus, one of the first acts of the Audit Commission for Local Government was severely to criticise the Government because it has frequently changed the basis on which it allocates grants to local authorities. The climate of uncertainty generated by nine major changes in the grant regime during Mrs Thatcher's first term of office had, according to the Commission, cost ratepayers some £1.2 billion – the amount which local authority Treasurers had felt obliged to hold in balances in case the grant rules were suddenly changed again (Audit Commission, 1983, see Elcock, Jordan and Midwinter, 1989).

2. Secondly, the persistent demands made by the central government for spending reductions for most of the period since 1976 have produced

reduced commitment to strategic planning, sometimes together with panic reactions to demands for cuts. When organisations are faced with immediate demands to reduce their spending, they are likely to lose interest in processes which tend to generate new proposals for spending and whose activities have only a limited relationship to the immediate pressure to retrench. In consequence, plans may be abandoned or shelved and planning staff may be diverted to more immediately pressing tasks. The most dramatic example of immediate pressure driving out strategic planning was the abandonment of the National Plan in the face of a sterling crisis in the summer of 1966.

Before the 1964 general election, the Labour Party had become committed to the establishment of a Department of Economic Affairs (DEA) which would remove the planning and development of the British economy from control by the Treasury, with its penchant for short-term economic and financial management, as well as its eternal preoccupation with saving money. The new DEA was charged at its creation with preparing a National Plan, which duly appeared in 1965 after major – and remarkably quick – data collection and analysis. The National Plan (Department of Economic Affairs, 1965) set out a growth path for the British economy which would produce an economic expansion of 25 per cent by 1970. It identified what needed to be done in various sectors to achieve this target in the form of a series of checklists, as well as the possible impediments – including a projected manpower gap in the last two years of the Plan period which might have to be filled by increased immigration. This National Plan was launched with a flourish in 1965 but in July 1966, a major sterling crisis occurred which presented Harold Wilson as Prime Minister with a choice between abandoning the Plan (and much else besides) or devaluing the pound. Almost without hesitation the Plan was jettisoned (see Budd, 1978; Smith, 1979; Wilson, 1971). The demands of short-term economic management prevailed over longer-term attempts to improve the country's economic performance.

Examples of the debilitating effect of resource constraints on strategic planning now abound. The senior managers of one local authority in the north of England developed a community plan in the early 1980s but they were compelled by resource pressure to relegate it to the background. Significantly, by the end of the decade they were seeking to revive it (Elcock, Fenwick and Harrop, 1988). Again, the role of 'think tanks' tends to alter from developing strategies to coping with immediate crises (Norris, 1989). In all these ways, retrenchment has tended to reduce the role of strategic planning and those people and organisations chiefly concerned with it.

This tendency may be accelerated if politicians or senior managers press the panic button. Faced with demands for spending cuts, strategic planning will be attacked (along with other 'overhead' costs) because it makes no direct contribution to immediate service provision. Strategic plans and planners easily fall victim to such a mood. Many county councils have disbanded their planning departments because since 1981 they have been deprived of most of their development control functions and Structure Planning has been relegated to a low priority by the Department of the Environment. Strategic planners may therefore find themselves moved to less congenial working environments, as well as being required to assume day-to-day administrative responsibilities rather than considering long-term developments. Again, central policy units become increasingly preoccupied with short-term, 'fire-brigade' trouble-shooting roles. Because the *Zeitgeist* is hostile to strategic planning, resources are short and immediate problems are pressing, strategic planning is likely to be largely abandoned. At worst, the result is the cry of despair: 'Planning is impossible.' (Elcock, Fenwick and Harrop, 1988, p. 22)

However, such a reaction ignores the possibility that not only may strategic planning be desirable; it can also assist hard-pressed public service managers to cope better with the incessant demands for resource reductions which nowadays constitute their daily lot. A leading advocate of strategic planning in business, John M. Bryson (1988) has argued that strategic planning produces 'a disciplined effort to produce fundamental decisions and actions that shape and guide what an organisation is, what it does and why it does it.' (1988, p. 11) He argues that strategic planning enables the organisation to:

- Manage the exercise of discretion by its employees and ensure its responsiveness to customers;
- Develop strategies to deal with changing circumstances;
- Develop a coherent, defensible basis for decision-making;
- Implement its policies, including resource cuts, in a truly efficient manner. (Ibid, p. 11)

Thus strategy should improve control, increase managers' ability to cope with change and procure more coherent decision-making at all levels within the organisation. However, he also urges that organisations should move towards their objectives by a series of steps: a series of 'little wins' can add up to a 'big win'. Hence, 'Strategists should seriously consider the advantages of winning small – time after time – instead of trying to win big once.' (Ibid., cf. Lindblom, 1965, 1979)

We can explore these issues in greater detail in the context of organisations' use of corporate strategic planning to cope with external demands and internal pressures and then focus more specifically on how they have used strategic planning to respond to the persistent fiscal pressures imposed on them in the 1980s.

STRATEGIC PLANS: THE EXTERNAL AND INTERNAL DIMENSIONS

It is not surprising that strategic planning has enjoyed something of a renaissance in the last few years because it may offer a means to deal with fiscal pressure while minimising the damage it causes to services and staff. In the emergence of this renaissance, strategic planning in the public sector has become linked to developing ideas about business planning (Bryson, 1988, Greenwood, 1987). One major theme is how organisations respond to pressure from their outside environments, as well as to the need to improve their internal management. Royston Greenwood (1987) classified a sample of local authorities into four groups, depending on their responses to internal pressures as well as to their external environments. The categories are:

Type A: Defenders. These authorities prefer stability to experimentation, concentrate on providing statutory services, seek stability and are determined to become more efficient.

Type B: Analysers. These authorities seek to learn from other authorities but do not try to develop unproven ideas on their own.

Type C: Prospectors. These authorities seek new opportunities and challenges. They will experiment and accept that some of their experiments will be unsuccessful. Innovation is preferred to stability.

Type D: Reactors. The largest category in the study were authorities which value stability but introduce changes as circumstances require (Greenwood, 1987, pp. 310–11).

Clearly, a central theme running through these categories is how far a particular local authority looks outwards to other organisations and its general environment to stimulate development, or looks inwards and seeks to ensure its own stability and efficiency. Types B and C are more outward-looking than Types A and D.

A similar classification emerged in the Northern Network for Public Policy study of senior public service managers in the north-east of England, which showed that they prepare plans and policies in response to two sets of issues (Elcock, Fenwick and Harrop, 1988; Fenwick, Harrop and Elcock, 1989). The first set of issues is similar to those raised in Greenwood's study of local authorities and concerns whether the organisation focuses mainly on its external environment or its internal management: whether it is mainly inward- or outward-looking. The second set of issues concerns whether the organisation's members are more concerned to influence its environment or respond to the demands others make upon its members: whether it is proactive or reactive. Thus the categories defined in Table 5.2 may be summarised as follows:

Type A organisations (Outward-looking/Proactive) carry out consumer research and marketing. They subscribe to the Public Service Orientation (Stewart, 1986; Clarke and Stewart, 1988) in that they wish to be sensitive

Table 5.2   Managerial Stance

Relationship to environment	Proactive	Reactive
Outward-looking	A	B
Inward-looking	C	D

to community needs and demands. Their structures will probably be decentralised. Thus, one local authority in the study had decentralised its service provision and set up a public limited company to buy up a large number of surplus houses in order to retain them for rent. It was making a variety of land deals in order to promote the area's economic development and was preparing a Community Plan. A second local authority was preparing a three-year Economic Development Plan and was consciously seeking to apply the Public Service Orientation to its services in order to make them more customer-responsive. However, this authority found that government pressure for spending reductions was 'the basic over-riding factor' in its policy-making, which was inhibiting its strategic planning to some degree.

Type B organisations (Outward-looking/Reactive) seek to influence their environment but – often because of the nature of their roles – have to spend much of their time responding to its demands. The classic outward-looking but reactive organisation might be a fire brigade, which must respond to emergency calls while at the same time trying to promote fire prevention measures. Health authorities also tend to be in part reactive because they too are responsible for emergency services, as well as more generally because they must deal with the patients who present themselves for diagnosis and treatment. One health authority manager complained of heavy pressure from the Department of Health but felt that his authority had to be outward-looking because it saw its role as not only curing the sick but also promoting better health.

Type C organisations (Inward-looking/Proactive) may respond to problems imposed from outside by restructuring themselves (see Chapter 3). In order to secure acceptance of such changes, they should seek to motivate and reassure staff, in order to develop a consensus in support of such restructuring. This will include developing close relationships with trade unions to secure their co-operation. Such organisations will not usually attempt to plan very far ahead but they will seek to protect their staff and activities. Hence, they will monitor their staffing levels and try to avoid redundancies. Thus a local authority in the Northern Network study saw a need to develop its use of information technology rapidly, in particular to cope with the demands of the Community Charge.

Type D organisations (Inward-looking/Reactive) constrain their budgets within externally set limits. They therefore tend to follow 'compliance' or perhaps 'shadow-boxing' budgetary strategies (see next section, also Midwinter, 1988; Elcock, Jordan and Midwinter, 1989). They will probably not attempt much strategic planning but will seek to preserve their activities and the employment of their staff. They will therefore monitor their staffing levels and seek to avoid redundancies. Thus the managers of an organisation which was under especially heavy pressure from the government because Ministers were determined to expose its services to maximum competition, felt that its managers could only 'make the best of a bad job'. One manager said that the first thing he asked when a demand was made was: 'Is this worth a strike?' Others were preoccupied with internal efficiency and reducing manpower levels: with 'running the job as a business'. A civil servant said that he and his colleagues were 'purely operational...servants of the Government'.

We must note that most organisations contain elements of several or all of these orientations and that any organisation's location in Table 5.2 is determined as much by the nature of its responsibilities as by managerial attitudes or decisions. There is no necessary moral or other virtue in being located in one box rather than another, although it is valuable for managers to consider whether they should attempt to move the organisation into another box.

COPING WITH FISCAL PRESSURE

Here we consider some examples of how various public bodies have responded to fiscal pressure by developing strategies, by which we mean coherent, long-term generalised approaches to the need to respond to financial stringency. They have demonstrated the usefulness of strategic planning for developing methods of retrenchment which minimise damage to their members, services and customers. Arthur Midwinter (1988) has argued that local authorities have adopted one or other of three budgetary strategies in response to the Thatcher Governments' continuous effort to make them reduce their spending (see also Elcock, Jordan and Midwinter, 1989). The first and most common are compliance strategies, under which local authorities accept, sometimes albeit reluctantly, that they must try to meet the government's requirements.

One form of compliance strategy, which was common among the 17 local authorities involved in a study of their 1985–6 budget-making (Elcock and Jordan (eds), 1987) was the 'Standstill Strategy'. Early in the budget-making cycle, the authority's leading officers and councillors assess the resources likely to be available during the coming financial year. Some authorities in the PAC Study made such assessments as early as May (for the financial year commencing the following April), although considerable uncertainty existed about government grant allocations, which are not announced until near the end of the budgetary cycle. This resource assessment would be followed by issuing an instruction to departments and committees that they must prepare their estimates on the basis of no overall spending growth in real terms. Any new growth items must be paid for by making reductions elsewhere in the estimates. However, in practice such 'standstill' strategies tend to produce creeping expenditure growth because the reductions offered to pay for new growth never fully compensate for the cost of the latter. None the less, such strategies have reversed the first two stages of the traditional budgetary process (see Hepworth, 1984) under which estimates are prepared and then trimmed back when, inevitably, it becomes apparent that the resources available are insufficient to meet the cost of all the proposed expenditure (Greenwood *et al.*, 1980; Elcock, Jordan and Midwinter, 1989). Under a 'Standstill' strategy, an assessment of resource availability is made first and estimates are – or at any rate should be – prepared within the parameters of the resources declared to be available. A still more stringent strategy was developed by one local authority in the north-east of England which has prepared a three-year plan to make its income equal its expenditure without suffering grant penalties from overspending (Elcock, Fenwick and Harrop, 1988).

Midwinter's second type of strategy is 'Brinkmanship', under which the local authority's members decide their political position and announce their determination to defend that position against all comers, including the Government. In the early 1980s, many Labour-controlled local authorities adopted such strategies in the form of a pledge of 'No Cuts in Jobs or Services'. Some added a promise not to increase rates or rents either. In consequence, councillors in Liverpool and Lambeth came into direct conflict with the law. Such 'Brinkmanship' strategies initially involve increasingly complex and daring creative accountancy measures (see Parkinson, 1985; 1986; 1987a) but have sometimes caused councillors to topple over the brink of illegality. Delays by Liverpool and Lambeth in setting their rates were ruled illegal by the District Auditor and the Courts, with the result that the majority of councillors on these two authorities were surcharged and disqualified from holding public office. Labour councillors on several other authorities have narrowly avoided suffering the same fate. In Sheffield, a legal budget was passed in 1986 only after a split in the Labour Group (Morris and Haigh, 1987). The danger of 'Brinkmanship' is that you may fall over the cliff. Liverpool and Lambeth did; Sheffield and Islington teetered on the edge but did not fall over.

The third strategy is 'Shadow Boxing', where a local authority accepts the need to prepare a budget which takes account of the government's policies but seeks to avoid expenditure reductions which will affect service levels or cause redundancies. Such authorities do this through a range of expedients to reduce their apparent spending otherwise than by making cuts, including 'creative accountancy' measures such as refinancing loans at lower rates of interest, selling properties and sometimes leasing them back, or moving expenditures from one financial year to another in order to reduce the severity of grant penalties (Parkinson, 1986; Elcock and Jordan (eds), 1987; Elcock, Jordan and Midwinter, 1989). Harold Wolman (1984) provides many examples of such 'shadow-boxing' strategies in an international comparison of local authority budgetary processes (see chapter 6 and Tarschys, 1984). Here, 'damage limitation' is the order of the day (Midwinter, 1988, p. 24).

Many local authority Treasurers would argue that the development of a strategy for coping with fiscal pressure enables them to minimise the damage that spending reductions cause to their authorities' services and customers but some admit to having thrown in the towel. They argue that service cuts have to be made as and when they become necessary. These pessimists are confirmed in their view by the vagaries of the grant system. Thus Lancashire County Council prepared a budget for 1986–7 based on three assessments of its likely grant allocation, only to find that its eventual allocation was smaller than its most pessimistic assumption! A few weeks later, however, the council was allocated an extra £4 million, by which time the budget was virtually complete and it was too late to allocate the extra money rationally (Barlow, 1987). Certainly, many public authorities have abandoned the financial planning strategies developed in the 1970s and where such strategic plans are still prepared, time horizons tend to be relatively short (Elcock, Fenwick and Harrop, 1988, Table 1, p. 21).

The other major difficulty which besets strategic planners is obtaining agreement on the objectives the plan is seeking to achieve. Some writers would argue with Michael Oakeshott that setting objectives is an entirely inappropriate task for governments to undertake; their duty is to keep the ship of state afloat, not to steer it in any particular direction (Oakeshott, 1962). Equally, if the best means of producing good public services is deemed to be to expose them to competition and market forces and see whether they survive, developing strategies for their development becomes inappropriate since the main preoccupation of public organisations must be to respond to the actions of their competitors in the market place (Friedman and Friedman, 1980).

Even if one does accept that governments, local authorities and other public organisations should set themselves goals, as is commonly prescribed by writers on public management, it is more difficult to secure agreement on what those objectives should be now that the post-war political consensus has disappeared (Elcock, (ed.), 1982). Many of the strategic planning processes discussed here place a considerable emphasis on consultation and securing agreement, both on the objectives to be achieved and on the steps needed to achieve them (see, for example, Bryson, 1988). For instance, two former local authority chief executives argue that councillors should set 'Directions' within which the authority's staff should work; they say little about how to deal with or resolve the political disputes that any attempt to set such directions entails (Barratt and Downs, 1988). On the other hand, in regions or localities where the level of consensus is relatively high, it may be possible to secure agreement both on objectives and the way to achieve them, even when some of the objectives are unpalatable. Thus in the north-east of England, where nearly all the local authorities are Labour-controlled and therefore relations with trade unions tend to be relatively close and less conflictual than elsewhere, reaching agreement on changing work practices and abolishing restrictive practices is relatively easy (Fenwick, Harrop and Elcock, 1989). However, such agreement is likely to prove impossible where there are major ideological differences or conflicts of interest. Thus there is no longer agreement, for example, that integrated passenger transport systems are desirable. Rather, the different transport modes should compete with one another and with the private car. No wonder, then, that strategic planning in government is in eclipse and that a much narrower view of the role of planners and managers is now taken than was the case before 1979. Their major preoccupation is now with the management of resources and to improve economy, efficiency and effectiveness.

CHAPTER SIX

Resources

THE IMPORTANCE OF RESOURCE MANAGEMENT

One way in which the focus of public management has become narrowed during the Thatcher years is a concentration on improving the use public servants make of resources. As strategic planning has become more difficult and less valued; as public service has been devalued and government has come to be regarded as a residual which exists to perform only those functions which cannot be performed by the private sector, so resource management has tended to become the principal preoccupation of Ministers, councillors, civil servants and local authority officers. This has produced valuable improvements in resource use but it has also impoverished public management by causing other issues to be neglected.

This is not to argue that resource management should not be one of the major concerns of public administrators. Public authorities control budgets of millions or billions of pounds. Their budgets are larger than those of all but the biggest private enterprises at the local, regional and national levels. Furthermore, levels of national and local taxation are constantly criticised and economy is demanded in order to keep tax rates down. The Government hopes that the introduction of the Community Charge will increase this pressure on local authorities by ensuring that high expenditure will hit all adults' pockets and hence arouse their opposition to high-spending councillors. Public authorities are also major employers of labour: often the local authority is the largest single employer in its city or county: even the European Commission, which is often criticised for appearing to be a vast bureaucracy, only employs about the same number of people – about 15,000 – as a medium-sized metropolitan district council. Personnel management has therefore become increasingly important in the public sector in the last two decades or so. Lastly, public authorities own large amounts of land and property – again, local authorities for example are often the largest landowners in their areas. Land in public ownership not only constitutes a valuable resource but also provides public authorities with development opportunities which they may take, or which they may offer or deny to others. One of the purposes of the 1980 Local Government, Planning and Land Act was to put pressure on local authorities to sell land which they hold but are not using.

Central to all discussion of resource management in the public sector must be the content of public servants' accountability for the resources of which they dispose. That accountability has been heavily scrutinised in recent years and has been extended beyond its traditional parameters. Long-standing anxiety to ensure that funds are not misappropriated and that land transactions are not corrupt has extended increasingly to trying to ensure that resources are also used efficiently and effectively. We therefore need to begin our exploration of the issues posed by resource management in the public sector by offering a brief account of the objectives that are sought in seeking accountability for resource use (see Robinson, 1969; Gray and Jenkins, 1985; Day and Klein, 1987). These objectives can be grouped under four headings: Fiscal Accountability, Efficiency Accountability, Programme Accountability, and Process Accountability. We shall now explore each in turn.

- *Fiscal Accountability.* The oldest form of resource management is to demand that those who have been entrusted with resources should be required to render an account of how they used those resources, together with vouchers proving that each receipt or disbursement has been correctly executed. The traditional role of auditors (internal or external) is to examine each unit's record and assure themselves that resources have not been mis-spent or used for corrupt or illegal purposes. In English local government one of the District Auditor's roles has always involved checking that no funds have been spent illegally. Furthermore, any ratepayer has had the right to inspect the local authority's accounts and challenge any item of expenditure recorded therein. If a decision is found to be illegal, the District Auditor (or such other auditor as the council appoints) may surcharge those councillors who voted for it with their share of the amount involved. He may also disqualify those councillors from holding public office. This power was invoked against the Labour members of the Clay Cross Urban District Council because they voted to refuse to increase council house rents as was required under the Housing Finance Act, 1972. More recently, this power was used against the majority councillors on Liverpool City Council and Lambeth London Borough Council in 1987 because councillors had delayed setting a rate beyond the legal time limit. These councillors were therefore held to have defaulted on the trust vested in them by their election and oaths of office.

• *Efficiency Accountability.* Definitions of efficiency are still somewhat controversial but most people would accept that efficiency denotes a concern to achieve the most advantageous possible relationship between the cost of an activity and the results it produces or to secure the most benefit possible for the cost incurred. In recent years, several methods of encouraging efficiency have been developed, including the publication of 'league tables' which indicate where local authorities or health authorities rank in terms of their expenditure per unit of service. Such indicators include how much each local authority spends on a specified service per head of its population (CIPFA, annual; Elcock, Jordan and Midwinter, 1989) or how long patients are kept in hospitals after particular surgical procedures (Pollitt, 1985). The development of performance measures and indicators has become a major growth area in public management in recent years and is discussed more fully in Chapter 7. Another means to encourage efficiency is to publicise examples of 'good management practice' so that others can copy them: an activity in which the Audit Commission has become extensively involved. Local authorities have been encouraged since the Bains Report (1972) to establish performance review sub-committees to monitor their departments' efficiency and promote changes in management which increase efficiency. Councillors, therefore, have been encouraged to take an active part in promoting efficiency.

• *Programme Accountability* entails ensuring that resources are being used to promote the achievement of the organisation's objectives. However it may be difficult or impossible to assess or measure such achievements, especially in the short or medium term. There are several reasons for this difficulty. The first is that public authorities have a wide range of differing, often conflicting, objectives. Furthermore, these objectives, or at least their relative importance, may change when a different political party, which holds different values, wins office. Secondly, the effects of public policies – both those intended by their formulators and the unanticipated consequences of the policies – may not become apparent for a long time. Thirdly, it may be impossible to determine how far apparent success has been the result of public policies rather than other circumstances. It is notoriously difficult, for example, to demonstrate

111

whether the undoubted improvements in the longevity and health status of the British population are the result of improved health care (including the establishment of the NHS) or of improvements in diet and housing conditions (Brown, 1975). In consequence, those responsible for the management of public resources have often taken refuge by presenting their achievements in terms of the fourth objective.

- *Process Accountability.* Here, achievement is assessed in terms of information which is relatively easy to collect and present but which may not provide a true guide either to past achievements or future requirements. Thus, it is relatively easy to demonstrate that the number of mental illness beds per thousand of the population of a region has been increased over (say) the last five years. However, it is more difficult to demonstrate that such an increase has resulted in a happier, mentally fitter population! By the same token, the statistics may show that the next door region has more hospital beds per thousand of the population than ours does but it does not follow that this leads to an improvement in that region's population's health status relative to that of our own region. However, producer lobbies in the health care sector will use such comparisons as a means to persuade policy-makers to give more resources to their sector or service. The policy-makers themselves will claim credit for putting more resources into public services regardless of whether or not doing so improves either the service or the condition of its clients. Much incremental policy-making is flawed because of its reliance on process measures: 'If flying 200 bombing missions a day fails to subdue the Vietcong, then fly 400 missions tomorrow' would be a typical statement of such logic. The American defeat in the Vietnam War was proof positive of the inadequacies of such process accountability logic.

Dissatisfaction with the results of public policies, coupled with increasing demands for efficient resource use, have recently heightened interest in the problems of resource management. The most prominent problems are concerned with the management of money but efficiently deploying and developing staff and making good use of land are important too. Indeed, some public managers suggest that constraints on personnel are more significant than monetary restrictions. We now discuss the management of the three main resources in turn.

THE MANAGEMENT OF MONEY

Public authorities dispose of approaching half the Gross National Product – even after ten years of 'Thatcherism'. In 1988, central and local government spent £4,178 per head of UK's adult population (Public Finance Foundation, 1988, p. 3). In that year, total public spending was planned to be £183 billion or 42.1 per cent of the Gross National Product (Ibid, p. 2). The management of these vast sums entails not only ensuring that it is spent efficiently; it also involves the making of choices about how much money shall be spent on what. In consequence, one of the main policy-making and management processes in which every public service organisation must engage is the preparation of its budget. In theory, the allocation of funds ought to be related to the organisation's objectives and monitoring their use ought to be related to the achievement of those objectives. In section 1 we have already explored some of the difficulties inherent in this process and studying the realities of public sector budgeting reveals further major problems about such rationalistic views of what the budgetary process is or ought to be about.

The Budgetary Process

In exploring the nature of budgetary processes in modern government, we need first to recognise that its nature is fundamentally different from that of a private firm. In the private sector, expenditure plans will be prepared on the basis of a forecast level of output but if demand for the firm's products exceeds expectations, production will be increased to meet the extra demand if at all possible, because extra sales generate increase profits. In the public services, by contrast, budgeting entails the distribution of limited resources among competing demands. It must therefore include making choices about which activities to promote and which to restrict, as well as rationing the resources available to support the organisation's various functions or provide services for each of its clients. Thus Michael Clarke and John Stewart have declared that 'The budget in the public domain is an act of political choice...The budget sets out the choice as to the desirable level of taxation and expenditure and the choices made on the allocation of that expenditure.' (Clarke and Stewart, 1988, p. 3) Those choices cannot be made purely on the basis of economic rationality; they will be influenced by politicians' judgements about the wishes of the electorate, which in turn may produce a cycle of severe budgets after an election, followed by generous ones as the next election approaches (Downs, 1957). They will also be influenced by pressure groups and the demands of the professional service workers employed by the organisation to provide the services for which it is responsible. Other government agencies will impose further constraints, as will the country's overall economic prosperity or otherwise.

There are five main groups of issues to be discussed in any examination of the resource allocation processes which generate a public organisation's budget and which we need to explore in what follows. They are:

- Whether the budget should be resource-led or demand-led;
- Over what time-span budgets should be prepared;
- What is or what ought to be the relationship between those responsible for providing services and those responsible for financial management;
- How far public services budgetary processes can be anything other than incremental and whether or not they should be made increasingly rational;
- How budgetary processes change as a result of fiscal pressure and whether that pressure has produced better budgets.

Demand-led or resource-led? In many public authorities, including both the central government and local authorities, the budgetary process has traditionally commenced with the preparation of spending estimates by those responsible for service provision. Thus the initiative has initially rested with those who know the needs of the organisation's clients and who are subject to pressure from the lobby groups who claim to speak for those clients. The demands which are reflected in the estimates are therefore commonly generated in the policy communities (Richardson and Jordan, 1979) which constitute the pattern of influence from which public policies – including budgets – are generated. We can explore the implication of this in a number of contexts, beginning with the central government.

The budgetary process of the central government is illustrated by Figure 6.1. The most significant dates in the cycle are the presentation to Parliament of the Chancellor's Autumn Statement on Public Expenditure each November and the announcement of his Budget the following March. The process leading up to the presentation of the Autumn Statement begins with the preparation by government departments of their estimates followed by negotiation about their content and cost in a series of bilateral meetings between each department's Principal Finance Officer and Treasury officials, overseen by the Chief Secretary to the Treasury (Heclo and Wildavsky, 1974). Heclo and Wildavsky have described the delicate nature of these negotiations, which must be conducted on a basis of trust between the departments' Principal Finance Officers and the

The Treasury Year

	Mar Apr	May	June	July	Aug	Sept		Nov Dec	Jan	Feb	Mar Apr	May	June	July
Major statements	Budget							Autumn forecast			Budget			
Forecasts	IAF													
			Summer forecast			Autumn forecast		IAF		Winter forecast	IAF			
Public Expenditure	Survey							Main estimates White Paper			Survey			
Legislation		Finance Bill										Finance Bill		

Table 6.1   The Treasury Year

Treasury representatives. For example, departments must decide how far they should 'pad' their estimates. Some funds over and above the department's clearly established needs must be included in the estimates, for two reasons. The first is to insure against unexpected demands for spending in the coming budgetary year; the second is so that during the negotiations with the Treasury some proposals can be surrendered without imposing any real threat to the service. These surrenders hence constitute 'fairy gold': you give up items whose inclusion in the budget was never realistically expected. However, if during the bargaining process reductions are accepted too easily by the department, the Treasury will suspect that department put an unduly large amount of 'padding' into its estimates in the first place. On the other hand, the Principal Finance Officer must at the same time maintain the trust of his or her colleagues in the department. They may accompany him or her to meetings with Treasury officials 'so that they can see you are not selling them down to the river to the Treasury' (Ibid, p. 124). An Accountant-General told Heclo and Wildavsky that 'I act as a bridge between the Treasury and the department. One has to some extent a dual loyalty.' (Ibid, p. 118) Remaining disputes, which cannot be resolved among officials, must be referred to the Ministers and in the last resort to the Cabinet – the only forum where determined dissenters can be finally overridden. Usually these final stages of bargaining followed by decisions are carried out by a small group of non-departmental Ministers with a senior Cabinet member in the chair, known as the 'Star Chamber'. For many years this role was played by Lord Whitelaw but he has now been succeeded by Mr Cecil Parkinson as the holder of this poisoned chalice.

This budgetary process is characterised by a conflict between the demands of the service departments and their policy communities for increased spending and the Treasury, whose duty is to restrain expenditure in order to limit the demands made on the public purse and hence on taxpayers. We have already noted Wildavsky's (1979) classic analysis of public sector budgeting, in which he called the first groups the 'Advocates', the second the 'Guardians'. The budgetary process begins with the Advocates articulating their demands, which will be resisted by the Guardians and modified as negotiations proceed and the expenditure budget is assembled. Only when the expenditure totals have been completed can the first assessment of their implications for taxation be prepared. The Chancellor of the Exchequer's Budget judgement is, of course, based not only on expenditure totals but also on the national economic outlook and the policies he and the Prime Minister wish to pursue. Budget-making for the Chancellors is not conducted on the basis of Mr Micawber's equations where happiness is an excess of income over expenditure and misery the reverse. None the less, clearly increasing expenditure must at least entail consideration of whether an increase of income and hence taxes ought to result from it.

The traditional local authority's budget also begins with the preparation of estimates by the service departments; hence the Advocates are again the first actors to appear on the stage. Thus the standard textbook on local government finance (Hepworth, 1984) tells us that a local authority's departments prepare their estimates separately, these being brought together only around Christmas to be aggregated and trimmed to match the available resources. At this point, a percentage cut across the departments' estimates will probably be demanded in order to prevent the council having to raise its rate or precept by an excessive amount (Hepworth, 1984, pp. 214 ff). Connolly and McChesney (1987) tell us that Belfast City Council's budgetary process begins with individual Chief Officers collecting the information required to prepare their departments' estimates. Hence, '...the present structure and attitudes are not conducive to the establishment of a corporate approach.' (Connolly and McChesney, 1987, p. 239)

Under pressure of demands from the central government for ex-penditure reductions, however, local authorities have increasingly sought to increase the importance of resource availability as one of the formative influences on budgets. When Denis Healey demanded spending cuts in 1976, local authorities sometimes responded by trying to reverse the first two stages of the budgetary process by making an assessment of the resources likely to be available next year near the beginning of the budgetary cycle and then instructing departments and committees that they must prepare their estimates within the limits indicated by that assessment. Such a resource-led approach is axiomatic in the development of a 'standstill strategy' of the kind described in Chapter 5. One consequence is likely to be a strengthening of control over the preparation of the estimates by individuals or group of councillors and officials at the centre of the authority, who will play Guardian roles, who are committed to increasing the coherence of the authority's financial strategy as well as their control over its policies and priorities. In consequence, the Leader of the Council and other members of the ruling party group, together with the Chief Executive and the Treasurer, all play a part in determining resource availability and demanding that departments and committees take account of it when they prepare their bids for resources (Greenwood *et al.*, 1980; Greenwood, 1983; Elcock and Jordan (eds), 1987; Elcock, Jordan and Midwinter, 1989). In other words, the roles of the Guardians must be strengthened relative to those of the Advocates. In the mid-1980s a study of local authority budgets found many authorities determining in their budgetary cycles that estimates should be prepared in the context of 'standstill' strategies under which new growth must be paid for by making reductions elsewhere – which in practice is a recipe for incremental expenditure growth (Elcock and Jordan (eds), 1987). None the less, the importance of assessing the resources likely to be available as a guide to preparing estimates alters the balance in the budgetary process: it becomes more resource-led and less demand-led. Furthermore, control over the process becomes more centralised, as will be seen below in the discussion of incrementalism.

Is financial planning possible? A second traditional feature of budgetary processes is their annual nature: their preoccupation with setting expenditure and taxation levels for the fiscal year immediately ahead. In central government this process leads up to the Chancellor presenting his Budget to the House of Commons each March – an occasion anxiously awaited by all taxpayers and many others. In local authorities, annual budgeting is demanded because only very limited transfers of money from one financial year to the next are permitted by the law. A local authority may retain in its balances only such amounts as the District Auditor may judge to be reasonable and prudent. There is in consequence a tendency to spend unused funds towards the end of each financial year, often without having much regard for their efficient and effective use, in order not to lose the money when the financial year ends at the end of March. The inefficiency caused by this rule was to some extent recognised when the National Health Service was reorganised in 1974 because the new health authorities were allowed a limited right to carry funds over from one year to the next (Elcock and Haywood, 1980, p. 30). However, overspending this year is also charged against next year's allocation and the carry-over was restricted to 1 per cent of health authorities' budgets (Ibid, p. 35).

Furthermore, the Government allocates grants annually to local and health authorities alike, a process which has become more than somewhat unpredictable in local government in recent years because the rules for grant allocation are frequently changed and grants allocated only late in the financial year. This uncertainty has had adverse consequences for local authority financial management. It makes the early predictions of resource availability by local authorities difficult and unreliable (Audit Commission, 1983; Elcock and Jordan (eds), 1987). None the less, many attempts have been made to extend the period over which public expenditures are planned. Most immediate spending decisions have implications for more than one year ahead (Jordan, 1987). Equally, the consequences of past decisions commit resources and hence reduce policy-makers' freedom of manoeuvre in the present year.

In 1961, the Committee on the Control of Public Expenditure, chaired by Lord Plowden, published its report (Cmnd. 1432, Plowden, 1961) which recommended the establishment of a five year financial planning system which became known as the Public Expenditure Survey (PES). It is managed by a committee of senior civil servants commonly known by the acronym PESC. However, although initially the development of the PES was linked to the economic planning exercises which were attempted in the early 1960s and which included the creation of the National Economic Development Council (NEDC) in 1962 and then the Department of Economic Affairs (DEA) in 1964, it has become incremental. The process of preparing the annual PES White Paper, which set out five-year forward projections of Government expenditure, has always been dominated by the traditional bilateral bargaining process between the spending departments and the Treasury (Heclo and Wildavsky, 1974; Gray and Jenkins, 1985). This bargaining now ends with the resolution of intractable disputes by the 'Star Chamber' and the publication of the PES White Paper by the Cabinet for presentation in the Chancellor's Autumn Statement. In practice, therefore, the PES process has become both annualised and incremental. Incrementalism was simply projected forward for five years ahead and that period has now been reduced to three years.

Local authorities have also sought to develop financial planning systems, often attempting to project the consequences of current spending and taxing decisions up to three years into the future. After local government reorganisation, such financial planning was attempted by many local authorities (see Elcock, 1986a, pp. 188 ff) but it has been rendered difficult by the lateness with which the central government announces its grant allocations to local authorities. This uncertainty has been greatly increased by the frequent changes in the grant regime made by the Thatcher administrations; in the first five Thatcher years there were nine major changes and many more smaller alterations in the grant allocation system.

The Audit Commission estimated that the need for local authorities to retain extra balances to cope with the possibility of the grants regime being changed to their disadvantage had cost ratepayers £1.2 billion between 1979 and 1984. (Audit Commission, 1983) The extra rate levies which resulted were hence caused by central policies rather than local authorities themselves but this responsibility was never acknowledged by Ministers.

This climate of uncertainty seems to have destroyed most local authorities' enthusiasm for financial planning. Only one of the seventeen local authorities whose budgetary processes were studied by members of the Public Administration Committee in 1985–6, Oldham Borough Council, was attempting financial planning beyond the immediately forthcoming financial year (Elcock and Jordan (eds), 1987). In any case, in Oldham financial planning played a marginal role in determining the authority's budget compared to the struggle between Advocates and Guardians to reconcile the estimates with the resources available (Barberis and Skelton, 1987). A recent series of interviews with public managers, including a number from local authorities, revealed widespread scepticism about the usefulness in current circumstances of financial planning, when government policies and regulations are frequently changed (Elcock, Fenwick and Harrop, 1988). In consequence, most local authority budgetary processes are still essentially annualised and incremental, as is the PES procedure in Whitehall.

Incrementalism seems inevitable. Over the last 20 years, many attempts have been made to develop new approaches to budgeting which should enable resources to be allocated more rationally to projects and services than is possible by the traditional incremental process of adding or subtracting money at the margins. The best known such devices are: Planning, Programming, Budgeting Systems (PPBS), and Zero-Base Budgeting (ZBB).

Weighty tomes have been written about both these devices, so here only a brief summary of each will be offered. The principle underlying both systems is to secure scrutiny of continuing or 'base' expenditure, rather than only examining proposals for new projects or services while existing services or projects continue to be supported without undergoing scrutiny to determine whether they are still useful and giving value for money. Thus C. L. Schulze advocated 'careful identification and examination of goals and objectives in each major area of government activity …the analysis of alternatives to find the more effective means of reaching basic programme objectives' (Schulze, 1968) in order to develop PPBS.

PPBS is therefore conceptually related to H. A. Simon's advocacy of administrative rationality under which public administration is assumed to be goal-directed; goals or objectives should be identified and then the best means of implementing them should be sought (see Hogwood and Gunn, 1984, pp. 153–4 and 187 ff; see also document 11). A number of problems arise, some of which are similar to those encountered by those who have attempted to apply rational models of the policy processes. Among these problems are:

- First, that even the notion that government should be concerned with achieving goals may be disputed; it would be rejected by both Edmund Burke and Michael Oakeshott (1962), who argued that politics is a practical activity concerned with 'the pursuit of intimations', not with the rationalistic (for him a pejorative term) pursuit of goals (see Greenleaf, 1966).

- Even if one admits the validity of identifying goals, the process of doing so is fraught with difficulties. In multi-party systems, the various parties will press different goals, so that the goals being pursued by the government may change, possible radically, each time an election is held. Furthermore, lobby groups will compete to get goals favourable to their members' or clients' interests adopted. Richardson and Jordan (1979) have amply demonstrated that government policies are not coherent sets of measures to achieve objectives but the more or less contested results of negotiations within and between policy communities.

- Thirdly, even if parties and policies communities can produce a coherent set of goals, the cost involved in identifying and analysing the different possible means of achieving them quickly becomes horrendous. Programme Analysis and Review (PAR) in British central government which was introduced in 1970 as part of Edward Heath's effort to improve management in government, might be described as a limited form of PPBS. (Hogwood and Gunn, 1984, p. 188) It was an attempt to review in detail the usefulness and value for money being achieved by government programmes but its vitality quickly declined once Prime Ministerial patronage was withdrawn from it. One reason for PAR's decline was the amount of time and manpower required to carry out PAR reviews. These demands seem to have been widely resented among civil servants: 'The refrain, "PAR is not designed to help me," is heard everywhere.' (Heclo and Wildavsky, 1974, p. 283) Hence PAR languished in obscurity and was abolished in 1979 (Gray and Jenkins, 1985, p. 104–16).

- Lastly, PPBS may challenge vested interest within government who will seek to restrict its use or destroy it. Again, PAR provides a good example, in that its introduction was opposed by the Treasury, who saw it as a challenge to its own role of controlling public expenditure. The Treasury first secured control over PAR as the price for accepting it and then ensured that its operations remained on a small scale (Heclo and Wildavsky, 1974; Gray and Jenkins, 1985).

Zero-Base Budgeting (ZBB) has more modest objectives than PPBS but it has suffered some of the same problems. ZBB may be defined briefly as 'A budgetary system involving the scrutiny of all existing policies and commitments as well as proposals for new expenditure.' (Stephenson and Elcock (eds), 1985, p. 176) It consists of three main phases: Designation of decision units, which may be sections within departments; Formulation of decision packages for each unit; Ranking the decision packages in order of priority (see Hogwood and Gunn, 1984, p. 189).

ZBB should therefore ensure that existing as well as new activities are subjected to scrutiny before the resources needed for them are provided in the budget. However, the principal problem that ZBB causes is that it generates a very considerable volume of information, which must be absorbed by decision-makers if all the organisation's programmes are to be reviewed fully. A Scottish district council which introduced a limited version of ZBB in the early 1980s found that its central policy-makers were expected to read, comprehend and make decisions about the contents of a document of some 600 pages. This 'certainly proved excessive for most elected members'. (Charlton and Martlew, 1987, p. 182) In consequence, the scope of the ZBB system had to be reduced and the policy-making process became concentrated on a small group of leading members and senior officers – the Budget Scrutiny Group – who undertook the considerable task of reading the departments' Action Plans and discussing them with each committee convenor and departmental Chief Officer in turn. The experience of PPBS and ZBB may well lead one to the conclusion that budgeting is inevitably an incremental process because the alternatives demand too much work and generate too much conflict; certainly recent studies of local authority budgeting lead one inexorably to that conclusion (Elcock, Jordan and Midwinter, 1989). The pressures of time, events, and crises force policy-makers back to managing the margins, looking only at new or controversial expenditure and otherwise permitting existing activities to continue undisturbed and unchallenged. None the less, the pressure of demands for spending reduction may force at least some extensions of scrutiny.

Advocates versus Guardians. One feature of budgeting which is crucial for explaining why incrementalism is so prevalent is the tussle which always develops between those who are responsible for providing public services and those who must control overall demands on resources – Wildavsky's (1979) Advocates and Guardians. The tension between them arises for three main reasons, which are related to wider discussions about the balance between differentiation and integration in public service organisations.

The first is that the roles which the two groups of actors are expected to play are fundamentally different. Those official and politicians who are responsible for service provision are in contact with the organisation's clients or customers and hence are aware of their needs and demands. These needs and demands make their impact directly on the 'street level bureaucrats' (Lipsky, 1980) who deal directly with members of the public. These include social workers, teachers, clerks in benefit offices, policemen on the beat and a great many more. They transmit these needs and demands up to the hierarchy and they constitute collectively a constant demand for increased expenditure. The members of the service departments are anxious to provide the best possible service for citizens, as well as being conscious of large numbers of urgent needs which ought to be met and of the political controversies which may result if they are not met.

However, these service workers can have little conception of the overall resources available to the organisation, or of the resource constraints imposed on it. Resource management has traditionally been the responsibility of 'topocrats', officials responsible for the management of the organisation as a whole who report to elected members. Among elected members – Ministers and councillors alike – there are likely to be a small number who accept 'topocratic' roles or have them thrust upon them. In the central government, the Treasury has long played and proudly asserted its role in the management of public expenditure. 'Treasury Rules' dominate much financial management in the public sector. One all-pervading influence of Treasury control is its long-standing insistence that public organisations must budget their income and expenditure year by year and may not be permitted to 'carry over' funds from one year to the next. It is often alleged that this leads to wasteful spending towards the end of the financial year (see Chapman, 1978). When health authorities were allowed to 'carry over' 1 per cent of their budgets in 1974, this was regarded as a major innovation.

Again, the Chancellor of the Exchequer and the Chief Secretary to the Treasury assert control over expenditure decisions at the Ministerial level, especially during the PES process. For both the Treasury and its Ministers, the bilateral bargaining processes with the Advocate spending departments ensure that the Treasury alone and its Ministers are aware both of the overall pattern of resource availability and of the nature, as well as the intensity, of the competition for resources among the various departments.

In local authorities, the Treasurer and his or her department similarly seek to maintain overall control over resources and expenditure but the Treasurer may nowadays have to share this role with the Chief Executive Officer. At member level, there will probably be a finance committee or sub-committee with a Chairman who will have a role in the budgetary process but he or she is likely to play second fiddle to the Leader of the council, perhaps working with one or two other senior politicians. Such central groups have become increasingly important in recent years (Elcock and Jordan (eds), 1987). They work in informal groups to control the budgetary process and influence the preparation of estimates by the authority's departments. Apart from public pressure, which will be reflected both through the demands made on the 'street-level bureaucrat' and the pressures exerted on politicians, a second pressure generated by advocates which they impose on 'topocrats' stems from professional workers. This pressure is probably most relentless in the National Health Service because the high status of the medical profession coupled with doctors' role in dealing with sickness and disability produces incessant demand from hospitals, general practitioners and the public alike for increased health care spending. Doctors can and do freely engage in the practice of 'shroud-waving', being able to make a convincing case that refusal to increase NHS spending will result in needless deaths and suffering (Eckstein, 1957; Haywood and Alaszewski, 1980; Klein, 1983; Ham, 1985).

In local government too, professionalism generates demands for increased spending, not only to meet perceived needs but also to maintain established professional standards or ensure good professional practice. Here, accountability outwards to professional colleagues, including that to professional regulatory bodies, generates demands for extra spending in order not to expose professionals to criticism of their services by professional colleagues in the same or other authorities (see Elcock, Jordan and Midwinter, 1989, chapter 5) Again, these demands may be difficult for politicians to resist especially if they are supported by expressions of concern from the Press or members of the public. Central government is less directly exposed to such professional pressure, both because many of its activities do not affect citizens in their daily lives to the same extent as do those of local authorities and the NHS and because of the dominance of Civil Service policy advice by generalist administrators. They are able to maintain a more detached view of professional concerns and may therefore be sterner Guardians than local authority departmental officers who share their colleagues' professional interest and concerns. Even the Treasurer's men and women who work with the spending departments may 'go native' and support the professional Advocates in their arguments with the Guardians in the Treasurer's Department (Rosenberg, 1984).

Thirdly, political demands presented by constituencies, parties or pressure groups for higher spending may conflict with resource limitations, to the embarrassment of politicians. Political demands arise from election commitments or party policies which demand higher spending on favoured services or projects. They are also generated by constituency pressures on MPs or councillors. This tends to cause a role tension among Conservative politicians, who favour retrenchment in general terms but frequently plead for an exception to be made in favour of their own constituents. When such pressures become public, opposition parties will accuse Conservative members of hypocrisy. More charitably, the apparent inconsistency arises from a tension between Conservatives' general policies in favour of cuts and councillors' responsibility to protect and promote their constituents' interests. Ward pressures produce a series of demands for expenditure which appear small when taken in isolation but which can soon add up to considerable sums. Larger demands come from organised groups within the policy communities with whom public organisations must deal and whose demands are also hard to resist, both because of the public pressure they can bring to bear and the sanctions, such as industrial action, which they may be able to impose. The conflict between the Advocates and the Guardians thus occurs in each politician's individual breast as well as in collective debates.

Responses to fiscal pressure. We can summarise this section on the management of money by considering the nature of the effect that some fifteen years of pressure to reduce public spending and taxation has had on the financial management of public authorities. First, there has been little tendency for budgetary processes to become more rational, in the sense that such methods as PPBS and ZBB have made little headway. Incrementalism, the management of marginal or new expenditures, is still the prevailing approach. However, public authorities have generally sought to avoid actions which would entail them having to reduce the level of services they provide or make some of their employees redundant.

The best evidence that considerable ingenuity is used to avoid real reductions in services and employment comes from national and transnational comparative studies of local authorities (Tarschys, 1984; Wolman, 1984; Elcock and Jordan (eds), 1987) which demonstrate that local authorities are forced more or less reluctantly up an escalating 'ladder' of actions, each successive step of which may pose an increasing prospect of damaging services or staff. Such a 'ladder' is illustrated in Box 6.1 This is not an invariable order of proceeding but it is typical.

The first stages essentially involve gaining time by conceding reductions which will have little effect – including items which have been included

---

i. *How to Avoid Cuts*
'Fairy Gold' (Buy Time)
'Sore Thumbs'/'Shroud-waving'
Increase Charges
Sell Assets
Cut Capital Spending (Export unemployment to the local building industry)
Make Efficiency Savings: 'Cut bureaucracy'
Use private contractors or volunteers (shift costs)
Impose cash limits …

but if all these fail:
Impose service cuts and voluntary redundancies.
Impose service cuts and compulsory redundancies.

Box 6.1 How to Avoid Cuts

only so that they can be taken out later – and pressuring politicians to provide extra resources on pain of adverse consequences developing. The next stages may well be to increase revenue by increasing income charges such as those for entrance to municipal facilities, hire charges and fines for the late return of library books. However, some increases may have distributional effects which will be unacceptable to politicians, since they may penalise the poor or exclude them from using public services which they need or ought to be able to enjoy. Property or other assets may be sold to raise funds. Until recently, assets could be sold to British or foreign banks and leased back (Parkinson, 1986).

Cutting capital rather than current spending preserves current service levels and the jobs of the local authority's staff but may 'export' unemployment to local builders and result in the authority's stock of buildings becoming increasingly shabby. An across the board reduction in administrative expenses will attract favourable publicity while appearing to do little harm in the short term. However, severe damage may result if supervision is inadequate, so that inefficiency and corruption creep into service provision. Also, the quality of the authority's communication with the outside world may deteriorate. Private contractors or voluntary agencies may be able to provide services at lower cost than the authority itself can but they must be supervised. Finally, cash limits may be imposed as a part of a 'standstill' budget strategy but, as we have seen, this may in practice produce incremental growth in expenditure (see Chapter 5).

What is significant is that even after ten years of consistent pressure on resources, no British local authority seems to have been forced onto either of the final two rungs of the 'ladder', which involve real service reductions coupled with redundancies. Two local authorities have announced mass redundancies: Liverpool City Council in 1985 and Bradford City Council

125

in 1988 but in both cases these were the consequences of deliberate political choices by councillors and were not forced on them by outside pressure (Parkinson, 1985, 1987a).

Liverpool City Council announced its intention in 1985 to make all its 31,000 employees redundant in the hope both of putting pressure on the government to increase its grant to the council and to unite the unions behind its stand against government-imposed cuts. This tactic failed on both counts and the redundancies were withdrawn. In Bradford, the Conservatives won control of the city council in the autumn of 1988 after winning a by-election and were able by the use of the Lord Mayor's casting vote to impose a package of spending cuts, privatisation measures and redundancies which they had promised in their election manifesto. However, despite frequent warnings from many quarters that the day of reckoning is at hand, much recent research demonstrates that by developing a wide range of measures ranging from the conventional to the ingenious and unorthodox, local authorities and indeed most other public agencies have maintained their services and work-forces mainly intact (Elcock and Jordan (eds), 1987; Elcock, Fenwick and Harrop, 1988). Furthermore, local authority budgets are still almost invariably prepared by making incremental adjustments at the margin of their expenditure and income (Elcock, Jordan and Midwinter, 1989).

We have already discussed other changes to budgetary processes brought about by fiscal pressure. These have included making budgets resource rather than demand-led and centralising control over the preparation of budgets. However, while these changes have not removed from staff in spending departments the constant pressure for cuts, they have also not eliminated the constant demands from professional staff, 'street-level bureaucrats' and their clients for increased spending. Hence, the relationships between citizens, interest groups, the public service professionals and elected represented are still conflictual and the resolution of those conflicts in accordance with the ideologies of national and local ruling parties is still at the centre of programme and process accountability. Even in times of financial stringency, politicians are expected, as far as possible, both to pursue their parties' ideals and promote their constituents' interests. In addition, fiscal pressure has increased interest in developing greater efficiency in public services, which has been further encouraged in local government by the work of the Audit Commission in preparing 'league tables' of local authority performance and disseminating examples of 'good management practice'. The wish and need to increase efficiency have both extended the role of auditors well beyond their traditional preoccupation with fiscal accountability and encouraged the adoption and development of several techniques which we shall consider in Chapter 7.

Meanwhile, we turn to examine the second major resource controlled by government in its many manifestations: personnel.

FROM ESTABLISHMENT WORK TO HUMAN RESOURCE MANAGEMENT: THE PERSONNEL FUNCTION

We have already remarked that public organisations are among the largest employers of labour (in its widest sense) at the local, regional and national levels. Not only are public organisations very large compared to most private companies, but also much of their work is by definition labour-intensive – so much so that attempts to increase productivity may reduce the quality of the service if the number of staff allocated to a particular activity is reduced. Increasing student–staff ratios in schools or colleges may reduce the quality of the education they provide. For example, increased numbers of students may mean that the pastoral care offered to them declines, so that in turn student withdrawal and mental illness rates increase. Again, if social workers' case-loads are increased too far, they may not be able to devote sufficient time to each client to recognise the signs of an approaching catastrophe, such as child abuse. One particular problem about these examples and many other public sector jobs is that one cannot easily identify at what point increasing student–staff ratios or social work case-loads becomes counter-productive.

In consequence of the size of public organisations, the nature of their work and their ultimate accountability to elected politicians, personnel management in public services is and must be different in several respects from that in private firms, although there are common needs and problems too. The differences and similarities of personnel work in private firms and public authorities can be discussed in terms of a development from concern with issues of fiscal accountability to an almost total preoccupation now with improving public employees' performance.

Traditional Establishments work was concerned above all with ensuring that the public services were, as nearly as possible, incorruptible. Also, Establishment Officers are concerned to ensure that the number of staff employed and their grading conform to the regulations in force and the approved total. Establishments Work is therefore essentially concerned with fiscal accountability as defined earlier.

Richard Chapman has well described the nature of such Establishments work in the Civil Service. Its nature stems from the Treasury's responsibility for the preparation of the annual estimates and establishments work used not to enjoy a very high status:

127

> Some Establishments staff in Departments of government…tended to be rather unexciting officials, sometimes those who were a bit worn out by previous work, sometimes those promoted from the executive class and generally people not expected to rise higher in the civil service. Establishments was, essentially, a type of work aptly referred to in civil service terminology as a form of management as distinct from administration because it tended to be at arm's length from the political environment and the development of policy, for both of which the really outstandingly able staff were always in short supply.
>
> (Chapman, 1988a, p. 51)

Senior civil servants have always regarded themselves as being first and foremost the Minister's advisers on policy, with the management of their subordinates constituting very much a secondary aspect of their duties, an order of priorities which was severely criticised both by the Fulton Committee (1968, 1) and the Management Consultancy Group which advised it (Fulton, 1968, 2). One of the Report's major themes was that senior civil servants should devote more attention to management in order to improve the efficiency of the Service. In consequence, personnel management has slowly gained a higher place in the Civil Service's order of priorities (1968, 1, para. 18, p. 12; Garret, 1980).

In local government likewise, personnel management has become important only relatively recently. When the Mallaby Committee on the Staffing of Local Government reported in 1967, it criticised the absence of the personnel function from most local authorities' management structures, although the Hadow Committee more than thirty years earlier had urged local authorities to create Establishment Committees to take responsibility for personnel matters (Poole, 1978; Elcock, 1986a, pp. 196–7). However, as in the Civil Service at the time, such responsibilities were perceived largely as consisting of controlling the size of an authority's departments and scrutinising applications from them for new posts.

Thus, the traditional view of what Personnel (or rather Establishments) should consist of is closely related to the maintenance of the bureaucratic hierarchy, in which the duties, status and remuneration of each post must be clearly defined by general, detailed rules (Weber, 1947; Haynes, 1980). It is also related to fiscal accountability: ensuring that new posts are created only when the need for them has been proved and the appropriate grade decided. The values thus promoted are economy and probity. Public services will be provided by the minimum possible number of staff, who must be appointed to posts whose grading and remuneration have been approved as being appropriate to the duties involved.

Over the last thirty years, however, such an approach to personnel management has been widely recognised as being inadequate. Thus in relation to local government, the Bains Committee declared that:

The human problems of management in local government are in no way different from those in industry or the Civil Service. The resources devoted to the solution and more important the prevention of those problems in local government are in our view generally inadequate.

(Bains, 1972, para. 6:14, p. 67)

In the Civil Service, the Fulton Committee was severely critical of personnel management:

...civil servants are moved too frequently between unrelated jobs, often with scant regard to personal preferences or aptitudes. Nor is there enough encouragement and reward for individual initiative and objectively measured performance...

(1968, para. 20)

In the years since these two reports appeared, enormous changes have taken place in both the content and the status of personnel management in government organisations, although the status of personnel managers is still uncertain (Elcock, 1986a, pp. 199 ff). Change has occurred because of a wide range of pressures and opportunities, which we can consider in turn. There are three main sources of pressure and three areas of opportunity to discuss.

Pressures

1. The first source of pressure is continuing and increasingly insistent demands to procure economy and value for money in the public services. The wasteful use of under-employed manpower is a perennial complaint of saloon-bar bores and the editors of tabloid newspapers alike. This complaint was highlighted in particular by Labour Ministers after local government reorganisation had been carried out by a Conservative government in the early 1970s. The Prime Minister (Harold Wilson) declared in 1975 that some of the new local authorities had 'more chiefs than Indians', while the Secretary of State for the Environment, Anthony Crosland, bluntly told local government that 'The party's over.' More recently, Margaret Thatcher and her colleagues have repeatedly declared their determination to transform government agencies into 'leaner, fitter organisations'. (Parkinson, 1987b, p. 1) The pressure to make more efficient use of staff has, of course, been rendered much greater by the fiscal stringency of recent years. Indeed, many public service managers appear to feel that pressure to reduce staffing is a more severe constraint than the financial one, according to one regional survey (Elcock, Fenwick and Harrop, 1988, p. 43). Public managers have

often in consequence become more interested in the range of opportunities to improve the use of personnel which are now available, although many of them involve immediate increases in spending in the expectation that the organisation's performance will be improved in the future. Some managers have simply become increasingly defensive, reluctantly cutting staff at the margin by recourse to early retirement schemes and voluntary redundancies.

2. A second source of pressure to improve personnel management is a constant source of demands for more money: the development of increasingly active and militant trade unionism in the public services. This in turn involves personnel managers in extensive, difficult negotiations, as well as developing new benefits for staff which will render them less likely to leave or go on strike. Union pressure also produces more demands for training for staff. In the late 1970s, however, a wave of industrial action in the public services undoubtedly contributed to the growing public disillusion with them which was one of the main reasons for Mrs Thatcher's general election victory in 1979. (Butler and Kavanagh, 1979, pp. 333 ff) Hence, industrial relations is now a major preoccupation for personnel managers in government organisations.

3. The third source of pressure on personnel managers which is often generated by trade unions, are the policies and legislation adopted in the last two decades to secure equitable treatment at work for women, members of ethnic minorities and the disabled. The passage through Parliament of successive Race Relation Acts, together with legislation to promote women's rights, have combined with the consequent establishment of the Equal Opportunities Commission (EOC) and the Community Relations Commission (CRE) to impose new responsibilities on personnel managers to ensure that recruitment, training and promotion procedures give women, the disabled and members of ethnic minorities full opportunities to compete on equal terms with white people and men. Thus recruitment and promotion procedures, work practices and training schemes must be carefully scrutinised in order to ensure that they do not fall foul of equal opportunities legislation or that they will not give rise to action in the courts or the industrial tribunals (see *Public Administration*, Spring, 1989: a special issue on Equal Opportunities) This pressure is especially acute in the public services, above all because government organisations are commonly expected to set an example to others by scrupulously observing the law and because many politicians, especially in the Labour, Democrat and Social Democratic Parties, are enthusiastic supporters of equal opportunities policies who will

demand the implementation of those policies in the organisations which are accountable to them as MPs, councillors or health authority members.

These pressures have all increased the necessity for public services to develop increased capacities for effective personnel management by appointing officers with appropriate skills and attributes to negotiate effectively with trade unions, secure the implementation of equal opportunities policies and improve the value for money obtained from staff. The number and the scope of responsibility of personnel officers have been vastly increased; fortunately so too have the means available for them to carry them out.

Opportunities.

Three main opportunities for improving personnel management have emerged since 1950, which have both improved the status and content of public sector personnel management and increased managers' ability to cope with the pressures we have just discussed.

1. The first is that an increasingly wide range of management techniques became available to personnel managers from the 1950s on, including Organisation and Methods (O and M), and Work Study. The development of these techniques has in turn produced specialist staff who can apply them to public organisations.
2. Secondly, more attention is now paid to securing coherent training and career development for public service staff. In local government, for example, increasing emphasis is put on providing training courses in management or public administration to supplement the specialist professional courses which traditionally have provided the main, usually the sole focus for training in local government. In the Civil Service, the Civil Service College now offers a wide range of training courses in management, the use of information technology, managing priorities and time, as well as negotiating skills. These courses are 'tailored to the needs of civil servants and some (training) is specifically to support the management reforms and central initiatives of recent years.' (Civil Service College, 1987, p. 1) For less senior staff, the College, together with other academic institutions, now provides a wide range of courses for civil servants which lead to the acquisition of appropriate professional qualifications.
3. Lastly and at a much higher level of generality, the nature and importance of personnel management have changed as a result of the work of the 'Human Relations' school of personnel management.

This originated with the famous 'Hawthorne Experiments' which demonstrated, among other things, that informal peer-group relationships are more important in determining how hard and well workers work than formal, hierarchical relationships. Hence if performance is to be improved, attention should be given to improving their working environments, rather than by simply increasing the pressure put on them by superiors to work harder. (Rethlisberger and Dickinson, 1939; see also Brown and Steel, 1978). Such a shift of focus is especially hard to achieve in government, with its tradition of accountable hierarchies but it has gained ground as the number of personnel managers employed in government has increased and their status has improved (Poole, 1978). In consequence, the traditional role of Establishments Officer has been changed into a much wider personnel management role, which encompasses human resource management, industrial negotiations, the organisation of training programmes and much else besides.

LAND AND PROPERTY

Many writers of textbooks on public administration forget that as well as managing large budgets and employing many people, public authorities also own large quantities of land and property. Its management has largely been left to specialised Estates and Property Officers, who have often been left largely unnoticed to manage land and property without being subjected to anything more than occasional and cursory supervision by politicians or other senior officials. Little regard seems to have been paid until relatively recently to land management in the public sector. For example, when new local authorities took over their predecessors' property holdings in 1974, some were unable to discover at all precisely what land and property they owned. This led on the one hand to acrimonious disputes between county and district councils over the ownership of particular properties. On the other hand, if a local authority was ignorant of owning a particular piece of land it could not use it and if that ignorance continued for long enough, someone could acquire squatter's rights to it. In consequence, time and money had to be devoted to the preparation of terriers: complete records of the land and property which was in the council's ownership.

The management of land and property involves close contact with the private sector since its value can be determined only in the light of local and regional market conditions. The relevant profession of valuation and estate management therefore crosses the divide between the public and private sectors. Two developments in particular have increased its importance in public administration in recent times.

- The first was the passage of the Community Land Act in 1975, which required local authorities to manage the disposal of all land for which planning permission for development had been granted. Reduced to its essentials, the Act required each local planning authority to buy such land at its current use value and then, if it chose, to sell it for development at its higher value with planning permission for development. Hence increases in the value of land and property which resulted from a decision by a public authority (a grant of planning permission for development) would accrue to the public purse rather than to private gain. Although the Community Land Act was too short-lived (it was repealed in 1980) for many such purchases to take place, its effects were to increase the importance of valuers in local authority decision-making processes and to push them into closer relationships with their colleagues in planning departments, because the system established by the Act was 'planning-led' (see Elcock, 1986a, p. 195).
- Although the Thatcher Government repealed the Community Land Act soon after it won office, it replaced it with an obligation on local authorities to dispose of land which they were not using, with a power vested in the Environment Secretary to enforce such disposals. Hence, local authorities must now ensure that they are making efficient use of the land they own or risk being deprived of it.

The current emphasis on the free market in land, coupled with fiscal pressure and the requirement to dispose of surplus land, have produced controversial changes in land management. For example, many local authorities in rural areas have disposed of their smallholdings estates, which often provide young farmers with the only means to acquire a small farm at a rent they could afford in order to establish themselves in agriculture (Elcock, 1986a, pp. 193–4). Also, some municipal airports are now owned and managed by private firms. Under recent legislation, the management of housing has been subjected to radical changes with the introduction of council tenants' right to choose their future landlords from among the council, housing associations and private firms. This has, of course, been added to their existing right to buy houses at a substantial discount. It seems likely, therefore, that the land holdings of public authorities will be substantially reduced – mainly in local government, although health authorities have also been pressed by financial pressure into disposing of substantial amounts of hospital land for private development. Furthermore, pressure for the efficient management of those land and property holdings that remain in public ownership has been considerably increased.

CONCLUSION

In general, the traditional concern of those responsible for the administration of publicly-owned resources with fiscal accountability: with ensuring that funds are properly spent and not wasted, that appointments and promotions are made on the basis of impersonal criteria and that land dealings are honest, has widened to include efforts to secure greater efficiency, as well as to secure better performance in accomplishing public authorities' objectives and purposes. These changes have occurred because fiscal pressure has led politicians and officials alike to seek ways to maintain or if possible improve public services while the resources available to pay for them have shrunk, as well as because politicians and the public have become more aware of the inadequacy of management systems which pay insufficient attention to improving the efficiency and effectiveness of government organisations. Not the least spur to such developments, however, has been the availability of an increasing range of techniques to assist in increasing efficiency and improving performance. These are the subject of the next chapter.

However, this discussion of resource management should end with a warning. Preoccupation with the 'Three Es' – Economy, Efficiency and Effectiveness – may exclude consideration of other important issues. On the one hand, we may be in danger of forgetting that some of the traditional values of public administration also continue to be important. These include, for example, the elimination of corruption from the public services and the ability of officers in central and local government to advise politicians of all parties (see Widdicombe, 1986). Also, public servants have a responsibility to ensure that citizens are treated equitably in the distribution of benefits and taxes, as well as in the enforcement of laws and regulations. Richard Chapman has repeatedly warned, for example, that these values are threatened by recent changes in the management of the Civil Service. Thus secondments of private sector managers to the Civil Service, as well as the appointment of recently retired civil servants to company boards of directors may render the relationship between government departments and outside contractors open to possibly corrupt influences. Also the appointment of 'people who think like us', to use the Prime Minister's phrase, to senior positions in the Civil Service may render it hard for those top civil servants objectively to advise a government of another party should one be elected (Chapman, 1988b and c).

On the other hand, concentrating on the 'Three Es' may exclude consideration of other important values. Lewis Gunn (1988) has suggested that the 'Three Es' should properly be five; that Excellence and Enterprise should also be included. In Chapter 2 we noted that the debate about applying the 'Principles of Excellence' (Peters and Waterman, 1982) to the public services. Equally, public authorities need to be enterprising in forming partnerships with private companies or competing with them, while being aware of the dangers of corruption that may arise. What Nicholas Ridley, when he was Secretary of State for the Environment, dubbed the 'Enabling Local Authority' because its role will be to enable others to provide public services rather than providing them itself, may need also to become the 'Enterprising Local Authority' if its departments are to compete for the right to continue providing those services themselves. All these may change patterns of accountability but not remove the need to be accountable, or destroy the importance of longer-standing values in public administration.

CHAPTER SEVEN

Applying techniques

INTRODUCTION

The new student of public administration will meet during his or her studies a bewildering array of initials and acronyms whose meaning he or she will probably be left to discover alone. Teachers and peers will assume that students know what the acronyms mean without being told; students themselves are reluctant to reveal their ignorance. A few textbooks offer glossaries (for example Stephenson and Elcock, 1985, p. 176) but they are rare. Hence, the student is confronted by rows of letters like AIDA, IT, PPBS, ZBB and the like to interpret. Many of them refer to techniques which have been developed in the hope of improving management in both the private and the public sectors. They are intended to assist decision-makers and administrators to develop better policies and improve their performance. They are of many different kinds and often their intended use is not well defined, either by their inventors or their users. However, they can be considered under four main headings: Research, Finance and Resource Management, Information Technology, and Decision-making Aids. We can discuss each in turn and use a concluding section to discuss some techniques that do not easily fall into any of these four categories.

RESEARCH TECHNIQUES

A perennial problem which faces public policy-makers is the inadequacy of the information upon which difficult and controversial decisions must be reached. The Institute of Operational Research approach discussed in

Chapter 4 urged the systematic reduction of uncertainty of information by research as one of its three means to reduce uncertainty and hence increase the likelihood of policy decisions being sound (Friend and Jessop, 1969). The availability of an increasing range of social science research techniques has increased the amount of information available very considerably but policy-makers must be cautious about deploying it uncritically, for three main reasons.

1. First, much of the information collected, as well as the conclusions drawn from it, is based on probability. Although the probability that a sample survey, for example, is accurate may be as high as 98 per cent, there is still a slight possibility that conclusions drawn from it may be erroneous.

2. Secondly, information may be incomplete and the research may prove inadequate for the decision-maker to base secure conclusions on it. Furthermore, the cost of achieving a high level of accuracy or of probability that the conclusions drawn are correct is often prohibitive. Almost inevitably, therefore, the decision-maker cannot escape making a judgement based on experience and intuition as well as on the research information available; hence the importance attached by writers on policy analysis to such extra-rational judgements as those based on past experience, 'hunches' and so on (Vickers, 1965; Dror. 1973).

3. Thirdly, all research will have been carried out by researchers who are influenced by their own values and may be seeking to establish conclusions which support those values. Max Weber's view that social science could be value-free has proved to be an unrealistic chimera. All social science research is influenced by values. Charles Taylor has warned us that '...a *political* framework cannot fail to contain some, even implicit, conception of human needs, wants and purposes.' (Taylor, 1967, p. 25) We need, therefore, to be aware of the values that influence social scientists despite their claims that the application of rigorous scientific methods produces irrefutable data and conclusions (see Elcock, 1976, pp. 11–14). We also need to be value-critical, seeking to identify and scrutinise the values underlying social science research (Rein, 1976). Some social scientists wear their ideological hearts openly on their sleeves, as did SM Lipset when he declared at the end of his book, *Political Man*, that 'A basic premise of this book is that democracy is not only or even primarily a means through which different groups attain their ends or seek the good society; *it is a good society itself in operation.*' (Lipset, 1963, p. 403. Author's italics) Others are not so open and their work must be read

carefully in order to tease out the value assumptions that underlie their findings and conclusions (Rein, 1976). The author's assumptive world must be identified (Vickers, 1965).

Having thus given some general 'health warnings' about the use and possible misuse of the research techniques available to public policy-makers and their advisers, we can now explore some of the main techniques, considering both the ways in which these general problems manifest themselves and some specific difficulties which arise from the deployment of a particular technique. We consider four main research techniques: the sample survey, demographic projections, policy reports, and Critical Path Analysis (CPA).

The Sample Survey is now well established as a technique for exploring a wide range of the personal attributes or opinions of large numbers of people. Its usefulness derives from the impossibility of studying the entire population of a country or even a city. It is widely used by companies testing the success of their product ranges or the likely popularity of future products. Sample surveys are also used by newspapers and political scientists to identify patterns of electoral behaviour on the basis of which election results can be predicted. Some spectacular failures notwithstanding, opinion polls are now an established feature of the political scene in most liberal democracies.

The usefulness of the sample survey is predicated upon the high probability that a relatively small sample which is systematically drawn from the population at large will accurately reflect the attributes and opinions of the relevant population, at a fraction of the cost entailed in carrying out a census of the entire population (Kalton, 1966; Moser and Kalton, 1971). To ensure accuracy, careful attention must be paid to four aspects of the research design.

1. The first is that the sample must be drawn in such a way as to ensure that its members are likely to be representative of the population being studied. The samples used by some newspaper polls have been regarded as suspect because they include too many respondents who are likely to share the editor's political views. Again, the findings of telephone opinion polls may need to be treated with caution because relatively few working class people possess a telephone and hence they will not be contacted by the researchers, although a correction factor can be built into the analysis. None the less, only an approximation of the population's view will result.

2. Secondly, the questionnaire must be designed in such a way that it does not lead the respondents in particular directions. In this matter,

the survey researcher is in a similar position to the barrister in court, who is not allowed to ask leading questions. The questions must not guide the respondent in favour of one response rather than another and must be carefully scrutinised in the Popperian spirit of seeking to detect and avoid error (Popper, 1960). Also, the order in which the questions are asked may distort the response. For example, if you ask respondents how they voted in last week's general election and then immediately ask them how they voted in the previous one, you may encourage them to give consistent answers and thus conceal the extent of changes in party loyalties between the two elections (Benewick *et al.*, 1969). The questions should therefore be separated. A 'brainstorming' technique (see Section 5 below) should be used during the design of a survey questionnaire to pick up questions that are likely to produce unsatisfactory results. Also, a small pilot study is often carried out to test the questionnaire, so as to maximise the likely value of the final study.

3. Thirdly, wherever possible the answers required from the respondents should be capable of numerical classification, rather than requiring subjective interpretation by the researcher before they can be classified. However, this is not always possible, especially when the survey involves interviewing small groups of senior decision-makers (Elcock, 1978; Elcock, Fenwick and Harrop, 1988).

4. Finally, interviewers must be trained to administer the questionnaire in ways that do not produce distorted responses. They must take care that the response rate to the survey is maximised, for example by making repeated calls on respondents who were not in when the interviewer originally called.

If these four conditions are met and the response rate is sufficiently high, up to a 98 per cent probability that the results accurately reflect the attributes and opinions of the population may be achieved.

The sample survey as a technique is commonly used to study electorates and predict the results of elections. It may also be used by policy-makers as part of the public participation exercises required in the development of some major policy statements. Thus the 1968 and 1971 Town and Country Planning Acts required county councils who were preparing their Structure Plans to seek public views about their proposals. The difficulty of securing more than minimal participation (see Humberside County Council, 1976, Volume 3, for example) may render the sample survey a useful, although relatively expensive means to secure a systematic view of public opinion about the issues being tackled in the Structure Plan.

However, two major defects remain.

1. The first is that unless the survey is periodically repeated, it provides only a static picture of the state of public opinion: a 'snapshot' of what the respondents and hence the population thought at the time when the survey was carried out.
2. Secondly, if the wrong questions are written into the questionnaire or the researchers discover during the survey that matters which the respondents think are of great importance have been omitted, the survey's value may be limited and the only remedy may be to repeat it, which is a costly and time-consuming process. However, sometimes it does become apparent after a poll has been carried out that an important factor was neglected. Thus the importance of differential abstentions seems to have been underrated by the pollsters who failed to predict the Labour defeat in the 1970 general election (Butler and Kavanagh, 1971).

Demographic Projections. Using information collected by the decennial census, it is possible to predict changes in the balance or location of the population which have implications for public policies. Some such projections may have major, long-term consequences. For example, an increase in the birth-rate now will generate increased demand for primary school places five years hence, a demand which will work through secondary and higher education over the following 15 years or so. Twenty-one years hence there will be an increased number of graduates seeking employment. However, the most certain predictions concern pressure on primary and secondary education, when attendance for the new babies as they grow up will be compulsory.

One recent demographic change which has major policy implications is the increase in the number of old and very old (over 75) people in Britain and other developed countries (Sunter, 1986). Old people make particularly heavy demands on the health care and personal social services: the 'age explosion' has imposed a requirement that expenditure on the National Health Service must increase by approaching 2 per cent per annum, if the services available are to keep pace with the increasing demands imposed on the social and health services by increased longevity. Again, pension costs are increasing as more people attain the age at which they have the right to draw State and private pensions. Coupled with a declining birth-rate, this means that the increasing number of old people will have to be supported by a smaller number of economically active citizens. The consequences for public policy are hence considerable. In 1982, the Central Policy Review Staff warned the Thatcher government that it would soon have to choose between increasing taxes and radically reducing the level of welfare services available, because the current level of services could not be supported by the income being received. Increasing taxes was anathema to the government; reducing welfare services was unthinkable with a general election approaching, yet the demographic trend made the dilemma inescapable and abolishing the CPRS has not caused it to disappear (Blackstone and Plowden, 1988).

Demographic projections may produce spatial consequences too with which public policy-makers must deal. For example, an analysis of the 1971 Census data by Humberside County Council's Planning Department revealed that the number of elderly people living in the seaside resort of Bridlington was increasing very rapidly as more Yorkshire folk chose to retire there. The local health and social services were likely soon to be unable to meet the consequent demands which would fall on them unless the Health Authority and the Social Services Department took action to provide more personnel and facilities in Bridlington for the care of old people (Humberside County Council, 1976).

Such long-term changes in the structure and location of the population can more easily be detected now that large quantities of information can be analysed by computers (see below). The changes that occur are regular over long periods and may have major policy implications. They may, however, be disrupted by unexpected developments; for example AIDS may (or may not) have major implications for population projections into the twenty-first century. None the less, they usually provide a sound basis for policy decisions, especially long-term social investment decisions such as the location of new schools, hospitals or residential homes which take several years to construct and open.

Policy Reports. The analysis of demographic projections, possibly combined with the use of sample surveys and other techniques, may be used by official or unofficial persons or groups to indicate to the government that action is needed to resolve a particular problem. For example, in 1980 an official working party chaired by Sir Douglas Black published a report which demonstrated that there were substantial variations in the health states and life-chances of people residing in different parts of the country, which were the result in the main of differing levels of wealth and poverty, as well as of different standards of health care provision. People in the North of England were shown to be likely to be ill more frequently and die sooner than those living in the South-East.

The Black Report clearly indicated that substantial public spending was needed if health states and life-chances were to become more equal. However, increased expenditure was unacceptable to Mrs Thatcher's administration: Sir Douglas Black's working party had been appointed by the previous Labour government. Instead, Ministers exhorted citizens to adopt healthier life-styles. The Whitehead Report, which was published originally by the Health Education Council as its last act before its abolition in 1987, revealed that the variations in health states and longevity detected by the Black Report had increased in the seven years since its publication. For example, Table 7.1 shows that Standard Mortality Ratios (SMRs) are higher both in the more deprived parts of the country and among people in the lower social classes than they are in the affluent South-East and among the upper classes. Table 7.2 illustrates the differences in consumption of healthy and unhealthy foods between the best-off and the worst-off, clearly demonstrating that the poor do not eat healthy foods. The Government made a clumsy and unsuccessful attempt to suppress the Whitehead Report or at least restrict its circulation, because its findings showed that government policies had increased inequalities in health-states in ways which many citizens would find repugnant. Again, Ministers' responses were confined in the main to urging people to give up smoking, cut down their drinking, go jogging

Table 7.1   SMRs for all causes, 1979-80, 1982-83 by Region
(Men aged 20-64 and Women aged 20-59)

Standard Region/ Country	Men			Women		
	I & II	*IV & V*	*IV & V as % of I & II*	*I & II*	*IV & V*	*IV & V as % of I & II*
North	81	152	188	80	136	170
Wales	79	144	182	79	125	158
Scotland	87	157	180	91	141	155
North West	83	146	176	86	135	157
Yorkshire & Humberside	79	134	170	78	120	154
West Midlands	75	127	169	77	113	147
South East	67	112	167	71	100	141
East Midlands	74	122	165	73	110	151
South West	69	108	156	70	96	137
East Anglia	65	93	143	69	81	117
Great Britain	74	129	174	76	116	153

Note: SMR for all men and women, in Great Britain in 1979-80, 1982-83 is 100. Regions ranked by SMR for classes IV and V combined as a proportion of SMR for classes I and II combined.
Women classified on own, for husband's occupation.
Source: Townsend (1987) derived from OCPS data.

Table 7.2 Food Consumption by income group, Great Britain, 1976 and 1984
(oz./person/week)

Income Group	White Bread		Brown Bread inc. Wholemeal		Sugar		Total Fats		Fruit (Fresh)		Vegetables (fresh)		Potatoes	
	1976	1984	1976	1984	1976	1984	1976	1984	1976	1984	1976	1984	1976	1984
A	19.8	12.3	4.1	8.0	12.3	8.0	9.8	9.1	22.5	25.3	27.3	30.7	29.8	33.4
B	26.2	18.3	3.0	6.0	13.4	9.4	10.5	9.5	18.3	19.0	24.0	24.4	35.0	36.5
C	30.4	23.0	3.0	5.9	14.5	10.9	11.0	10.4	15.2	16.0	24.8	25.5	38.2	42.4
D	29.9	26.0	2.7	5.2	15.7	11.5	11.0	10.0	15.2	13.0	24.9	21.5	42.3	48.3

Source: MAFF: Household food consumption and expenditure for 1976 and 1984.

and eat healthier foods – the former junior Health Minister, Mrs Edwina Currie was particularly active in issuing such injunctions. However, the last in particular was unrealistic advice to give to most of those whose deprivation had been revealed by the Black and Whitehead Reports because they could not afford healthy but relatively expensive diets (The *Guardian,* 14 December 1988, p. 25). Hence, where the use of techniques – in this case demographic analysis – produced results which are firmly grounded in apparently incontestable evidence but are unpalatable to rulers, they will be rejected as a basis on which to make policy decisions. Alternatively, the government may try to change the basis on which official statistics are collected. Thus the basis on which the monthly unemployment figures are collected has repeatedly been changed to produce a reduction in the official total. Other statistical series have likewise been altered or sometimes dropped altogether to reduce the chances that they will produce information which will embarrass the Government (The *Guardian*, 15 March, 1989, p. 21). Research is only the preliminary to policy preparation: its presentation may not produce the results which politicians and its collectors hope for.

Critical Path Analysis. A final research technique has been borrowed from engineering. It involves identifying the stages involved in, for example, building a bridge, identifying which activity takes longest and what other activities can be completed in the meantime, so shortening the building period as much as possible. Similarly, it may be possible to project the stages involved in building, equipping and staffing a new hospital and by doing so accelerate its opening. Equally, a service or project can be planned so that the demands it will make on resources at each stage can be assessed and budgetary processes adjusted to ensure that the appropriate resources are available when they are needed, rather than too early or too late. At this point Critical Path Analysis may be combined with one or more of the financial techniques discussed next.

FINANCIAL TECHNIQUES.

In Chapter 6, we saw that budgetary processes in the public sector tend to be incremental and demand-led, although they may be becoming more resource-led as Treasurers try to cope with demands for spending cuts. They also tend to be annualised. These features produce two particular tendencies in public sector budgets which have been widely criticised. In consequence, radical proposals have been made for their improvement.

The first of these tendencies is that since expenditures are adjusted only at the margins, most of an organisation's activities continue to receive resources without being subjected to any scrutiny to determine their continued efficiency or usefulness. Stories abound of the filing clerk whose work is unnecessary because the need for it has passed but the work continues because no-one has noticed that it is no longer needed. Secondly, much public finance is planned only for one year or so ahead, although we have seen that both the policies on which money is spent and the problems these policies seek to resolve have predictable consequences for more – often much more – than one year ahead.

Two techniques have been proposed to address these problems, about which a great deal has been written and whose initials are firmly installed in the public finance and public administration languages: PPBS and ZBB. We have discussed both in the last chapter because they are intimately linked with the budgetary process: here we need only note that both entail scrutiny of continuing as well as new expenditures. Ideally, the budget should be built up from scratch each year but there is never sufficient time to do this. In any case, most public organisations are legally obliged to carry out many of their activities, hence review can be confined to seeing whether they can be provided more efficiently, thus freeing more resources for discretionary activities. At least 80 per cent of a local authority's budget, for example, is likely to be committed by such statutory obligations. However, PPBS and ZBB generate very heavy burdens for policy-makers and administrators. They are also likely to be resisted by vested interests if the continuation of existing activities is questioned. For both these reasons, attempts to introduce PPBS and ZBB have proved largely unsuccessful.

We have also discussed the difficulties inherent in financial planning, which have resulted in many local authorities abandoning it, as well as its modification (in the form of the PES) by the Civil Service to reinforce incrementalism. In any case, at present the climate of uncertainty in which public organisations must operate has made financial planning difficult, if not impossible, for most of them.

At a rather different level, we need to discuss further two other financial techniques which have become increasingly important in the 1980s. These are creative accountancy and efficiency strategies. Both have common origins as responses to the unremitting pressure imposed on the entire public sector by the Thatcher Governments to reduce spending and hence taxation. The first is a response which is intended to evade the government's requirements by making apparent savings without reducing expenditures on jobs and services; the second may, by reducing the cost of each unit of service, enable existing services to be maintained or create room for the provision of new or increased services.

Creative Accountancy. This technique has been developed mainly by local authorities, although it has been copied by other public sector organisations faced with the need to make restricted funds go further. Local authorities have resorted to 'creative accountancy' because since 1980, the financial relationship between the central government and local authorities changed in two ways. The first was an increase in central pressure to reduce spending as a matter of ideological conviction rather than, as had been the case after 1976, of economic necessity. The second was an attempt to restrain not only the global total of local government spending but also to restrict that of individual local authorities whom the government regarded as 'overspenders': these were almost all authorities controlled by the Labour Party. The Government therefore embarked on a whole series of measures directed both at restricting overall expenditure and controlling that of the 'overspending' local authorities. The need to do this was intensified, from the Government's point of view, as an increasing number of local authorities fell under Labour control from 1981 (which was somewhat of a Socialist *annus mirabilis*) onward.

We considered the overall consequences of the government's measures in the last chapter. Here we need only highlight some of the major stages in the cyclical struggle which has developed between the Thatcher Government and local authorities, which compelled many of the latter to resort to creative accountancy in order to avoid having to make major service and staff reductions. The Government has attempted to secure reductions in local government spending and many local authorities have been determined to preserve their services and employment levels. The adoption of 'creative accountancy' techniques by local authorities was one of the measures they took to evade the consequences of the government's spending policies. The principal stages in the government's attack have been:

- The 1980 Local Government, Planning and Land Act which introduced a new system for the distribution of the Rate Support Grant which would base an authority's grant allocation on the amount that authority would need to spend in order to provide its services at a 'standard' level. This calculation is the Grant Related Expenditure Assessment (GREA) and spending above the assessment attracts penalties in the form of progressively greater reductions in grant, to the point at which the cost of an extra pound of spending can cost a local authority's ratepayers up to £8 because of the steepness of the penalty slope, as illustrated in Figure 7.1.

Figure 7.1   Block Grant Profile 1987–88

Block Grant Profile 1987 – 88

The Table and diagram illustrate that as spending increases, the Council loses Block Grant, and vice-versa, at a rate of £642,000 grant per £1m of expenditure. Beyond the 'threshold' the fate of loss/gain becomes £1,240,000 grant per £1m of expenditure.

Oxfordshire County Council	Net Expenditure £m	Block Grant £m
Maximum Grant	94.1	94.1
Grant Related Expenditure (GRE)	195.6	28.9
Government's Assumed Spending Level	200.0	26.0
Budget	210.5	19.3
Threshold	221.1	12.4
Zero Grant	231.2	0

* excluding additional spending for Teachers' Salaries Restructuring

---

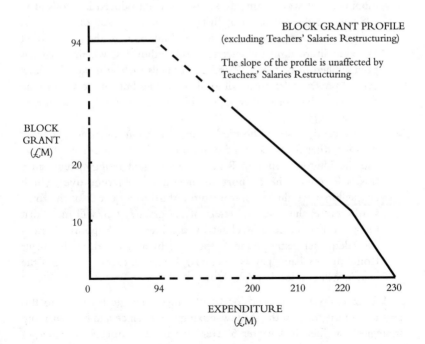

- At the same time as GREAs were introduced, the government announced an overall target for local government spending which was initially set at 5.2 per cent below the level achieved in the last year of the Labour government. Targets were introduced to bring spending down more quickly than would have occurred if reliance had been placed on the GREA system alone – in part because some local authorities were spending below their GREA and might therefore feel encouraged to *increase* their spending! However, targets were abolished in 1985 when the Government felt that GREAs and penalties would suffice to control spending.

- In 1982, local authorities' right to set supplementary rates was abolished, although it was rarely used, after an attempt to impose an obligation to hold a referendum before levying a supplementary rate was rejected by the House of Lords as an undesirable constitutional innovation.

- Two years later in England and Wales councillors lost a further right: that of setting what rate precept they chose subject only to the constraints of annuality and *ultra vires* including the prohibitions on deficit budgeting and carrying over excessive balances. 'Rate-capping', as it was commonly known, was introduced in Scotland in 1982 and in the rest of Great Britain by the Rates Act of 1984. This Act gives the Secretary of State for the Environment the power to set an expenditure limit for selected local authorities, which so far has been applied to between 12 and 20 councils each year. He also has a general power to 'rate-cap' all local authorities but this power may be exercised only after further approval by Parliament, which has not so far been sought.

- Most recently, local authorities' financial freedom of manoeuvre may be still further reduced by the substitution of the Community Charge and the Uniform Business Rate for the present rating system, since this will reduce the proportion of councils' income over which councillors have direct control from a third to a quarter of the total. Furthermore, the 'Gearing' effect of the grant system will mean that once the expenditure level set by the Revenue Support Grant is exceeded, each extra pound of spending by an authority will cost its Community Charge payers an extra £4. Hence, extra spending at the margin will cost local people dear.

We have already discussed local authorities' strategic responses to this pressure, in the form of the shadow-boxing, compliance and brinkmanship strategies described in Chapter 5. Here we need to discuss the range of techniques for avoiding having to translate fiscal pressure into redundancies and service cuts which are known collectively as 'creative accountancy'.

They constitute a rung on the ladder of responses to financial pressure discussed in the last chapter. The techniques are:

- The allocation of expenditures, especially on repairs, to capital rather than current budgets in order to avoid penalties.
- Adjusting the council's balances so that 'overspending' occurs in the budgets of financial years when penalties are less severe, which usually means transferring expenditure to an earlier financial year, since the government has tended to impose progressively more severe penalties in each successive year.
- Rescheduling debts to avoid repayments in the early years when they would attract penalties. However, deferring repayments stores up higher burdens in the future and is essentially a tactic of buying time in the hope that a Government more sympathetic to public spending will win office.
- Reopening the books in order, for example, to claim grants which have been left unclaimed.
- Varying the assumptions on which the Budget is based: more optimistic assumptions about likely grants or about contingencies may reduce 'overspending' relative to GREA and hence penalties. Reducing contingency allowances is a form of 'fairy gold' because it reduces the budget without affecting the authority's activities.
- Selling mortgages on council houses to banks or other lenders.
- Deferred purchases and lease-back arrangements: essentially selling the council's assets to a bank or other financial institution and then leasing them back.

Several of these techniques have either been made illegal by subsequent legislation designed to block loopholes discovered by ingenious local authority Treasurers, or their legality has been challenged by the District Auditor. However, the ingenuity of local government Treasurers' staff in finding new loopholes seems to be inexhaustible, so that a continuing cycle of evasion followed by legislation or court actions to close off new 'creative accountancy' measures has developed. Furthermore, we have seen that no local authority seems yet to have been compelled to make major spending and service cuts or impose compulsory redundancies.

Efficiency Strategies have been much in evidence in the central government, especially in the form of the successive initiatives which have been launched by the Prime Minister's Efficiency Unit and which we have already considered in some detail in Chapter 2 (see also Document 7). The Rayner Scrutinies were designed to identify and reduce waste. These were followed by MINIS and the FMI (see Document 6), both of which encourage cost-centre managers to use resources more carefully in order to provide the maximum amount of services for the resources available. The efficiency strategy which has the most far-reaching implications is the establishment of departmental agencies, whose Chief Executives will 'be given personal responsibility to achieve the best possible results...' (Efficiency Unit, 1988, Para. 22, p. 10). The objective is therefore to maximise the amount of service provided relative to the resources deployed to provide it but we have seen that the creation of agencies has extensive, possibly sometimes sinister implications for the development of the Constitution which range far beyond its declared purpose of increasing efficiency.

However, many of the measures developed by the Prime Minister's Efficiency Unit do seem to have reduced waste and encouraged increased efficiency. As such, many of these changes ought to be accepted and developed by Governments of other political hues if and when they gain office, as well as being considered by local authorities of all political complexions who are anxious to reduce waste. Local authorities have been encouraged to develop efficiency strategies by the Audit Commission. Again, liberating public sector managers from detailed control and supervision will encourage them to be more creative and enterprising in seeking to provide the best possible services as cheaply as possible. Some of the implications of *The Next Steps* initiative, such as the hint of the eventual privatisation of some agencies (para. 19, p. 9) are highly controversial but managerial devolution as a technique could be most useful to, say, a Labour government which wished to encourage the provision of more attractive services. Indeed, in the form of 'going local', we have already seen that it has been valuable in improving the accessibility and responsiveness of local government services (see Chapter 3). Care will need to be taken when a government led by a Prime Minister other than Mrs Thatcher wins office, that the new Ministers do not throw out useful managerial babies with what they will regard as a lot of ideological bath water.

INFORMATION TECHNOLOGY

Computers are now so much a part of our everyday lives that it is hard to remember that until relatively recently their impact on government was at most marginal. Their effect on public administration has become considerable but the nature of that effect has altered fundamentally since computers began to be widely deployed in government departments, local authorities and other public service organisations.

At first, computers were large, unwieldy but powerful machines which were most useful for the processing of large amounts of statistical information, such as the results of the Census, or the execution of repetitive routine operations involving large amounts of repeated data such as the administration of payrolls. Then, in the late 1970s and early 1980s, with the arrival first of the 'Virtual Machine Concept' and then of cheap, easily used micro-computers, not only did the range of computer applications become much more varied but also the implications of information technology for organisational structures changed fundamentally.

The 'Virtual Machine Concept' means that a user sitting at a terminal, which could be located many miles away from the mainframe processor, can operate as if he or she is the sole user of the machine, gaining access to information stored in it, inserting new material and carrying out analytical operations with it. The micro-computer offers full computing facilities on a desktop. Data can be obtained by the transfer of floppy discs or micro-computers can be linked to one another in networks. These may include a link to a large mainframe machine as well, when the micro-processor acts as a terminal linked to the mainframe.

The impact of these developments has been that, whereas the arrival of the mainframe computer centralised much activity on the department where the computer was located, the 'Virtual Machine Concept' and even more the micro-computer have decentralised control because 'street-level bureaucrats' and local offices can have easy access to the information and facilities available on mainframe and micro-computers. In consequence, some have argued that information technology is producing a 'polo effect': organisations with only holes at their centres because control is decentralised to the users of terminals or micro-computers. Simon Booth and Douglas Pitt tell us that, 'As IT increases the self-regulatory component of much lower-level work, each worker may become his own foreman. Deskilling of the middle-level supervisory function may presage the beginning of the end for first-line supervisors.' (Booth and Pitt, 1984, p. 33) A related change is the 'Heineken Effect', under which

> Information will begin to flow to those parts of the organisation previously inaccessible. As a consequence, some employees will be better placed to carry out an efficiency audit on their nominal superiors. Light will flood into the darker recesses of the organisational labyrinth. The conclusion seems irresistible that where light flows, power will shortly follow.　　　　(Ibid., p. 19)

Such dispersal of information and hence power to an organisation's periphery will support trends like 'going local' and the disaggregation of the traditional departmental hierarchies of all government bodies.

We can explore both the centralising and decentralising influences of information technology in a little more detail by considering some examples. The centralising effect relates chiefly to such major batch processing operations as the Driver and Vehicle Licensing Centre at Swansea, the Police National Computer and the National Insurance computer system, whose headquarters is at Longbenton, Newcastle upon Tyne. This last is responsible for issuing National Insurance Numbers and for the payment of insurance-related benefits, including the state pension. The Social Security system is being computerised, as is the Inland Revenue's Pay as You Earn (PAYE) system. All these operations involve the repetitive processing of vast amounts of data and employ large numbers of people: the Department of Social Security at Longbenton and its local outstations give employment to some 10,000 people in the north-east of England. Their work is largely routine and is concerned with the implementation of government policies through the National Insurance system, rather than with influencing their development. The DSS Central Office is soon to be given Executive Agency status under *The Next Steps* project.

None the less, these data-processing systems may have policy implications. In particular, their design may rule out possible future developments because their flexibility is limited. Thus Steve Matheson, commenting on the computerisation of PAYE, has written that

> Changes involve many man-months in specifying them, analysing the initial impact to see whether they are feasible in the timescale, making changes in the data dictionary, changing the design, programming, testing and operating. So making a change is not cheap. A major legislative change has just the same sort of parameters to it because once Ministers have decided what they want to do, the requirement has got to be specified. The user has to say what he wants. The peripheral users of a system need to say what they want. All that has to be agreed before the system can be changed. *There should not be too much change too quickly.*
> (Matheson, 1984, p. 103. My italics.)

It seems, for example, that the PAYE computer system does not include provision for the possible introduction of a local income tax, although such a tax was recommended by the Layfield Committee on Local Government Finance in 1976. This may render the introduction of a local income tax difficult if a government wishing to do it is returned to office. Local income tax has been adopted as a Labour Party policy but the cost of adapting the PAYE computer system to enable local income tax to be charged through it, together with the time it will take to adjust the computer system, may discourage the implementation of this policy.

Many other large data-processing installations exist in the public sector at all levels. Some of them provide extensive information which may constitute a threat to privacy and civil liberties, such as the extensive data held on many of us by the Police National Computer, which can be quickly accessed by any police officer through his or her personal or car radio.

Local authorities too possess large central mainframe computers which are used for processing financial data, payrolls and personnel data. The introduction of such mainframes was one of the reasons why corporate management became fashionable in local government in the late 1960s. They were too powerful and too expensive for each department to be given a separate machine. In consequence, departments have had to co-operate in developing uses for the computer and agreeing access to it. The largest single user is always the Treasurer's or Finance Department which therefore has almost invariably been given control over the mainframe computer.

The arrival of the 'Virtual Machine Concept' and then the micro-computer has, as we have noted, produced a move towards decentralisation. Neighbourhood offices can obtain lists of vacant council houses, records of social work cases and guidance on benefit rules, for example, at a local terminal or micro-computer, so that decisions can be made by local staff instead of having to be referred to the centre of the department at the Civic Centre or County Hall. The point of effective decision is therefore transferred to 'street-level bureaucrats' (Lipsky, 1980) and local offices: the 'Heineken Effect' thus disperses both information and power.

The decentralised control of computers and the data stored in them also provides a safeguard against the potential danger posed by information technology in the hands of the government to our privacy and civil liberties. If the information held on us in computers belonging to the banks, local authorities, health authorities, government departments and others were combined, privacy would cease to exist (Lynn and Jay, 1981, chapter 4). Although the telescreen would not be installed in everyone's living room, officials could know all about our debts, illnesses, relationships and criminal records. Furthermore, the ability to alter information and the possibility of false or erroneous material being held on our files makes George Orwell's MINITRUTH more than possible.

The technology imagined by Orwell in 1948 now looks old-fashioned compared to the potential of present-day computers and renders the development of a Thought Police more than possible. A plastic card could in theory give officials access to all the information held in computers about us. It should be remembered that it is not what is stored on the card itself that is dangerous but the information to which that card would give access through the ability it confers on whoever is in possession of it to delve into our personal records.

At present, we are protected to a degree from such invasions by the Data Protection Act of 1984. This gives us a right of access to information which is held on computers about us, together with a right to demand that inaccuracies be corrected. It forbids such abuses as the transfer of information held for one purpose for use for another. However, the Act only provides limited safeguards in respect of personal information held by government agencies. It is also salutary to remember that the Data Protection Act was not introduced because the Government was anxious about protecting the liberties and privacy of its subjects but because British businesses would be unable to secure foreign contracts if Britain's data protection laws were weaker than those prevailing in the rest of Western Europe (Elcock,1984). If foreign companies' assets were likely to be disclosed if they were processed in Britain because the law offered them no protection, much lucrative software and data processing business would be lost to British firms. Hence, the Data Protection Act was passed.

In addition, however, we are protected by the decentralised control of the computers on which personal information about us is held. Local authorities, government departments and others are unlikely to allow others to share access to their data and indeed would be committing an offence under the Data Protection Act if they did so. Still less are they likely to allow private firms access to public records; equally, banks and others guarantee their customers' confidentiality and risk losing custom if they do not protect it. The likelihood of connections being made which would destroy our privacy is therefore still remote. However, we must always be aware that a sovereign Parliament could destroy that protection, albeit for such apparently beneficial purposes as being able to sequestrate the proceeds of drug traffickers.

A last implication of information technology is that it encourages inter-organisational and international co-operation. It is producing increased international interdependence which is arguably reducing the risk of war. The Soviet Union's need to acquire Western computer technology has not been the least of her reasons for seeking peaceful co-existence with the West and more recently improving its human rights record in the hope of obtaining the lifting of trade restrictions. In Western Europe, technology developments are so rapid and so costly that multi-national consortia or co-operation arrangements like EUREKA and ESPRIT have been developed to ensure that Europe is not left behind by the United States and the Far East in the race to develop new information technologies (Peterson, 1989). At a lower level, organisations may collaborate in order to make the most efficient use both of expensive equipment and extensive data, such as common population databases which can be used by different local authority departments, including planning, education and social services, as well as by health authorities, to plan the location of developments and service provision. We have seen that such co-operation quickly developed in Humberside after local government and NHS reorganisation in the early 1970s (Humberside County Council, 1976, Volume I; Elcock, 1986a; Brown *et al.*, 1976). All these developments illustrate the tendency for information technology to generate inter-organisational and international co-operation.

AIDS TO POLICY-MAKING

Computers may also form part of several techniques which have been developed to assist policy-makers to improve the quality of the decisions they have to take. These techniques broadly fall into two categories: those whose inventors aspire to increase the rationality of policy decisions – an objective also sought by the advocates of PPBS and ZBB; and those which increase the creativity available to decision-makers – the objective of establishing 'Think Tanks'.

1. *Aids to Rationality.* Many attempts to render policy decisions more rational are based on Utilitarian theories of ethics and economics which are themselves based on an assumption that it is possible to identify, quantify and compare the benefits or harm which are likely to accrue from adopting different courses of action. It should then be possible to choose that course of action which will produce the most benefit for the least cost.

One such technique is Cost-Benefit Analysis (CBA), which seeks to quantify benefits and costs and thus allow policy options to be compared. Cost-Benefit Analyses were prepared for the Roskill Commission, which was charged to evaluate different locations for a third London airport in the 1970s, as well as for those responsible for determining how best to provide a public transport link between Heathrow Airport and central London. CBAs are also frequently used to determine whether and where new motorways or major roads should be built.

An interesting and rather different type of CBA has been developed for health care policy-makers by Alan Williams and colleagues at the University of York (Williams, 1985; Crisp, 1989). They propose that the efficacy of different medical procedures can be compared by developing a common measure of the extent to which they prolong life and improve its quality. This measure is the Quality Adjusted Life-Year (QALY). A healthy life-year counts as 1, death as 0 and impairment through ill-health or treatment is expressed in decimal fractions of 1. It then becomes possible to measure and compare the relative merits of, for example, a surgical procedure which gives a limited number of more or less healthy life-years and the treatment of a chronic disease which gives more years of life but of lesser quality. If resources are allocated to those treatments which provide the largest number of QALYs, so the argument runs, those resources will have been used to the best effect and produce the maximum amount of patient welfare.

Unfortunately, such attempts to measure the merits of different policy options have proved to lead to serious and in some cases insurmountable difficulties, which may render the results of such analyses of limited or even no value. Among the major problems are:

- Problems of Quantification. Ideally, a CBA requires that a numerical value should be given to all the variables of which account needs to be taken and this can present horrendous problems of judgement. For example, in the CBA prepared for the Roskill Commission an assessment of the value of a village church with a Saxon tower was needed because it would be demolished if one site was chosen. The analysts put a value of £50,000 on the church, which may seem high to a Philistine but which for conservationists and Church historians was 'a particularly ludicrous price tag'. (Aldous, 1972) CBAs prepared in relation to proposals for physical development abound with such problems. We may equally consider Jeremy Bentham's proposition that all forms of pleasure and pain can be quantified and compared, so as to determine accurately what constitutes the greatest happiness for the greatest number. In the end, subjective judgements about the worth of particular activities like pushpin and poetry must be made, just as a subjective judgement of the worth of an ancient building is an inescapable judgement for potential developers to make. Such questions of quantification therefore must in the end involve subjective, often controversial political decisions which are likely to be vigorously contested.

- Repugnant Conclusions. The analysis may produce a result which is politically or morally unacceptable. Thus Crisp has argued that the rigorous application of QALYs might produce the conclusion that we should terminate all support for the severely mentally defective so as to reduce the risk of non-defective people dying prematurely (Crisp, 1989 pp. 34-5). No Secretary of State for Health would dare to accept such a proposition. Equally, the site chosen for the third London airport by the Roskill Commission proved to be politically unacceptable and was rejected by the Heath Government. This led to a further decade of acrimonious debate about this issue, which was not resolved by the use of a CBA.

- Multiple Options. Even if the conclusions are not repugnant, the analysis may produce several conclusions which differ at most marginally in their desirability – which will in any case depend on the values supported by the decision-maker. There can be more than one Pareto optimum in a welfare economics calculation and the option selected will depend on the chooser's value-slope. Hence, the conclusions of the CBA may stimulate dissension rather than removing it. The decision to extend the Picadilly Underground line to Heathrow has not prevented British Rail from continuing to develop and press proposals for a link to the Great Western main line. Equally, Crisp (1989) points to the possibility that a QALY analysis may produce a dilemma between giving 100 people one extra life-year or saving two people for 50 years each.

- The Importance of Probability. Few if any public policy outcomes are certain. For example, a QALY analysis is invalidated if an operation is not successful and the patient dies or his quality of life is unexpectedly impaired. More generally, the problems inherent in assessing the probability of the consequences of a policy, as well as their extent, are notoriously difficult (see Keynes, 1923). Not only may expected benefits not accrue but unexpected problems and unanticipated consequences commonly develop, which may be so severe that they destroy or at least counterbalance the benefits the policy has produced. Many would argue that the virtual disappearance of the private rented sector must be set against the benefits that the 1965 Rent Act brought to tenants who have been protected by it from unfair rents and harassment by landlords.

One must conclude, therefore, that while techniques based on assessing costs and benefits may assist public policy-makers to reach beneficial conclusions, they cannot be substituted for value-judgements, nor should they be allowed to displace judgements based on precedent, experience or 'hunches'. (Vickers, 1965; Dror, 1973) Furthermore, although they may appear to present objective assessments of policy-problems, they do not eliminate the need to make value-judgements. Hence they will not eliminate political debate.

2. *Stimulating Creativity.* We noted earlier that the establishment of 'Think Tanks' was intended to increase the creativity available to policy-makers. There are also several techniques which have been developed to try and stimulate new thinking about an organisation's policies and the problems it

faces. Three such aids to creative thinking may be noted here:

- 'Brainstorming' involves a group of managers, executives or policy-makers being collected together, preferably away from their usual place of work, to discuss the issues they face individually and collectively. Each individual must speak freely, respond to the others' statements and hence stimulate one another to produce new ideas or procedures for tackling the problems with which they are dealing at work.
- Quality Circles were originally developed in Japanese industry. A group of workers or executives are asked to consider how the quality of the product could be improved. The application of this concept to public policy has been considered by Campbell and Peters (1989)
- The Analysis of Inter-Connected Decision Areas (AIDA) involves the careful tracing of the links between different organisations which are involved in taking a decision or implementing a policy. Identifying the links among the organisations involved indicates new approaches or procedures which will increase support for the policy across the organisations involved and hence render its successful implementation more likely. This technique may be employed by an individual or group who may come to play a reticulist role as discussed in Chapter 4.

CONCLUSIONS

There exists, therefore, a large, indeed a bewildering, variety of techniques which their proponents insist will enable public policy-makers and administrators to make better decisions and be more efficient. In general, however, the function of the techniques discussed in this chapter is to be the handmaidens of policy-makers, rather than displacing the judgements about values and interests which politicians and their senior advisers must make. Policy research generates useful information. Computers assist in its analysis and render its conclusions more easily accessible. Analytical techniques like PPBS, ZBB and CBA may assist in making assessments of rival policies whose fate might otherwise be determined incrementally. However, using techniques imposes costs too, which can be substantial in terms of money, manpower and the time needed to absorb large amounts of information.

In any case, the application of techniques in public administration is restricted because no politician, officer, manager or 'street-level bureaucrat' can act in isolation from colleagues in his or her own organisation or in other agencies, or from the demands of citizens and pressure groups. A policy may be adjudged to be cost-effective but if it is unacceptable to politicians or causes a public outcry, it is likely to be rejected. If it is inimical to the interests of pressure groups, its implementation will be impeded or even blocked. The public administrator at all levels cannot, therefore, escape from the interplay of actors and these relationships are the subject-matter of Part 3 of this book.

PART THREE

Relationships

CHAPTER EIGHT
Accountabilities

THE VARIABILITY OF ACCOUNTABILITY RELATIONSHIPS

Accountability has been a recurring theme of this book, just as it is and must be a central concern of academics and practitioners alike. We have seen that the individual accountability of Ministers to Parliament is no longer significant as a means of ensuring that Parliament can control the actions of the Executive, except on rare occasions. However, it has none the less been of great importance in forming civil servants' conception of their roles. It has produced the preoccupation with policy advice as opposed to management which was so severely criticised by the Fulton Committee (1968) and many others. It has also been used to justify the subordinate position accorded in the civil service to experts (Sisson, 1959).

Secondly, we have explored accountability in the context of the management of resources, considering the need to distinguish between the different forms of accountability for the use and misuse of resources: fiscal accountability, efficiency accountability, programme accountability, and process accountability. Furthermore, we have explored the balance that needs to be struck between the different directions in which public servants are held accountable. Thus they may be simultaneously accountable *upwards,* ultimately to politicians, *outwards* to professional colleagues and *downwards* to citizens. Specialist professionals may be held so strongly accountable outwards to their professional colleagues that accountability upwards and downwards may become attenuated.

In all these contexts, accountability is seen to constitute a set of relationships which for public service agencies and individual public servants alike, produce a range of dilemmas. The individual public servant, as well as departments, sections and trade unions, must seek to resolve these dilemmas in such ways as to maintain relationships with politicians, colleagues and the public alike. This balance is often not easy to achieve and one can argue that certain features of British government and the British political system may allow public servants sometimes to evade what might properly be considered their duty to account for their actions. Certainly, in recent years major controversies about accountability have developed in several contexts, apart from the perennial argument about just how ineffective the accountability of Ministers to Parliament is. Thus, for example, it has several times been argued that the police cannot be held effectively to account for their misdeeds. At one level, prolonged controversies about deaths in police custody, such as those of Liddle Towers and Blair Peach, have failed to produce sufficient reassurance for many of the participants in them that policemen did not use excessive violence on these two men and other people who have died in police custody.

The two cases were very different. Liddle Towers was arrested outside a working men's club in County Durham late at night after a long evening's drinking. He subsequently died while in the police cells. His family and friends alleged that his death had been the result of a violent and unnecessary attack by the police officers who were restraining him. Blair Peach was struck on the head with a police truncheon, which was alleged to have been weighted, during a demonstration near the United States Embassy in London. His friends subsequently alleged that the blow which caused his death had been both unnecessary and excessively severe. In both cases, despite repeated enquiries the men's friends and relatives were never wholly satisfied either that the full truth had been revealed or that the police had completely disproved the allegations made against them. Since these incidents, a Police Complaints Authority has been established to conduct independent investigations into complaints against the police but although its activities seem to cause considerable irritation to the police themselves (Stalker, 1989), there are still doubts as to whether the Authority can fully hold the police to account when misconduct has been established to have occurred – a point to which we will return later.

Further doubts about police accountability have been raised by the case of the former Deputy Chief Constable of the Greater Manchester Police, John Stalker, who was suspended from duty in somewhat obscure circumstances when he was close to concluding an investigation into an alleged 'shoot to kill' policy in the Royal Ulster Constabulary which had resulted in the death of an innocent youth (Stalker, 1988). Even more serious doubts have been raised about the accountability of the security services (Chapman Pincher, various; Wright, 1987).

Another major doubt concerning the effectiveness of accountability in British government concerns the question of whether Ministers and civil servants have used their discretionary powers to withhold information because its disclosure would be contrary to the interests of the State, in order to protect themselves from possible embarrassment rather than protecting the safety of the realm. Between 1942 and 1968, Ministers had an absolute discretion to withhold documents under their control from disclosure in the courts because of the interpretation which the House of Lords gave to the ancient doctrine of Crown privilege in the case of *Duncan v. Cammell Laird* in 1942 (see Elcock, 1969b).

In this case, the First Lord of the Admiralty, A.V. Alexander, had ordered that the hull and engine room plans of the ill–fated submarine *Thetis* should be withheld from production in court during an action in which relatives of the 99 crewmen lost when the submarine sank on trials were suing the builders for negligence. While protecting the plans of a major weapon was perhaps allowable in time of war, this case was used as a precedent to uphold refusals to disclose documents in circumstances where the justification for doing so was much less clearly evident. In 1954, Mr Justice Devlin (as he then was) criticised the use made of Crown privilege in a case in which a former prisoner was suing the Home Office for negligence. He warned that Crown privilege in this case, *Ellis v. the Home Office*, was being abused to avoid Ministerial embarrassment. By the mid-1960s, judges in the higher Courts, especially the Master of the Rolls, Lord Denning, had become sufficiently concerned about the use being made of Crown privilege to seek a means of restricting its scope. This was finally achieved by the House of Lords in 1968, in the case of *Conway v. Rimmer,* when their Lordships ruled that the Courts have residual right to overrule a Ministerial claim to Crown privilege where in the judge's view, a case cannot be justly tried without the documents for which the Minister is seeking protection and there are insufficient public interest grounds for withholding the documents. Furthermore, the judge may order the production of the documents to him in Chambers so that he may assess whether the claim to Crown privilege is justified or not (Elcock, 1969b).

Here, then, are two very different examples of anxieties which have arisen about the effectiveness of accountability and control in modern British government. In both cases, public concern led eventually to a strengthening of the means by which accountability could be enforced but by no means everybody is satisfied that either police misconduct or Ministerial concealment of information for insufficient reasons have been eliminated. Furthermore, we may note that these problems emerged at least in part because the unwritten British Constitution contains no guarantees of citizens' rights of the kind that exist in most other liberal democracies, as well as under at least some Eastern European regimes (Garlicki, 1987). The Thatcher years have greatly increased many observers' concern about the absence of constitutional guarantees as the traditional Constitution has, it is argued, been breached, for example to deny workers at GCHQ the right to join trade unions or councillors' right to levy such rate as they think fit (Jones and Stewart, 1984). There therefore seem to be particular problems about accountability and citizens' rights in the British system of government which we need to assess before discussing the means that are available to MPs, councillors and citizens to hold public servants to account.

THE BRITISH APPROACH TO ACCOUNTABILITY

Britain's unwritten Constitution permits three features in particular of our policy-making and administrative systems to exist which render our mechanisms of accountability peculiarly weak compared to those of the United States or our European neighbours, There are:

1. First, the sovereignty of Parliament, which permits 'The Queen in Parliament' to pass any legislation it thinks fit by its normal procedure of three Readings in each House, followed by the granting of the Royal Assent. Sir Ivor Jennings argued that if by this procedure, an Act of Parliament was passed which forbade smoking in the streets of Paris, that law could be enforced against a Frenchman who was seen smoking a Gaulloise in the streets of Paris who subsequently came to Folkestone on a day trip. More seriously, this sovereign Parliament was able to pass in a single afternoon the Official Secrets Act of 1911, which made it both an offence to disclose to anyone any information held by anyone in central government without specific authorisation, as well as to receive such information. The second offence was defined in the infamous 'catch–all' provisions of Section 2 of the Act. Furthermore, although Section 1 was modified to confine its scope to espionage, Section 2 was not amended until the passage of a new Act in 1989, despite repeated expressions of judicial and public concern about its use and abuse by Crown servants (see Williams, 1965; Hewitt, 1982, also Document 17). Other legislation also infringes the rights which Britons believe they hold; thus the 1936 Public Order Act in effect rendered the right to demonstrate exercisable only with police permission (Street, 1963).

    One consequence of the sovereignty of Parliament is that the Courts cannot intervene to protect citizens from legislation which is tyrannical in its effect, or from abuses of power under Acts of

Parliament, because they are bound by statutes passed by Parliament: there can be no equivalent of the power vested in the United States Supreme Court to strike down legislation as unconstitutional. Similar powers exist in most other European states. In comparison with other countries, therefore, the role of the Courts as controllers of the conduct of politicians and officials is curiously attenuated: judges can only correct abuses of power if a statute permits them to do so or it can be interpreted to allow such correction.

2. Secondly, by common law, statute and regulation the British confer very wide discretionary powers, which are often also of uncertain scope, on public servants. We have referred to one example already. The right to demonstrate – peacefully to assemble for the redress of grievances – is restricted by the common law principle that a citizen has a right only to pass and repass along the public highway in pursuit of his or her normal business. One may not stop or engage in activities not connected with one's normal business. This rule was used in the late nineteenth century against a person whom we would now call a hunt saboteur, who attempted to disrupt the Duke of Rutland's game shooting by noisily opening and shutting his umbrella (*Earl v. Bass*, 1894). The powers of the police to control demonstrations were increased by the 1936 Public Order Act (Document 18), so much so that the late Harry Street argued that organisers of demonstrations are in effect dependent on police goodwill:

> The right of public meeting…is dependent almost entirely on the police exercising their discretion in a reasonable manner. The promoter should co-operate with the police in the expectation that they will treat him fairly; if he proceeds in defiance of their wishes, conviction is likely.
>
> (Street, 1963, p. 48)

Another example concerns the power to intercept mail and tap telephones. Until 1985 this power was conferred on the Home Secretary as part of the Royal Prerogative. The means available to hold the Home Secretary to account under this system were – and still are – almost entirely dependent on the honesty of the Home Secretary and his officials. The Home Secretary is required to issue warrants authorising mail interception and telephone taps only in accordance with a set of rules laid down by the then Home Secretary, Sir David Maxwell-Fyfe, in 1957. These rules lay down that the power should be used only in the investigation of serious crime where other methods have been tried and either have failed or are deemed unlikely to succeed. However, the only means of checking how the Home Secretary is using the powers was to ask a Parliamentary Question, to which answers – complete or at all – are not always forthcoming.

The power to intercept mail and tap telephones has now had to be put on a statutory basis. Significantly, this was the result of a ruling by the European Court of Human Rights against the British government in *Malone's* case. In any case, the discretion conferred on the Home Secretary is still very widely defined and the means available to scrutinise its exercise are still feeble. The existence of so wide and uncertain a discretionary power can create considerable anxiety. In 1966, several left-wing Labour MPs noticed unusual noises on their telephones and set down a series of Questions to the Prime Minister asking whether their telephones were being tapped. This produced a limited assurance from the Prime Minister and an article in The *Guardian*, written by an anonymous wire-tapper, which stated that to suggest that tapping could be detected by noises on the line was an insult to the wire–tapping profession! (see also *MI5's Official Secrets*, Channel 4, 1985.)

One reason for the existence of such wide, uncertain discretionary powers is the failure of the British courts to develop a specialist body of administrative case-law until very recently, in part because of the non-existence of legally-enforceable basic rights. Dicey argued that the handling of administrative cases by the ordinary courts demonstrated that Britain did not need a specialist system of administrative courts but many Britons have looked increasingly enviously at, for example, the French *Conseil d'Etat's* principle of *détournement de pouvoir*, which lays down that an official may not use powers for purposes not related to those for which they granted.

3.   Lastly, the availability of redress when a citizen's interests have been damaged or he suffers injury as a result of the actions of public servants, is uncertain. There is, for example, no general assurance that if a person is injured or his property is damaged by public servants, he will receive any compensation. By contrast, the *Conseil d'Etat* has laid down that the State is liable for damage caused by officials at any time when they can be said to have been on duty.

THE MACHINERY OF REDRESS: HOW EFFECTIVE IS ACCOUNTABILITY DOWNWARDS?

We have already seen in several different contexts that the ability of MPs to hold Ministers to account for their officials' actions is uncertain in its effectiveness: hence an individual who complains about mistreatment to his or her MP is not guaranteed any redress. However, because MPs and councillors are elected to represent defined local areas, they are expected to pursue such complaints both informally through personal contacts and by using such formal mechanisms as Question Time and adjournment debates (Norton, various). As in many of the other fields explored in this chapter, the effectiveness of this method of seeking redress is largely dependent on politicians and officials taking complaints seriously and being willing to grant redress where wrong has been done. It must be said that they usually do respond reasonably to such complaints. Where they do not, it may be possible for an aggrieved citizen to seek redress by other means.

The Courts and Administration. The role of the Courts of Law is restricted, as we have seen, by the sovereignty of Parliament and was in any case further constrained for many years by acts of judicial self-restraint which indicated that the judges did not accept that they had a significant role to play in scrutinising the behaviour of politicians and officials. In particular, until relatively recently the courts largely excluded the propriety and fairness of administrative procedures from their purview. In 1915, the House of Lords ruled that when Parliament had decided that a matter should be decided by a government department rather than a court, the department should determine the matter through its accustomed procedures. Their Lordships said that in such cases, the department ought to 'act judicially' but did nothing to compel departments to apply judicial standards of procedure (*Local Government Board v. Arlidge*, 1915, Document 19). Similarly, in 1947 the House of Lords ruled that objectors to a proposal to build a New Town at Stevenage could not demand that the decision be quashed because the Minister had acted as judge and jury in his own case. A public inquiry into the proposal had been held but the Minister had made the final decision and Lord Thankerton stated that the public inquiry's sole purpose was 'to inform the mind of the Minister'. In consequence, his decision could not be challenged on the ground that the Minister had broken the rules of natural justice by acting as judge in his own cause (*Franklin and Others v. Minister of Town and Country Planning*, 1947).

In recent years, however, judicial concern to ensure that administrative procedures are fair has increased, which in turn has rendered it more likely that a public authority which has acted unfairly can be held to account for its misconduct before the courts. This increase in judicial militancy in protecting citizens against unfair procedures or actions by public bodies seems to have begun with two sets of cases in which the law was developed by judges in ways which impose new or more stringent obligations on the State and its servants. The first such set of cases was concerned with the interpretation of Section 12(1) of the Tribunals and Inquiries Act, 1958 which imposed a duty on administrative tribunals and Ministers deciding public inquiry cases to give the reasons for their decisions on request. This obligation enables us to scrutinise the validity or otherwise of the adjudicator's logic and his understanding of the case (Wasserman, 1961; Lucas, 1967). Mr Justice Megaw decided two cases in which he put a stringent interpretation on Section 12(1) of the Tribunals and Inquiries Act, which required that the statement of reasons must cover all the issues raised at the hearing and must give a full response to them (*In re Poyser Mills Arbitration and Givaudan and Co. v. Minister of Housing and Local Government*, A.C. See Elcock, 1969a, pp. 89–90). Thus the major change in the procedures of administrative justice which had been brought about by the Act was interpreted in a manner which imposed on tribunals and Ministers a stringent test of the validity of their decisions through having to give full reasons for them.

The second set of cases which initially indicated the change in the judicial mood culminated in the *Conway v. Rimmer* case which restricted the scope of Crown privilege. Previously, Lord Denning had been one of three judges in the Court of Appeal who had asserted that they had a right to overturn Ministerial claims to Crown privilege but chose not to exercise it in the instant case (see Elcock, 1969b). When *Conway's* case came to the Court of Appeal, two different judges refused to accept Lord Denning's view but his dissenting judgement led to a successful appeal to the House of Lords which resulted in the Ministerial discretion to withhold documents from the courts being restricted.

Since then, the Courts have intervened to impose higher standards of fairness in a long series of cases arising from a wide variety of administrative contexts. Lord Denning was involved in many of them and their cumulative effect has been made available to citizens who feel that they have been treated unfairly by public servants to a right to seek judicial review of both the procedure followed and the decision reached. A few examples drawn from different fields of administration will demonstrate the importance of these developments (see Griffith, 1977; Drewry, various).

- *Central-Local Government Relations.* In 1976 the Court of Appeal, including Lord Denning, ruled that the Secretary of State for Education and Science had acted unreasonably in interfering with the political decision of a local authority. In that year, Tameside Metropolitan Borough Council, near Manchester, was about to introduce comprehensive secondary education. The scheme was to take effect in September but in May, the Conservative Party won control of the Council at the local elections and decided to retain selective schools, in accordance with a pledge they had given in their election manifesto. The Secretary of State decided to insist that the comprehensive scheme be implemented because he believed it was unreasonable to reverse it only three months or so before it came into effect. In issuing this instruction, the Secretary of State made use of a discretion conferred on him by the 1944 Education Act which permitted him to reverse local education authority decisions which in his view were unreasonable. However, Lord Denning and his colleagues in the Court of Appeal ruled instead that it was the Secretary of State himself who had acted unreasonably and the Court ruled that Tameside Council was acting within its powers to reverse the comprehensive scheme, which had been a major issue in the local elections (*Tameside Metropolitan Borough Council v. Secretary of State for Education and Science*, 1976).

However, in 1982, Lord Denning took a very different view of the status of party election manifestos when he and his colleagues in the Court of Appeal struck down the Greater London Council's 'Fares Fair' policy of making a 50 per cent reduction in London's bus and Tube fares. The Court ruled that the Council had failed properly to strike a balance between the interests of travellers and those of the ratepayers, who would have to pay for the extra subsidies needed to reduce the fares. According to the Court, a claim by councillors to be implementing an election manifesto commitment to reduce fares was not a valid argument for doing so without considering the extra payments which would be imposed on the ratepayers. The comparison of judicial attitudes towards Conservative and Labour election pledges revealed in the *Tameside* and *Bromley v. Greater London Council* cases supports J. A. G. Griffith's contention that the judiciary displays a bias in favour of the Conservative Party (Griffith, 1977; see also Pannick, 1989). The most important point for us to note here is the requirements imposed on public authorities to act reasonably and to consider the interests of all the classes of citizens who will be affected by their decisions.

- *The Treatment of Students.* In the *Aston University* case, Lord Denning and his two colleagues, again sitting in the Court of Appeal, ruled that a decision by the authorities of a university to expel two students who had failed examinations without giving them a chance to appeal against the decision or the opportunity to retake the failed examinations, was invalid. All students now have a right to appeal against such decisions or to take resit examinations.

- *Competition.* In the *Laker Airways* case, the Court of Appeal ruled that the Secretary of State for Trade, Peter Shore, had been unjustified in refusing to issue a licence for Mr (now Sir) Freddie Laker to operate his cut-price 'Skytrain' service across the Atlantic.
- *Immigration.* A series of cases has evoked judicial criticism of the fairness of Home Office procedures for dealing with immigrants who are refused entry to the country or who are threatened with deportation as illegal immigrants. In a recent case, for example, the court ruled that an immigrant must be regarded as a legal immigrant until he or she can be proved to have entered the country illegally.

What all these cases have in common is judicial criticism of the behaviour of politicians and public servants over their exercise of discretionary powers, together with the imposition of increasingly rigorous procedural requirements on the way public authorities exercise their discretion. So significant have these rulings become that the Treasury Solicitor has produced an advice pamphlet for civil servants on how to avoid falling foul of the procedural requirements laid on them by the courts. It is evocatively entitled, *The Judge Over Your Shoulder.*

The procedural impact of these cases must be distinguished from their outcomes when one attempts to assess their implications. Thus members of left-wing parties might welcome the results of some of the cases involving students and immigrants while those on the right would welcome the outcome of the *Laker Airways* and *Tameside* cases. However, a distinct set of issues which concern all those involved with the protection of civil liberties − whether on the left or the right − must also be assessed: the limitations which all these cases have imposed on the use and abuse of official discretion. Here we are concerned with evaluating the justness or otherwise of administrative procedures, in which the courts have increasingly seen fit to intervene. Citizens or organisations who feel aggrieved about the manner in which politicians or officials have exercised their discretion have surer remedies than were available 20 years ago, in the form of seeking the judicial review of their cases, albeit that the extent of the protection it accords them still leaves a lot to be desired. Not only does protection depend on the attitudes of the judges hearing the case; if Parliament legislates to restore discretionary powers after they have been limited by the courts, the judges must accept the views of a whipped majority in Parliament.

None the less, it could now be argued that Britain has developed a system of administrative law − a development which has been further encouraged by the rulings of the European Court of Human Rights. Since the United Kingdom became subject to the Court's jurisdiction, the British Government has been arraigned before it more frequently than any other European Government and has lost almost all the cases which it has been forced to defend in Strasbourg.

For anyone who is concerned that citizens' rights of redress against the public authorities have been poorly protected in Britain, all these developments must be welcome. However, as a means of holding public servants to account the courts have serious drawbacks. Going to law is expensive and the procedures are formidably opaque for the lay person (Pannick, 1989). The time taken to get a result is considerable and becomes massive when an appeal to the European Court of Human Rights is involved: then at least five years will elapse before the case is decided and of course, you may not win! Although the courts may be the only forum in which to resolve major issues and establish the principles of administrative law, they are not suitable fora for resolving many more routine disputes which none the less have important implications for the lives of those citizens who are affected by them. The courts' value as an instrument of accountability downwards to citizens is therefore important but limited, as has been recognised by the creation of administrative tribunals and public inquiries, which we discuss next.

The Machinery of Administrative Justice. The need to supplement the Courts of Law with other avenues of redress which could, in theory at least, provide quicker, cheaper and more appropriate means to resolve disputes between the State and its citizens, was not consciously or systematically recognised in Britain for many years. None the less, such machinery was brought into existence piecemeal as a result of the need to develop procedures to cope with the new pressures which have resulted from the vast expansion in the State's role which has occurred in the twentieth century. More specifically, new fields of conflict between state and citizen have developed in three areas.

1. The first is the decision of marginal or disputed claims to State benefits. As the State accepted responsibility to support those who are unemployed, ill or who have grown old, it has become necessary to provide adjudicators where disputes arise about denials of benefit or payment level. Such cases are dealt with by National Insurance Local Tribunals, Social Security Appeal Tribunals and Medical Appeal Tribunals, among others.
2. Secondly, the State increasingly intervenes to regulate various means of earning a living, in order to ensure the safety and well-being of the public. Thus if anyone wishes to open a public school, drive a taxi or

run a cinema, for example, they must obtain a licence to do so from the appropriate public authority, which must in turn assess his or her suitability to offer these services to the public. In some but not all such cases, an appeal may lie to a tribunal or other body against the refusal of a licence. Examples of such appellate bodies are the Public Schools Appeals Tribunal (which rarely meets) and the Civil Aviation Authority.

3.   Lastly, the State has acquired increasing rights to restrict what we may do with our property. It may even deprive us of it, albeit after paying compensation. We may not build a house or change the exterior of an existing property without obtaining planning permission from the local planning authority. If planning permission is refused, we have the right to appeal against that decision to the Secretary of State for the Environment, who will usually order that a Public Local Inquiry be held. Appeals against refusal of planning permission constitute by far the largest number of Public Inquiry cases but the Public Inquiry procedure is also used when landowners appeal against a local authority's decision compulsorily to acquire their properties, and to consider objections to major public building schemes such as major roads, power stations and airports. Lastly, a Public Inquiry is held when people object to the British Railways Board's proposal to close a passenger railway service.

The development of the machinery of administrative justice to assist in the resolution of disputes in these three areas has been classically incremental. No overall decision was ever taken to establish administrative tribunals or public inquiries; equally no attempt was made to define their status or lay down rules of fair procedure for them. In consequence, suspicions as to their fairness increased. By the late 1920s, the then Lord Chief Justice, Gordon Hewart, was warning, in somewhat hysterical terms, of the emergence of a 'New Despotism'. (Hewart, 1929) He warned that Ministers were acquiring too many discretionary powers and that the means of redress when they were misused were so unsatisfactory as to offer citizens no protection against abuses of power. Around the same time William Robson urged that administrative justice needed to be regularised through the establishment of a system of administrative law (Robson, 1928 and several later editions). In 1954, a study of tribunals and inquiries carried out by a group of lawyers at the London School of Economics and Political Science revealed that they were generally unsatisfactory and at the worst were travesties of justice (Pollard (ed.), 1950).

The machinery of administrative justice took, as we have suggested, two main forms, which are:

- *Administrative Tribunals,* which are adjudicatory bodies in the full sense. They usually consist of three members and hear disputes over, for example, a refusal to pay Social Security benefits, the assessment of rents and rejections of applications for licences. The chairman and members of the tribunal hear the arguments and evidence, after which they retire and announce their decision. A right to appeal to a superior tribunal may exist, as well as to the courts, at least on matters of law. Most tribunals deal with disputes between officials and citizens but some, such as Rent Tribunals and Agricultural Lands Tribunals, deal with disputes between citizens, here landlords and tenants, which are regulated by laws, setting fair rents and conferring security of tenure, which must be applied by the tribunal.

- *Public inquiries* are not, at least in principle, adjudicatory at all. We have already quoted Lord Thankerton's statement in the *Stevenage* case that their purpose is 'merely to inform the mind of the Minister.' The Inspector who conducts the inquiry will hear the objections to the public authority decision (for instance to refuse planning permission) or proposal (to build a road or close a railway). The Inspector then writes a report for the Minister, who must determine whether to uphold or overturn the original decision, although this is almost always done in practice by senior civil servants. However, most planning appeals are now delegated by the Secretary of State for the Environment to the Inspector to determine. Hence, the Inspector is in practice but still not in principle, responsible for adjudicating these appeals.

Radical changes occurred in the machinery of administrative justice after the Crichel Down case. One of the government's responses to the concern aroused by that case was, somewhat illogically, to establish a committee under the chairmanship of Sir Oliver Franks (now Lord Franks) to review the machinery of administrative justice. This was an illogical outcome of Crichel Down since administrative justice was not directly brought into question during the controversy which led up to Sir Thomas Dugdale's resignation. The Committee's Report was published in 1957 and most of its recommendations were enacted in the Tribunals and Inquiries Act of 1958. It laid down three principles against which administrative justice should be assessed and which would provide guidelines for future reforms, including the Committee's own recommendations. These principles were those of Openness, Fairness and Impartiality. (See Document 20.)

The Committee's most significant achievement was to secure the provision for the first time of a common framework within which the procedures involved in administrative justice could be developed. Its principal features are:

- First, the creation of a Council on Tribunals which has oversight over the entire system of administrative justice. The Council must be permitted to comment on all proposals to establish new tribunals or to lay down new procedural rules governing tribunals. Its members carry out annual programmes of inspection of tribunals and inquiries. The Council also deals with the complaints made by members of the public about tribunals and inquiries. It has no formal powers but its opinions are rarely rejected or ignored by Ministers.

- Since the 1958 Act, almost all administrative tribunals have been chaired by lawyers, usually appointed by the Lord Chancellor instead of, as previously, by the Minister whose department's decisions are the subject of the tribunal's case-load. This has produced two benefits in respect of the rules of natural justice. First, the tribunal is seen to be independent of the department whose decisions are being challenged before it. Secondly, lawyers can shape the proceedings, however informal they are, in such a way that all parties are able to explain their cases and ask questions of the other parties. Lawyers are experts in ensuring that procedures are fair (Elcock, 1969a).

- The reports of Inspectors on public inquiries must now be published, despite the plea made to the Franks Committee by the Ministry of Housing and Local Government, that the imposition of such an obligation might reveal to the public the awful truth that some Inspectors cannot spell. Now, the Inspector's report can be compared with the Minister's final decision, which must also state the reasons for it.

- All tribunals must now give the reasons for their decisions in writing on demand. A similar requirement is imposed on Ministers determining Inquiry cases. We have already seen that an early indication of increased judicial militancy in matters of administrative procedure was Mr Justice Megaw's stringent application of this requirement, which demands that all the points raised at the hearing must be examined in the statement of reasons. However, some observers have criticised the restriction of tribunals' obligations to the giving of reasons on demand, since not all persons appearing before tribunals will be aware of their right to demand reasons. Many tribunals in practice automatically give statements of reasons but they are not required to do so.

While it would be somewhat overstating the case to say that the 1958

Act brought order to chaos, it did for the first time provide the means whereby administrative justice could develop coherently, both because of the supervisory role accorded to the Council on Tribunals and through its other requirements. The Act's impact can be assessed by comparing the results of the LSE lawyers' study of tribunals and inquiries in 1954 (Pollard (ed), 1954) with a study carried out in the late 1960s (Elcock, 1969a). The results give an indication of the state of affairs before and after the Franks Report and the 1958 Act. They can be briefly summarised by saying that the earlier survey found that the system of administrative justice was in the main unsatisfactory, although sometimes procedures were fair and decisions just, whereas the later one revealed that most tribunals and inquiries are fair but occasional problems, even the odd travesty of justice, remained.

Some significant problems remain and new ones have developed in recent years, including the following:

- The resources available to the Council on Tribunals are very limited and probably inadequate. Although the Council's achievements in ensuring consistency throughout the system are impressive, it has no means of enforcing its decisions. However, since the Council's recommendations have nearly always been accepted, this is not perhaps as serious a problem as appears at first sight. More significantly, however, may be the Council's membership which is voluntary and part time, supported by only a small staff. This may limit the effectiveness of its supervisory role, although the programme of visits carried out by Council members has increased over the years. One other trend to be noted is that the proportion of its time that the Council has to devote to dealing with complaints from the public has declined from about a third to a quarter (Elcock, 1969a; Council on Tribunals, *Annual Reports, seriatim* since 1959).

- Secondly, the roles played by lawyers in administrative justice need close examination. The effect of engaging lawyers to take the chair at tribunals has undoubtedly been beneficial in that they give a coherent shape to the proceedings without rendering them unduly formal. Most tribunals are still more like a chat around a table than an intimidating court hearing. However, as advocates at tribunals and inquiries the value of lawyers' contribution is more questionable. It has long been alleged that barristers appearing at public inquiries both force the procedure into excessive formality and have rendered it extremely difficult for unrepresented lay people to present their cases, although enabling them to do so is one of the main purposes of holding a public inquiry. Pollard quoted a lay person who protested to an Inspector: 'Sir, I've never been in a place like this before!' More seriously, Denys Munby argued in the 1950s that

It should be perfectly possible to adopt a reasonable procedure which allows for full discussion of all the issues, critical examination of the case put up by the public body in question, elucidation of new facts and the presentation of relevant evidence and argument, without the full legal procedure of the law courts in the matter of the hearing of 'witnesses', formal rules of evidence and formal cross-examination and without turning a public inquiry into a forum for the display of counsels' eloquence. (1956, p. 184)

He concluded that if this were not done, 'it is to be feared that the question recently raised, "Are public inquiries a farce?" must be answered, "Yes because the lawyers have made them so."' (Ibid.) More recently, this problem reached great proportions at the public inquiry into the proposal to build the Sizewell B nuclear power station, which lasted 18 months and at which most of the objectors could not afford to maintain a continuous presence, let alone pay counsel to challenge those employed by the Department of Energy, the UK Atomic Energy Authority and the Central Electricity Generating Board. In consequence, the Inspector, Sir Frank Layfield, first requested that the government should assist the objectors with their costs. When this request was refused, he appointed a Counsel to the Inquiry one of whose duties was to assist objectors.

A similar problem now arises at Industrial Tribunals, at which it is now common for employers to have legal representation in cases involving redundancy, unfair dismissal and allegations of racial or gender discrimination. Appellants and the organisations supporting them may be forced to hire their own counsel at considerable expense or risk being unable fully to present their cases. Furthermore the proceedings at these tribunals are now highly formalised and can be lengthy; a case in 1989 which involved four women lecturers at Newcastle Polytechnic who claimed gender discrimination in an internal promotion procedure, lasted more than four weeks.

A person appearing before an administrative tribunal or public inquiry may represent him or herself or have any other person to act as representative: a friend, a trade union officer or a member of a voluntary organisation, for example. However, if the other side is legally represented the contest may become, or at least appear to be, unequal. Furthermore, lawyers who are not expert in the subject-matter of the hearing may cause difficulties for the tribunal. For example, at an Agricultural Lands Tribunal which was hearing a dispute over whether a tenant farmer should be evicted because he had not managed the rotation of crops competently, neither the solicitor representing the landowner nor the one representing the tenant understood the main issue at stake, which had to be explained to them by the members of the tribunal. (Elcock, 1969a, p. 66)

- The problems caused by the appearance of lawyers at tribunals and inquiries may be exacerbated by the non-availability of legal aid for advocacy before them. However, other representatives are likely usually to be sufficiently articulate, experienced and confident to counter the arguments put against them in most tribunal proceedings. The general introduction of legal aid would be excessively costly, as well as further damaging the informality of many tribunals but in some cases, such as the Industrial Tribunals, where the cases involve large sums of money or important issues and where legal representation is now the norm, there may now be a case for making legal aid available on grounds of equity. The problem at public inquiries may be countered by the Inspector appointing a Counsel to the Inquiry, as Sir Frank Layfield did at the Sizewell B Inquiry.

- Sir Frank's action was an ingenious solution to the problem that at the very lengthy public inquiries which have been conducted in recent years, it may be extremely expensive to procure adequate representation or even to maintain a presence at an inquiry which may last for months, even more than a year. Examples of such major inquiries include that into the proposed expansion of the Windscale (now Sellafield) nuclear reprocessing plant, the Sizewell B Inquiry and the inquiry into whether a fifth terminal should be built at Heathrow Airport or a second runway be built at Stansted in Essex. The Sizewell Inquiry lasted longest, at over 18 months but the other two lasted around a year.

- Another major problem about the machinery of administrative justice as a means of securing accountability downwards is what place policy should take in procedures whose purpose is to provide redress for aggrieved citizens. The legal rule is that any public body may have a policy, as long as in any case which it must decide, it considers whether an exception should be made to that policy. Thus a planning application may be rejected on the ground that it conflicts with a policy laid down by a local planning authority as long as the applicant is given the opportunity to challenge its application to his or her case. In consequence, at an appeal inquiry, the applicant may have to challenge either the entire policy or its application in the specific case. However, to challenge policy is not always easy.

  At several public inquiries into proposals to construct new major roads in the mid–1970s, a series of Inspectors attempted to rule out objectors' attempts to challenge the necessity of building the road at all, arguing that this was a policy decision taken by the Minister; the inquiry's role was confined to recommending the precise route the road should take in order to minimise its harmful effects on the objectors and their properties. In some cases, notably the public inquiries into the Aire Valley Trunk Road in West Yorkshire and the Archway extension of the M1 in London, the Inspector's attempt to rule arguments about the need for the proposed road out of order on the ground that they were policy matters for the Minister to decide, provoked such disorder that the inquiry had to be adjourned. Subsequently, the Department of Transport altered the rules to permit debate about the wider policy issues involved in major road schemes at public inquiries (Levin, 1979).

- Finally, the remedies available through the machinery of administrative justice are only available where provision has been made by statute for aggrieved citizens to be able to have recourse to a tribunal or inquiry. The Franks Committee pointed out that such provisions did not exist in many areas where disputes were likely to arise (Franks, 1957, para. 10). Such exclusions may appear to be without logic. For example, if you are refused permission to open a private school you can appeal to a tribunal, whereas no such right exists if you are refused a licence to operate a taxi or open a cinema. In the latter cases the only means of redress available would be to complain to MPs or councillors. The patchiness of the provision of redress identified by the Franks Committee was one reason why, in the late 1950s, pressure began to develop for the importation into Britain of the office of Ombudsman to provide a means of redress of general scope, especially where no alternative remedy existed.

REDRESS COMPLETED? THE OFFICE OF OMBUDSMAN

At this time, then, a number of academics and lawyers began to urge that the means available for aggrieved citizens to seek redress should be expanded by establishing officials whose task would be the investigation of such complaints, who have been popularly (if wrongly) dubbed Ombudsmen. In 1961 a committee of 'Justice' (the British section of the International Commission of Jurists) chaired by Sir John Whyatt, proposed the establishment of a Parliamentary Commissioner for Administration to investigate complaints of maladministration by public authorities (Whyatt, 1961). This proposal was dismissed by Harold Macmillan's Conservative Government as unnecessary because all such complaints could, Ministers argued, be dealt with under their individual responsibility to Parliament. However, the Leader of the Labour Party, Harold Wilson, took up the idea. A commitment to establish a Parliamentary Commissioner for Administration was included in Labour's election manifestos for 1964 and 1966 and was implemented after Labour was returned to office with a secure majority in 1966. The first Commissioner, Sir Edmund Compton, took up his duties on 1 April 1967 (Stacey, 1971).

Then and since, however, the office has been the subject of a good deal of criticism because of the constraints imposed upon it by the 1967 Act. When the Act was passed, several of the popular newspapers hailed the Commissioner's creation as an 'Ombudsboob' or 'Ombudsmouse'. More serious critics concentrated on several features of the office which they considered would limit its effectiveness, which included:

1. The 'MP filter'. Complainants can approach the Parliamentary Commissioner only through a Member of Parliament, although they need not use their own constituency MP to do so. Some MPs make more extensive use of the Commissioner than others; some use him rarely or never (Gregory and Hutchesson, 1975). MPs tend to be jealous of their own function of seeking redress for their constituents' grievances, not least because they believe, not without cause, that the diligent pursuit of constituency cases will increase their support at the next general election. When Local Commissioners for Administration were appointed in 1974 to investigate complaints about mal-administration against local authorities, complainants were required to seek access through a councillor sitting on the authority against which they wished to complain but this 'councillor filter' has now been removed. There is still criticism of the 'MP filter' and demands for its removal, so that citizens can have direct access to the Commissioner. However, not only would this probably considerably increase his case–load; also it might cause resentment among MPs, who could then see the Commissioner as a competitor for cases rather than as a weapon in their own armoury. Also the Commissioner can only act when he receives a complaint from an MP; he cannot initiate an investigation of apparent maladministration on his own initiative.

2. Secondly, the Parliamentary Commissioner is confined under the Act to investigating complaints of 'maladministration resulting in injustice'; he is debarred from investigating decisions properly taken under a Minister's discretionary powers. However, during the passage of the Act, the Leader of the House of Commons, Richard Crossman, explained that the term 'maladministration' covered a wide variety of administrative sins, including 'bias, inattention, delay, incompetence,

ineptitude, perversity, turpitude, arbitrariness and so on. It would be a long and interesting list.' (Quoted in Stacey, 1971, p. 75.) Since then, the Commissioner has ruled, with the support and encouragement of the Select Committee to which he reports, that he may assume that maladministration may have occurred where correct procedures appear to have been followed but the result is clearly a bad decision. Equally, where the application of a departmental rule produces bad or perverse results, he may also examine the matter to seek possible maladministration. The effect of these 'Bad Decision' and 'Bad Rule' rulings by the Commissioner and the Select Committee has been, according to Geoffrey Marshall, that '…it is, it seems, now possible to infer that if a decision has no merits at all there must have been maladministration in the way it was reached. Thus the stuffing was knocked out of s. 12 of the 1967 Act as it always deserved to be.' (Marshall, 1970, p. 123) In consequence, the restriction of the Commissioner's activities to 'maladministration resulting in injustice' probably imposes few practical restrictions on his investigations. The same clause has been inserted in the legislation establishing other Commissioners but has been similarly interpreted by them.

3. Complainants are barred from approaching the Commissioner when another avenue of redress, such as a tribunal or a court of law, exists unless the Commissioner judges that it is unreasonable to expect the complainant to use that other remedy. This power has been exercised by various Commissioners on a number of occasions. For instance, the Local Commissioners for Administration have investigated complaints by parents about the way in which Local Education Authorities have allocated their children to schools despite the existence of a right of appeal to the authority itself (Chinkin and Bailey, 1976).

4. Lastly and perhaps most fundamentally, the critics of the Parliamentary Commissioner argue that he has no power to compel Ministers to grant redress when their Departments are found to have been at fault. However, the precedent of the Council on Tribunals (on which the Commissioner has a seat *ex officio*) provides some reassurance. Furthermore, soon after his appointment, the Commissioner was given a case which enabled him to demonstrate conclusively that he could obtain results which had not been possible before his appointment.

The case concerned four ex-prisoners of war who claimed that they had been held in the extermination camp at Sachsenhausen, where they suffered in ways not normally expected for prisoners of war. They had therefore sought compensation from reparations paid after the war by the West German Government to compensate British victims of Nazi oppression. This claim had been repeatedly rejected by the Foreign Office when it had been pressed by the late Airey Neave, MP, himself an ex-prisoner of war who was one of the few to escape successfully from Colditz Castle. Immediately the Parliamentary Commissioner was appointed, Neave referred the Sachsenhausen case to him. The Commissioner carried out a detailed investigation into the men's claims and ruled that they had been wrongfully denied compensation. After some bluster from the then Foreign Secretary, George Brown, the former unwilling inhabitants of the Sachsenhausen camp received their compensation (Stacey, 1971, pp. 248–58). On a more general note, the Commissioner usually finds that maladministration has occurred in about a quarter of the cases he investigates – a figure which is arguably too high for comfort for either citizens or civil servants (Annual Reports of the Parliamentary Commissioner, *seriatim* since 1968. For an example of the Commissioner's work, see Document 21).

Since the creation of the Parliamentary Commissioner, several more similar offices have been created. In 1969, his functions were extended to Northern Ireland, as part of a package of measures designed to reassure the Province's Roman Catholic minority that they would in future receive fair treatment by officials there. At the same time, a Commissioner for Complaints was established to investigate complaints against local authorities and public utilities in Northern Ireland. He was given a specific remit to investigate allegations of discrimination on religious grounds (Elcock, 1971). His findings are admissible as evidence in subsequent court proceedings and must be accepted as true unless they can be proved false to the satisfaction of the court.

In 1973 a Commissioner was established for the National Health Service, charged to investigate complaints of maladministration by health authorities. However, matters involving clinical judgements are excluded from his remit. So far this office has been held by the Parliamentary Commissioner.

In 1974, Local Commissioners for Administration were appointed to investigate complaints against local authorities and regional water authorities. The second group of authorities have not attracted many complaints but complaints against local authorities have kept the Local Commissioners busy since their establishment. There are three Commissioners in England, one of whom is based in York and deals with complaints from citizens in the North of England. There is also a Commissioner for Scotland and one for Wales.

Like the Parliamentary Commissioner, the Local Commissioners have no power to compel local authorities to grant redress when they have been found to have been at fault but they can require a local authority to publicise their reports in the local Press. If the local authority does not grant redress to the Commissioner's satisfaction, then the Commissioner can issue a second report which the local authority is required also to publicise. Although most complaints that are upheld by the Local Commissioners are subsequently remedied, a few councils have proved recalcitrant and the Commissioners have expressed the view that they should be given a power to compel them to give redress when the Commissioners decide that this should be done.

The office of Ombudsman is therefore now an established part of the British administrative landscape; indeed it has been widely adopted around the world (Stacey, 1978). Despite the widespread criticism of the apparent toothlessness of the Parliamentary Commissioner and most of the other similar offices which have been established in Britain, they have won general acceptance as valuable means for aggrieved citizens to seek redress against the various agencies of the State.

One final body must be mentioned under this heading: the Police Complaints Authority. Until 1975, the police were themselves responsible for investigating complaints against them. The Deputy Chief Constable is the officer designated in each Police Force as responsible for investigating complaints. Serious complaints have long been investigated by a senior officer from another Force. The way in which complaints are dealt with is also carefully checked during each Force's annual inspection. However, for many years there was pressure for the establishment of an independent investigatory agency because it too often appeared that the police were acting as judge and jury in their own cause. Such pressure increased as a result of such cases as those of the deaths of Liddle Towers and Blair Peach. In 1975 an investigatory body, the Police Complaints Board, was established. It had the power both to refer complaints which it had investigated to the Director of Public Prosecutions (the DPP) for possible prosecution of the officers involved and to recommend to a Chief Constable that he take disciplinary action against officers whom the Board had found to have been at fault. In 1988 the Board's powers were extended and it became the Police Complaints Authority.

The Authority's effectiveness is limited, however. Complaints are usually examined by a single member of the Authority who is supplied with the official files on the case. Furthermore, the Authority has no independent investigators and must rely on the police themselves to investigate complaints on its behalf. Hence doubts are still expressed about the Police Complaints Authority's effectiveness, although recent attacks on it by the Police Federation may be taken as some reassurance that it is being effective.

The mechanisms we have discussed in this Section are concerned with strengthening the accountability of public servants downwards to citizens. They have all attracted a good deal of criticism over the years. Some have been radically reformed over the last thirty years and new ones have been created, yet doubts persist about the effectiveness of all of them and there are still those who look enviously across the Channel to systems of *droit administratif* and administrative courts. Perhaps the greatest single defect of many of these institutions is their lack of formal powers, yet few administrators who are found to have been at fault by the Council on Tribunals or an Ombudsman fail to grant redress and mend their ways. Ultimately, however, responsibility for ensuring that public servants are held accountable and that justified complaints are remedied lies with elected representatives and above all with Parliament.

PARLIAMENT AND ACCOUNTABILITY

This is not the place to give a general account of the functions and activities of Parliament (see Norton, 1981). It will suffice here briefly to identify its main functions which are: to legislate, to grant Supply and scrutinise the actions of the Executive and to seek the redress of citizens' grievances. Doubts have been cast on Parliament's effectiveness in executing all these functions. In the legislative process, Parliament influences but does not control the Executive (Norton, 1987). Its influence may have been increased because back–bench MPs have learnt how to express their discontent by voting against the government without bringing it down (Norton, 1981). In scrutinising the Executive, the means available to MPs have been considerably increased in recent years, especially with the extension of the Select Committee system in 1979 (Study of Parliament group, Richards and Ryle, 1987). In seeking redress for individual complaints, MPs have acquired the Parliamentary Commissioner in addition to the other formal and informal means available to them: letters to Ministers, local authorities and others, the Parliamentary Question and the Adjournment Debate, for instance. The Select Committee which receives the Commissioner's reports has, as we shall see, played an important role in developing the accountability of civil servants to Parliament.

Until the late 1970s the use of Select Committees was restricted chiefly to the scrutiny of government spending. The Estimates Committee, which was established in 1912, examined the government's spending plans and was involved – albeit somewhat half–heartedly – in the Public Expenditure Survey (Heclo and Wildavsky, 1974, chapter 5). Heclo and Wildavsky argued that through lack of interest among MPs, the House of Commons was missing an opportunity to become more involved in public expenditure planning. Of greater importance has been the Public Accounts Committee, which scrutinises what the Government has done with taxpayers' money and which from time to time uncovers noteworthy instances of waste and inefficiency. On several occasions, the Committee has discovered that private firms have been allowed to make excessive profits from government contracts. In consequence, sometimes part of the excessive profits have been returned to the Treasury and the Minister concerned has had to face severe parliamentary criticism.

In 1956, a Select Committee was established to monitor the nationalised industries. One result of the Attlee Government's programme of nationalisation in the late 1940s, had paradoxically been to reduce the accountability of these industries to Parliament. Under the wartime emergency legislation most of these industries had been placed under the direct control of government departments and were hence completely accountable to Parliament, so that for example, MPs could put down questions demanding to know why a train was late on a particular day. However, when these industries were transferred to public corporations under the nationalisation legislation, the responsibility of Ministers was confined to general control, with day-to-day management being reserved to the new Boards of the public corporations. In consequence, MPs were deprived of their previous right to ask detailed questions about the services the nationalised industries provided. The result was rumbling parliamentary discontent.

In 1955 the government proposed the establishment of a Select Committee on the Nationalised Industries (SCNI) but proposed that its terms of reference would restrict it to scrutinising the industries' annual reports and accounts. After a Parliamentary revolt, however, the Government agreed to give the new committee a general remit to scrutinise the industries and the Committee was set up in 1956 (Coombes, 1967). It proved itself an effective instrument for examining the deeds and misdeeds of the industries.

None the less, a major problem concerning the accountability of the nationalised industries remains: that although formally Ministers are excluded from interfering with their managements' day to day decisions, they none the less do so by 'back door' methods. Ministers can bring unfair pressure to bear on chairmen and board members who are appointed by Ministers and can be dismissed by them. This in turn has provoked criticism both that Ministers have acquired powers over the industries for which they cannot easily be held to account and that the ability of the public corporations to operate commercially has been damaged, even destroyed, by political interference. Commercial decisions are delayed or blocked because of their likely unpopularity (Fiennes, 1967). This occurred in a spectacular and generalised form in the early 1970s, when the Heath government required the nationalised industries to comply strictly with its price restraint policy. In consequence, most of the industries were driven into heavy deficit. 'Back stairs' influence on the nationalised industries was severely criticised by the Select Committee on the Nationalised Industries on many occasions (Coombes, 1967).

However, this problem is now declining in importance as successive nationalised industries are privatised. The Thatcher administrations have turned their backs on the nagging problem of whether or not it is possible to impose commercial pressures on nationalised industries with their political accountability; rather they are to be transferred to private owner-ship and hence to regulation by market forces, although regulatory bodies have been established to protect the public from misuse of their monopoly power, as well as from undesirable or unsafe practices.

The experience of the Select Committee on the Nationalised Industries, together with that of the Public Accounts Committee, encouraged the idea that Parliament's effectiveness in its scrutiny role could be increased by extending the Select Committee system to all government departments. This proposal was made by Bernard Crick in his book, *The Reform of Parliament*, which first appeared in 1962 and set the agenda for the debate about parliamentary reform for many years. Crick deprecated what he saw as the declining influence of Parliament and recommended the establishment of Select Committees to monitor the work of each government department, which would ensure that parlia-mentary scrutiny of the Government's activities would be both more extensive and more continuous. This proposal was extensively debated. Some observers and parliamentarians argued against the idea, arguing that the establishment of such Committees would transform the House of Commons from the 'Grand Inquest of the Nation' to becoming a collection of specialist auditors. Nevertheless, the Labour government of 1966–70 experimented rather gingerly with a small number of specialist Select Committees (Mackintosh, 1968; Crossman, 1977; see also the successive volumes discussing current parliamentary developments which have been published by the Study of Parliament Group: Hanson and Wiseman, 1970; Walkland and Ryle, 1977 and Richards and Ryle, 1987). The subsequent Heath Conservative government created an Expenditure Committee which spawned a series of specialist sub–committees (Walkland and Ryle, 1977). Finally, at the instigation of Norman St John Stevas when he was appointed Leader of the House in 1979, at the outset of Margaret Thatcher's premiership, Select Committees were at last established to scrutinise all departments and the power of Parliament to scrutinise the Executive and hold it to account was therefore strengthened.

The impact of these Select Committees on the accountability of civil servants to politicians in particular has been significant. Clearly the accountability upwards of civil servants to Ministers and hence to Parliament has been increased, because the number of occasions on which Ministers may now be required to answer somewhere in Parliament for their departments' deeds and misdeeds has increased. Furthermore, the relationship between civil servants themselves and Parliament has been changed.

This change began with the Select Committee on the Parliamentary Commissioner, which won the right to question civil servants who had been involved in the Commissioner's cases against civil service resistance. When the Commissioner and the Committee were established, the Head of the Civil Service argued that the only civil servants who could be required to appear before the Committee were the Permanent Secretaries, who are their Departments' Accounting Officers. This restriction was rejected by the Select Committee, however, with the result that a much wider range of civil servants are now called to appear not only before the Select Committee on the Parliamentary Commissioner but also before other Select Committees (Stacey, 1971, pp. 266–7; Marshall, 1970, pp. 121–2).

This in turn raises the possibility that, although when they appear before Select Committees civil servants are expected to put forward only the views of their Ministers, they are none the less likely to reveal more about the internal processes and decisions in their departments than would the Minister or indeed, the Permanent Secretary. This might in turn further weaken the Minister's own individual responsibility to Parliament because he is no longer its sole source of information about his department's affairs.

This dilemma may become still more acute as executive agencies are established under *The Next Steps* because their Chief Executives are more likely to be summoned before Select Committees and may well express views about the running of their agencies independent of or even at variance with, those of their Ministers (Fry *et al.*, 1988; Chapman, 1988b and c). The accountability of the Executive to Parliament may thus be being increased but the constitutional convention of Ministerial responsibility may at the same time suffer further damage.

CONCLUSIONS

Accountability to citizens thus continues to pose a series of problems in Britain, despite the repeated and sometimes radical changes introduced over the last twenty or thirty years. The machinery of administrative justice has been considerably improved, yet many still harbour doubts about its efficacy. In particular, many observers fear that public inquiries are no more than a chance for aggrieved citizens to 'let off steam' about decisions which will not be changed as a result of their representations. Ombudsmen are now an established part of the system of accountability but doubts still remain about their effectiveness, especially their lack of power to compel the granting of redress when they discover maladministration. Also, many argued that the 'MP filter' should be removed. Parliament may still not be effectively able to hold Ministers and civil servants to account for their misdeeds or inefficiency. Hence, debates about accountability seem likely to continue into the 1990s and beyond.

Such debates raise many important questions but they have been largely neglected in some recent approaches to public management and are not fully considered in such documents as *The Next Steps,* whose limited recognition of accountability issues is being severely criticised (Fry *et al.*, 1988; Chapman, 1988b and c). Accountability is a fundamental requirement of government in democratic polities but it does impose restrictions on the extent to which public organisations can be decentralised or public managers granted autonomy, however great the benefits of doing both may be in terms of stimulating enterprise and economy. A balance must be struck between the importance of maintaining accountability and improving performance; neither value ought to prevail to the extent of excluding the other.

CHAPTER NINE

The debates about power

POWER AND CONTROL

An accountability relationship is also a power relationship but contrary to common belief, it is not necessarily a simple superior – subordinate one. Jones may be accountable to Smith but he is not powerless relative to Smith. Ministers and civil servants do not have to disclose everything to MPs on demand, although they are accountable to them. Accountability is also multi-directional: upwards, downwards and outwards. Thus as we have seen, every individual, group or organisation is involved in a series of accountability relationships which will be of differing importance or impose different degrees of pressure on them. Some of these relationships are formal; prescribed in laws or constitutional conventions, while others are informal and unwritten but none the less important. All these relationships involve actors trying to control the activities of other actors but rarely does any one actor have anything like complete control over his or her fellows. Sometimes the means are simply insufficient, or (as is frequently the case in public administration) there are no sanctions available which are intermediate between the notional, such as a reprimand and the draconian – for instance, dismissal.

The lack of appropriate sanctions entails a limitation – perhaps a severe one – on the ability of superiors to control their subordinates. Indeed, the implication of Michael Lipsky's (1980) analysis of the position of 'street-level bureaucrats' is that staff at the bottom of the organisation, who actually provide services to citizens, determine its policies and priorities by the demands they make on behalf of their clients. Much of the literature on policy implementation is concerned with precisely this issue: whether policies are transmitted downwards from the politicians who formally decide them and the senior officers who advise them, or whether in practice policies are decided by the demands made at the 'street level'. Furthermore, policies determined at the top of the hierarchy may be distorted or obstructed by the staff lower down the hierarchy who are responsible for carrying them out (Barrett and Fudge (eds), 1982; Hill and Barrett, 1985).

Power is, however, a most elusive concept, as the interminable debates about power among pluralists, elite theorists, corporatists, Marxists and others demonstrate (see Parry, 1969; Lukes, 1977; Furlong, Page and Cox, 1985). However, we can establish some pointers towards making sense of the power relationships which bind politicians, officials and citizens together in the networks of relationships which constitute the political and administrative systems of the modern state.

A first set of such pointers is offered by a beguilingly simple series of definitions offered by John Lucas (1967). He suggests that:

- A man, or body of men, has *power* if it results from his saying, 'Let X happen', that X does happen;
- A man, or body of men, has *authority* if it follows from his saying, 'Let X happen', that X ought to happen.
- A man, or body of men, has *influence* if the result of his saying 'Let X happen', is that other people will say (perhaps only to themselves), 'Let X happen.' (Lucas, 1967, p. 16)

The first of these definitions is a simple descriptive statement to the effect that a power-holder is able to obtain compliance with his or her instructions. However, one of the recurring themes of this book has been that power is rarely, if ever, absolute even when responsibility for a policy or service is clearly located. Indeed, Harry S. Truman warned that his soldier successor would find the exercise of political power deeply frustrating: 'Poor Ike! He'll sit here and say Do this! Do that! And nothing will happen. And he will wonder why.' We have seen that although the Secretary of State for Health has complete responsibility for the National Health Service and the Service is funded almost totally from the central government, successive Secretaries of State have had difficulty in securing implementation of their major policy initiatives, such as the RAWP and Priorities exercises of the 1970s (Elcock and Haywood, 1980, 1981; Haywood and Alaszewski, 1980; Haywood and Elcock, 1982). Again, under the Caravan Sites Act of 1968, county councils were given a duty to provide camp sites for all people of nomadic habit residing in or resorting to their areas but they do not have the power to authorise and establish sites. To do so, they have to obtain the co-operation of the district council where the site is to be established, other public authorities and possibly private landowners, all of whom are likely to come under intense pressure from local objectors not to co-operate. In consequence, a site can only be established after a long and wearying series of negotiations and attempts at persuasion. Thus early in its existence, Humberside County Council established that to comply with the law's demands it needed to create eight gipsy sites but in its first eight years of existence it only managed to open two (Elcock, 1979b). Where power is inadequate, persuasion and the offer of inducements to co-operate are needed if policies are to be implemented and legal obligations discharged. Hence the pre-occupation of many policy analysts with the management of inter-organisational relationships (Friend, Power and Yewlett, 1977) and with understanding power relationships (Wildavsky, 1980).

Authority is crucial to many of the issues discussed in Part Two and our second set of pointers is Max Weber's famous definitions of traditional, legal-rational and charismatic authority. Traditional authority is probably of little relevance in modern states but the other two are crucial. They all involve acceptance of the right of one person to prescribe or command: the acceptance that that person is an authority or in authority on the matter in hand (Winch, 1967).

- *Legal-rational authority* is a central pillar of the bureaucratic hierarchy: authority is vested in the office, not the individual holding it. It may be signified by, for instance, a title, the wearing of a uniform or the thickness of an office carpet. Obedience is required because the law prescribes that the holder of the office is entitled to it, regardless of his or her personal qualities or deficiencies.

  We may illustrate this type of authority by referring briefly to the apparently strange notion that officers or bodies which are given no formal powers, such as the Council on Tribunals and the Parliamentary Commissioner for Administration none the less usually achieve compliance with their recommendations because politicians and public servants accept that they ought to comply with them.

- *Charismatic authority,* by contrast, results from the personality of its possessor. There can be no denying that the shift in the culture of the Civil Service since 1979 which has led to increasing attention being paid to ensuring that it is managed efficiently, has resulted from the personal insistence of Mrs Thatcher that established ways had to be changed. Beginning with her injunction to Permanent Secretaries not to be so 'wet', such initiatives as the Rayner Scrutinies, the FMI and *The Next Steps* have been implemented because the Prime Minister has insisted they must be. Indeed, *The Next Steps* proposals were resisted by the Treasury and they might never have seen the light of day but for the Prime Minister's insistence on the report's publication (Fry, *et al.*, 1988). The weakness of charismatic authority is, of course, that its holder is both physically and politically mortal: we shall consider in the last chapter what is likely to occur when Mrs Thatcher retires or loses office.

POWER AND ITS LIMITS

Any account of the policy processes of governments in Western democratic countries and increasingly in those of Eastern Europe as well (Kolankiewicz and Lewis, 1988), leads to the conclusion that the power of governments and governors is restricted. Such a conclusion is axiomatic for pluralist students of how decisions are made (Banfield, 1961; Dahl, 1962). Such a view is amply confirmed by many of the instances given in this book. However, elite theorists and Marxists argue that these processes serve to conceal the control of government by all-powerful but largely invisible ruling elites or classes. The problem is that the existence of such cohesive, conspiratorial and controlling elites or of ruling classes is extremely hard either to prove or disprove. The methodology used by Floyd Hunter (1953) to identify the elite in 'Regional City', has been widely criticised, as has that of other 'reputational' researchers. The methodology depends on the making of a series of subjective judgements either by the researcher or the subjects of the research about who wields power. Furthermore, to inquire, 'Who rules this town?' is to invite a dogmatic, simplistic answer (Popper, 1960). Studies of how decisions are reached which trace the process through documents and meetings as well as interviews, usually indicate that power is spread among a range of actors.

Edward Banfield's (1961) studies of how major decisions were made in Chicago were carried out when Mayor Richard J. Daley and his Democratic 'Machine' were at the height of their domination of the political system of Chicago (Royko, 1971), yet Banfield's studies revealed a fragmented power-structure in which coalitions of support had to be built for decisions to be taken and implemented. Robert Dahl's (1962) study of decision-making in New Haven, Connecticut revealed the existence of 'a pattern of petty sovereignties' in which a person's influence was almost invariably confined to a single issue-area. Even within the issue-areas of education, political nominations and town planning, coalitions of support for major decisions had to be assembled to secure their acceptance and implementation. The flavour of these analyses can be caught from

Banfield's definition of influence:

> By influence is meant ability to get others to act, think or feel as one intends...
> To concert activity for any purpose – to arrange a picnic, build a building or
> pass an ordinance, for example – a more or less elaborate system of influence
> must be created; the appropriate people must be persuaded, deceived, coerced,
> inveigled or otherwise induced to do what is required of them. Any co-
> operative activity – and so any organisation, formal or informal, ephemeral or
> lasting – may be viewed as a system of influence.   (Banfield, 1961, p. 3)

Examinations of political events reveal pluralistic influence structures,
which must be accepted as constituting reality, just as G.E. Moore (1939)
argued that his Royal Academy audience had no alternative to accepting
the existence of his two hands; they knew that two hands were being held
up before them and to argue that they only believed this and that therefore
they might be wrong, was absurd.

None the less, although elite theorists' and Marxists' theses concerning
the existence of invisible controllers ought to be dismissed in the light of
the realities of government in modern states, their writings still offer
valuable insights into the nature of power. First, not all persons or groups
are equal: to argue that pluralism consists of a free competition between
contenders who are even roughly equal in their influence is as unrealistic
as the economists' model of perfect competition, to which it bears a strong
resemblance (Galbraith, 1963). Some persons or groups will be excluded
from the competition entirely or their interests will be given little weight.
The issues which concern them will be kept off policy-makers' agendas by
processes of non-decision-making (Bachrach and Baratz, 1962, see
Documents 15 and 16) and the mobilisation of bias. Thus the needs of the
poor tend to be excluded from policy debates unless they are pressed by
organisations which tend to act on their behalf rather than being formed
by the poor themselves: the 'poverty lobby', most of whose activists
cannot themselves be regarded as being poor. Minority groups like
coloured people, homosexuals and gipsies have little power and are likely
to suffer discrimination unless others take up their causes. This was a major
activity of the 'New Urban Left' in the early 1980s (Gyford, 1984), who
used local authorities to promote the interests of such minority groups and
encourage them to participate in running their local communities
(Islington, 1987).

At the other extreme, a form of political oligopoly may develop, with
some groups being drawn deeply into the processes of government and
hence becoming identified with them. S.E. Finer (1956) described how
trusted interest groups become linked with government departments in
ways which are mutually beneficial. Each side obtains information and
advice from the other; in addition the department may obtain assistance

from interest groups in administering its policies, while the groups are able to ensure that the policy is administered in a manner acceptable to their members. Studies of the medical profession (Eckstein, 1957) and of farming (Self and Storing, 1958), among many others, have demonstrated the importance of such symbiotic relationships.

In the 1960s and 1970s, such co-option of interest groups into government was extended to macroeconomic management through the establishment of the National Economic Development Council in 1963 and the Prices and Incomes Board in 1964. Through these bodies and in less formal ways, employers and trade unions became involved with the government in a tripartite process of decision-making. Later, the Labour government and the trade union movement established the 'Social Contract' which between 1975 and 1978 enabled the Government to regulate wage increases in return for adopting policies sympathetic to the unions. (Smith, 1979 Budd, 1978) At times, this tripartite relationship seemed to be so dominant that some observers argued that it prevented the Government from taking economic initiatives and was therefore in danger of producing industrial and economic stagnation (Hayward, 1975). At this time, corporatism became a fashionable academic analytical tool for explaining how public policies were made and implemented (Pahl, 1970, 1975; Saunders, 1979). Government and interest groups work together in their common interests and although tension exists among the incorporated groups when their interests conflict, they will retain their unity to protect and promote their common interests.

In 1979, Jeremy Richardson and Grant Jordan produced an analysis of power-relations in the British system of government which provides a powerful tool for explaining the processes by which public policies are made and executed. Their concept of the policy community allows us to absorb both the notion that the various actors work together in their common interests and that they come into conflict when their interests are opposed to one another. A policy community is an issue-area or policy field, such as education, health care, local government or fire protection, in which a number of actors are involved and must maintain relationships with one another – however conflictual those relationships may sometimes be. Thus the education policy community includes the Department of Education and Science (DES), the local education authorities and their representative bodies, the teachers' unions, parent groups and campaign groups. This policy community is therefore likely to contain relatively loose relationships and be conflictual. By contrast, the fire service policy community includes only the Home Office, the local fire authorities and the two unions representing the members of the fire brigades and thus is able to maintain a relatively high level of consensus most of the time (Rhodes, 1987a; Elcock, forthcoming).

One policy community identified by Richardson and Jordan is that of local government. It consists of the government department which is principally concerned with the affairs of local government – in England the Department of the Environment – the local authorities themselves, the trade unions and professional bodies which represent local authority staff and a wide range of other interested parties.

The local government policy community provides a particularly good illustration of the limits which exist on the control Ministers can exercise over the development and execution of public policies in modern states. Central–local government relations have long been controversial and there have been many warnings that the central government is about to squeeze the life out of local government (for instance Glen, 1948; Griffith, 1961). However, R.A.W. Rhodes (1980, 1987a) has argued that central–local government relations constitute a process of exchange in which the actors involved deploy one or more types of resources to protect their own interests, promote their policies and resist encroachments by other actors in their area of activity. Here we can consider only the basic argument: that local authorities and the central government alike possess four types of resources, which they can at need deploy against the others. Rhodes defines these four types of resources as follows:

1. *Constitutional-Legal resources* are the grants of powers and functions by Parliament to local authorities. The latter can only derive their powers from statute but having been granted those powers and duties, they can resist central interference in how they carry them out. Thus in the *Tameside* case, the new Conservative majority on the council denied the Secretary of State the power to prevent it abandoning the previous Labour council's school reorganisation scheme.

2. *Financial resources* include the power to levy rates and taxes, which is available to the central government and local authorities alike. They also include the power of virement (the transfer of expenditure between budget headings), which often enables local authorities to carry out schemes for which money could not initially be included in the budget. This is only one of a range of 'creative accountancy' measures now available to local authorities.

3. *Political resources* are available to both sides in the process of exchange because both Ministers and councillors can claim the authority which comes from having been elected by the people. They also include influence exercised through the internal structures of the political parties.

4. Finally, both sides control *information resources*. Central departments and local authorities hold information the others need and it may be withheld in order to protect either side's position. For example, the Greater London Council and the metropolitan county councils refused to give the Department of the Environment the information it needed to prepare new forms of local government after they had been abolished.

However, this last example makes the point that the central government alone possesses *hierarchical resources*, because ultimately Governments control a sovereign Parliament which can change the powers and functions of local authorities, reorganise them or abolish local government altogether. In practice central–local relations characteristically consist of a cycle of Ministerial attempts to impose their will on local authorities, by legislation or otherwise, being resisted by local authorities who wish to pursue their own policies and protect the interests of their areas. Central policies are therefore seldom entirely implemented and this in turn produces a further attempt to oblige local authorities to comply with Ministerial wishes (see Elcock, Jordan and Midwinter, 1989).

Local government is an especially interesting policy community because in England at least, most national policy-making is done through a London-based policy community consisting of the Department of the Environment together with the Treasury and more marginally, other government departments such as the DES which have local government interests. They talk with the local authority associations – the Association of County Councils (ACC), the Association of Metropolitan Authorities, (AMA) and the Association of District Councils (ADC) – which represent the three main types of local authorities (Isaac-Henry, 1980; Rhodes, 1987a). Individual local authorities play only marginal roles in these 'centre–centre' relationships within the English local government policy community, a trend reinforced by the establishment of the Central Council on Local Government Finance in 1975.

In Scotland, Wales and Northern Ireland, however, contact between individual local authorities and the central government in the form of the three territorial Ministries (The Scottish, Welsh and Northern Ireland Offices) is more frequent, leading to better communication and closer co-ordination between central departments and local authorities than occurs in England (Elcock and Jordan (eds), 1987; Elcock, Jordan and Midwinter, 1989). However, in these countries too there are representative organisations which act on behalf of local authorities collectively in their dealings with the three territorial Ministers.

The variation in the relationships of the actors in policy communities has been further elaborated by Grant Jordan (1982) in the form of a continuum at whose extremes are 'iron triangles' and 'elastic nets'. The extent to which a policy community is coherent or diffuse, consensual or conflictual, depends on three factors: the number of actors engaged in the policy area; the nature of the relationships among them; and the extent to which the policy area is one which provokes partisan disagreements.

The smaller the number of actors involved, the less conflictual relationships are likely to be although conflict will still occur. Thus the fire service policy community contains few actors but there is a long history of disputes between the Fire Brigades Union (FBU) and the local fire authorities which went to the extent of the FBU calling a major strike in late 1977. None the less, the FBU has a unique status among public trade unions in that it has membership of the Service's main administering body (Rhodes, 1987a). Consensus is reinforced by the consciousness that all concerned are involved in the need to reduce the danger both to the public and to firemen themselves from carelessness or incompetence. Furthermore, the fire service is seldom the subject of political controversy because no politician would wish to be portrayed as being opposed to the provision of effective fire cover.

Such 'iron triangles' may, of course, maintain their consensual nature by excluding those who wish to disturb it. The Home Office and the Chief Constables, for example, sometimes appear to be determined to minimise the role of the local police authorities to which all police forces outside London are formally accountable. The formal powers of Police Committees are more limited than those of other local authority committees and a Chief Constable may refuse to answer questions from councillors on matters which he defines as being operational (Elcock, 1986a). In the event of a dispute, the Chief Constable can appeal to the Home Secretary, who almost always supports him in his refusal to disclose information to members of the local police authority or answer their questions. The police have long been resistant to extending their local accountability because they argue that this would increase the risk of improper political interference in their operations; however, it also restricts their obligation to account to anyone for their activities or their use of resources (Marshall, 1965).

Other policy communities include large numbers of actors, hence relationships among them will be loose and conflict may be frequent. We have already referred to the large number of actors who are involved in the education policy community. They also act on behalf of diverse, indeed divergent, interests in a policy field which in recent times has provoked acute political controversy both centrally and locally (Jennings, 1977; Kogan and van der Eycken, 1973). Even the teachers' unions themselves are chronically divided about the best way to represent the interests of the profession. There are four main teachers' unions: the National Union of Teachers (NUT), the Association of Schoolmasters/ Association of Women Teachers (NAS/UWT), the Assistant Masters and Mistresses Associations (AMMA) and the Professional Association of Teachers (PAT). They are divided in how best to represent the interests of primary and secondary teachers, on the extent to which teachers should or should not take industrial action, corporal punishment and many other matters. When one adds to the teachers' unions the multiplicity of school governors, parents and campaign groups, we see that the education policy community is and must be relatively loose: indeed, the problem is how to prevent it becoming chaotic (Richardson and Jordan, 1979; Rhodes, 1987a; Jennings, 1977; Kogan and van der Eycken, 1973).

The nature of the policy community is also one determinant of the structure of Whitehall departments. Their structures vary in relation to the nature of their tasks. Hence the Acton Society Trust argued in its evidence to the Fulton Committee that there is a 'continuum of bureaucratic modernity'. (Acton Society Trust, 1968) At one end lie such departments as the Home Office, whose functions are mostly of long standing and are concerned with the traditional role of the State to maintain the Queen's peace. At the other extreme are such departments as the then Department of Economic Affairs and Ministry of Technology, whose roles were both newer and more innovative. Hence, their structures are likely to be less hierarchical and to include more posts outside the established Civil Service structure than that of the Home Office. They also contained more people appointed from outside the Service, including substantial numbers of 'Irregulars'. (Brittan, 1969) The latter departments also had more varied relationships with outside members of the appropriate policy communities than the Home Office, which maintains a certain detachment from outside groups in carrying out its regulatory functions.

Later on, the Wardale Committee (1981) found that the structures of departments both do and ought to vary in relation to the extent to which they have operational responsibilities. This will also affect the extent of departments' contacts with outside organisations – the policy communities. Hence, the Treasury has few operational responsibilities and outside contacts and its structure is very different from that of, say, the Department of Education and Science because much of that Department's work involves dealing with local authorities and other outside organisations (see Elcock, 1985; Rhodes, 1987b). Again, Andrew Dunsire and his colleagues have demonstrated the variety of departmental structures and related that variation to other factors including the nature and extent of their contacts with outside interests (Dunsire *et al.*, 1981).

When we consider the complexities of such policy communities, it becomes easy to accept both the necessity for and the usefulness of the consensus-building, reiterative policy-making processes discussed in earlier chapters. Policies must be made by processes of communication and consultation among the groups involved in the policy community. They will need to be revised as new problems appear or opinions change. However, those who are formally responsible for the policy direction of the issue-area, ultimately Ministers and councillors, must be able to ensure that their values are reflected in the policies, routine decisions and administrative actions through which the policy community provides public services and allocates public resources. Some observers have questioned whether, in view of the many influences that are exerted on public policies, it may make any difference which political party is in office (Rose, 1974).

POLICY-MAKING IN THE 1980S: THE TOP-DOWN APPROACH?

For Richardson and Jordan it was both good luck and bad fortune that their book appeared in 1979. It is a valuable account of the policy process in British government as it then existed but in that year Margaret Thatcher won office and proceeded, many would argue, fundamentally to alter the manner in which public policies are made in Britain. She has sought to control the entire mechanism in order to implement her values throughout the public sector. Hence, one could argue that she has tried to change power-relationships in government to give her and her Ministers greater control over public policies. However, it would be vastly to exaggerate and over-simplify any account of the last ten years to argue that Mrs Thatcher's domination of the governmental system has become so great that no members of any policy community can prevent the implementation of her values and policies. Her ability apparently to dominate the governmental scene rests essentially on two features of the power structure: the sovereignty of Parliament and the position of the Prime Minister.

● The sovereignty of Parliament enables a government which commands more than a very small majority in the House of Commons to push legislation through largely regardless of the Opposition. In the last ten years, many would argue that this power has been used fundamentally to alter the balance of the Constitution. The Greater London Council and the six metropolitan county councils have been abolished. The right of local councillors to strike their rates or precepts at the level they choose has been abridged by rate-capping. The powers and privileges of trade unions have been reduced.

However, the sovereignty of Parliament does not confer absolute, untrammelled power on the Head of Government, for two main reasons. The first is that the Prime Minister and Cabinet must retain the support of their party's back-benchers and in recent times that support has become increasingly conditional, because MPs have learnt that they can defeat the government on specific matters without forcing a general election (Norton, 1981). In consequence, the Thatcher Government has suffered defeats in the Chamber and (more frequently) in the committees upstairs. It is also apparent that Mrs Thatcher and her Ministers have taken great care to maintain close contact with their back-benchers and to avoid putting forward proposals which would antagonise large numbers of them, as well as uniting the Opposition in and outside Parliament. The step-by-step approach to industrial relations reform initiated by James Prior and maintained by his successors, for example, has avoided uniting the entire Labour movement against the government in the manner which rendered the 1972 Industrial Relations Act ineffective within two years. (Elcock, (ed.), 1982, chapter 13)

Secondly, the House of Lords has by no means always been compliant with the Government's wishes, despite its built-in Conservative majority. There have been some notable Lords revolts. One occurred over the proposed abolition of children's right to free school transport if they live more than three miles from their schools. Because this proposal would have particularly damaged the interests of Catholic children, who tend to live further from school than others, a successful revolt against the proposal was led by the Duke of Norfolk. Again, the House of Lords refused to accept the imposition of referenda before local authorities levied supplementary rates. Their Lordships also rejected the replacement of Labour councillors by government nominees to control the GLC and the metropolitan county councils in the last year of their lives. Instead, the existing councillors' terms of office were extended for a further year.

Parliament is not, therefore, a compliant tool in the Prime Minister's hands and this reminds us that a Prime Minister can hold office only for as long as he or she commands the support of a majority in the House of Commons. (McKenzie, 1963; Jones, 1965) Mrs Thatcher's position is very dominant but other dominant Prime Ministers have lost their influence and their offices very quickly when they have made mistakes or the course of events has turned against them. Once David Lloyd George became 'A Prime Minister without a Party', his days in office were numbered (Beaverbrook, 1963). Harold Macmillan destroyed his authority by an ill-judged Cabinet reshuffle in the summer of 1962. Harold Wilson's reputation quickly became tarnished through repeated economic crises to which his governments seemed to have no effective answers. The Westland affair demonstrated that Mrs Thatcher is likewise not safe from such dangers.

However, the British Constitution gives the Prime Minister very considerable powers. In particular, Mrs Thatcher has made ruthless use of the Prime Minister's patronage powers to appoint 'people who think like us' to positions in many parts of the public services. Her influence is apparent in her selection of Permanent Secretaries, which some fear may have compromised the political neutrality of the Civil Service (Chapman, 1988b and c). Appointments to health authorities have been heavily influenced by Mrs Thatcher's wish to ensure that her values and policies are implemented. In addition the system of annual review meetings between the Secretary of State, RHA chairmen and their subsequent meetings with DHA chairmen has been introduced. She has also surrounded herself with personal advisers who share her views, of which the best known was her economic adviser, Professor Alan Walters. She has removed from her Cabinet most of the 'Wets' who challenge her policies.

Yet another indication of Margaret Thatcher's determination to dominate British government has been the erosion of the 'buffer' principle which formerly protected such institutions as the universities and the BBC from political interference (see Document 4). The BBC has been repeatedly attacked for bias by Mrs Thatcher and her senior colleagues; both the BBC and the independent broadcasting companies are now subject to scrutiny by a Broadcasting Standards Council, appointments to which clearly reflect the Government's views about what the proper content of broadcasting should be. Again, appointments to the Arts Council and other such bodies reflect the Government's views to an extent which previous governments avoided. Finally, the replacement of the University Grants Committee by the Universities Funding Council is intended to render the universities more subject to pressure to provide the teaching and research which Ministers consider relevant. Academic freedom was granted some degree of protection only after pressure was exerted on Ministers by eminent academics of all parties who hold seats in the House of Lords. Hence the need to respect limits on public servants' accountability to the Government in order to preserve freedom of opinion, which we discussed in Chapter 1, has not been greatly respected in recent years.

Corporatism now seems very dated, therefore. Policies come from the top down and trade union leaders are never now invited to No. 10 for consultations on economic policy; members of the CBI are seldom invited either. The NEDC still exists but its role is now marginal.

All this looks like a formidable case for arguing that Britain has become a highly centralised, authoritarian society in which pluralist analyses of policy communities have little relevance. One argument to the contrary is the paradox that although the Government's values and policies have been extremely consistent and have sought to follow Bentham's advice that 'The request which industry, manufactures and commerce make to Government is as simple as that of Diogenes to Alexander: Stand out of my sunshine', their implementation has often been difficult. One characteristic of the Thatcher years has been the development of a cycle of evasion followed by legislation to block loopholes. This has produced for many public managers a climate of uncertainty which makes planning or even coherent management extremely difficult (Elcock, Fenwick and Harrop, 1988). The Government's attempts to secure spending and staff reductions in the public sector have been consistently unsuccessful – or at best partially successful – and in consequence further measures keep being introduced which have not enjoyed much more success. One sees this vicious cycle (from the Government's point of view) especially clearly in the field of local government, where over 40 Acts of Parliament have been passed since 1979.

Again, the vigorous campaigns mounted in the mid-1980s against rate-capping and the abolition of the GLC won very considerable public and Parliamentary support. The abolition Bill only scraped through the House of Lords with a majority of six. Local authorities' campaigning powers have now been restricted but are still significant, as the campaigns being mounted against the Community Charge have shown. The local authority lawyers have advised councillors how they can continue using public funds to mount anti-government campaigns despite restrictive legislation. In the NHS, competitive tendering has been accepted, albeit reluctantly, but a vigorous campaign is being mounted against Kenneth Clarke's plans to reform the Service. Again, the Lord Chancellor was compelled considerably to modify his proposals for the reform of the English legal profession by concerted opposition from judges and barristers, especially to allowing solicitors to act as advocates in the higher Courts. Their ability to do so will now be in effect controlled by the four most senior judges. Again, a policy community has forced considerable concessions from the government, despite the Prime Minister's known determination to weaken traditional monopolies such as those which exist in the practice of the law.

All these examples demonstrate that the accountability and control relationships in British Government are still multi-directional. The Government possesses considerable powers but these still do not suffice to prevent resistance to its policies or to ensure that it always obtains the results it wants. Furthermore, if this is the case for a Government with a three-figure majority in the House of Commons and a Conservative Party which is still largely united behind a formidable Prime Minister, we can legitimately enquire what will occur when Mrs Thatcher leaves the stage and more opportunities for dissent and resistance occur. The policy communities are still present and active; their members can set out an agenda for public administration for the post-Thatcher era. In the last chapter we attempt the somewhat risky task of suggesting what that new agenda might contain.

CHAPTER TEN

The future agenda

THE MANNER OF HER GOING

Margaret Thatcher has been in office for more than a decade. She shows no sign of wanting to retire yet, although she is now in her middle sixties. However, Mrs Thatcher is neither politically nor physically immortal and we can expect that she will retire from the leadership of the Conservative Party within the next five years. Furthermore, the Labour Party seems now to be more or less united behind its Policy Review, which itself sets a comprehensive agenda for a future Labour government, which will take at least two terms of office to implement. As Labour's electoral chances improve and Mrs Thatcher grows older, we need to explore the likely concerns of the teachers and practitioners of public administration as we approach the turn of the millennium. The items that appear on the agenda for the 1990s are easy to identify and will be important whoever is in office. What is much less clear is the relative urgency of each item and the extent to which it will be dealt with by whatever government comes to office after the next general election. The major agenda items are:

1. The future of public management:
    i. Privatisation;
    ii. The assertion of accountability
    iii. The preservation of probity

2. A new territorial settlement:
    i. Devolution for Scotland and Wales;
    ii. Regional government in England;
    iii. The future of local government.

3. The future of the unwritten constitution:
   i. Arrangements for the new territorial settlement;
   ii. Defining the place of local government in the Constitutional order;
   iii. The erosion of the 'buffer principle';
   iv. The guarantee of basic rights and freedoms;
   v. European integration.

4. Environmental issues, including:
   i. The future role of the town and country planning system;
   ii. Intervention to prevent global warming and pollution;
   iii. Energy policy.

5. Social policy issues, notably:
   i. The 'age explosion';
   ii. The decline in the workforce.

The last two sets of issues are of much wider concern than the first three but they have major implications for how public administration will and ought to be conducted in the next ten or twenty years, so they must receive some consideration later.

Although the issues which appear on this agenda are relatively easy to identify, their significance will be determined by the circumstances in which power changes hands. Thus if, for example, the Thatcher Government were to fall after a major scandal in the City which involved improper conduct by Ministers and civil servants, the relative importance attached to the traditional concerns of public administration, notably accountability and probity, would be reasserted at the expense of the 'Three Es'. If the government escapes such a scandal these issues will remain important but will be less urgent.

They will remain important because the value-slope of the Thatcher administrations has been remarkably one-sided. A fundamental belief is that private enterprise provides efficient, attractive services. Efficiency and customer satisfaction alike are best ensured by exposing public services to the disciplines of free competitive markets. Hence, the public sector should be a residual category, reduced in size as far as possible and subjected to the disciplines of the 'Three Es'; this will both ensure its good performance and reduce the threat posed by government intervention to economic and political liberties alike (Hayek, 1944; Friedman and Friedman, 1980). Hence privatisation is the preferred approach, the residual public services being then exposed to business efficiency methods. Other values, including other 'Es', such as excellence and enterprise, tend to be neglected (Gunn, 1988). One might add one more – equity – which has long preoccupied public servants.

Another possible event which might change the order of our agenda would be further major disasters which demonstrated beyond doubt that deregulation of markets in, say, public transport, had unduly lowered safety standards. Such charges have repeatedly been made, for example after the King's Cross fire and the *Herald of Free Enterprise* capsize but the charges have not yet wholly stuck. A further major tragedy in which the role of deregulation in reducing safety margins was demonstrated beyond reasonable doubt could bring regulation of the supply of goods and services back into fashion.

These other values still arouse concern; they have been thrust into the background but not removed from the scene. We may instance:

- Concern about the accountability of the Police, the City, the Civil Service and other powerful groups to the public and their representatives;
- The weakening of the means available to ensure that public servants behave honestly and properly (Chapman, 1988b and c);
- The neglect of equity: for example the government seems to have been little concerned so far about the regressive distributional effects of the Community Charge;
- The need for regulations to ensure public safety;
- The need to protect rights and liberties, even when their existence is inconvenient to Ministers.

As the neglect of these issues stores up future problems and crises, so the potential for a shift of emphasis in the agenda becomes greater. Furthermore, sooner or later the Conservative Party will lose power and the balance of the agenda will then change.

ACHIEVEMENTS OF THE THATCHER YEARS

Even Mrs Thatcher's doughtiest opponents ought to admit, however, that important gains have been made in the management of government, especially in rendering public services more efficient, as well as more responsive to public attitudes and needs. These gains ought not to be lightly discarded and ought not to be matters of political controversy. Thus increased efficiency can be used either to reduce expenditure and hence taxes, or to free resources for use elsewhere. The use to which the resources produced by increased efficiency are put is a proper matter for political debate; the benefits obtained from the increase in efficiency are, however, incontrovertible. There is a danger that an incoming Labour government may discard, for example, the Financial Management Initiative or the Executive Agency programme, either because they are part of the Thatcher legacy or because vested interests such as trade unions demand their abandonment. However, to dispense with these initiatives without thought will entail discarding babies with the bathwater – a regrettable consequence of adversarial politics. Instead, the ways in which the initiatives' results can be diverted for different ends, which are more in line with the new Government's wishes, should be considered. Likewise, the developing concern of public authorities to attend to the opinions and requirements of the people for whom they provide services is welcome, whether it comes in the form of 'going local', marketing exercises or consultation procedures. It is, however, important to ensure that the views thus elicited do influence policy-makers and managers. If consultation exercises or public inquiries are seen merely as opportunities for citizens to feel they can have an influence when their views are in practice not heeded, or if the efforts of neighbourhood committees have no effect on the local environment and services, cynicism will soon prevail.

Above all, any consideration of how public management should develop in the rest of the century must determine whether what is desired is primarily market solutions or collectivist solutions (Hoggett and Hambleton, 1987). Consumerism and decentralisation, for example, can be applied in either context. Thus the establishment of an Executive Agency under *The Next Steps* programme could be either a step on the way towards privatisation or an attempt to improve both the creativity of its management and its responsiveness to its customers while retaining it in the public sector (see Document 7). Equally, a competitive tendering exercise is likely both to encourage public service workers to become more efficient – collectivist benefit – and possibly result in the transfer of the service to a private company – a market solution.

Another major concern for public administrators must be to correct one of the reasons for Mrs Thatcher's accession to power in the first place: general public perceptions of the public services as 'massive, alienating bureaucracies' (Parkinson, 1987b) which are authoritarian, unfeeling and inefficient. Again, such methods as decentralisation, consumer research, consultation and competitive tendering can all be employed to involve citizens more in determining what services are provided and how, regardless of the ultimate ideological goals being sought by political leaders. In all these ways, then, politicians, managers and not least trade unionists must be aware of the usefulness of the Thatcherite managerial legacy and not destroy it when they win the opportunity to reverse those features of modern government that they find objectionable. Institution-alised inefficiencies and restrictive practices must not reappear, otherwise public disillusion will once again lose public servants their constituency of support and expose them afresh to demands for market solutions to the perceived deficiencies of public administration.

THE MAJOR ISSUES

Having considered what should be preserved from the past ten years, we can now discuss some of the issues which are likely to dominate politicians' and officials' agendas in terms of changing the system of government.

Devolution

The first is likely to be increasingly insistent demands for a new territorial settlement. Devolution dominated the political agenda and almost monopolised Parliament's time in the late 1970s. It was then summarily dismissed from those agendas, first because devolution as then proposed failed to win the endorsement required from the peoples of Scotland and Wales in the referenda held on St David's Day, 1979. Secondly, that failure led directly to the defeat of the Callaghan government and his replacement as Prime Minister by Margaret Thatcher. Although she is an economic radical, she is a constitutional conservative, resistant to changes in the institutions of the country required by devolution or electoral reform. Jim Callaghan himself was then replaced by Michael Foot, who shared Mrs Thatcher's unwillingness to break with constitutional traditions. Devo-lution therefore fell through the oubliette after the referenda.

However, all the Opposition parties are now firmly committed to reviving devolution. The Labour Party's Policy Review (1989, pp. 18–19) contains firm commitments both to grant devolution to Scotland and Wales and to establish regional councils in England. The Liberal Democrats, as well as the Social Democrats, have made similar commit-ments. Their eagerness to do so has undoubtedly been increased by other factors. The most important of these is the increasing divergence in electoral behaviour among the countries and regions which make up Great Britain. Thus the Conservative Party suffered massive electoral rejection in Scotland, both in the 1987 general election and the 1989 European Parliament elections. Furthermore, they have lost control of most of the

Scottish Regional Councils. Although this rejection has not been accompanied by an unambiguous improvement in the fortunes of the Scottish National Party, it has damaged the authority in Scotland of a government whose support is concentrated in southern England, making demands for Scottish self-government more convincing.

The same can be said of many of the English Regions. In the north-east of England only five out of 30 constituencies returned Conservative MPs in 1987. After the 1989 county council elections, the Conservatives controlled none of the region's 26 local authorities, while Labour controlled 19 of them. Hence, like Scotland, the North-East is being governed by a party which has suffered massive rejection by the region's voters over the last few years. For all these reasons, the claim that fairness demands the establishment of devolved government throughout Great Britain is now very strong. The same would be the case in Northern Ireland if a means to ensure the involvement of all citizens in that Province's government could be developed that is acceptable to Protestants and Catholics alike.

A further reason why a new territorial settlement will need soon to be considered is the problematic position of local government. The abolition of the Greater London Council and the six metropolitan county councils in 1986 has left London without any form of city-wide government – the only capital city in Western Europe not to have such an authority. There are increasing suggestions that the remaining English county councils, as well as Scotland's Regional Councils, should also be abolished in the interest of simplifying the local government structure and increasing the powers of the district councils. The Labour Party has assumed that the creation of the regional councils in England entails the abolition of its remaining county councils. The pressures which produced the proposals for 'Organic Change' have also not disappeared. On the other hand, most people involved in local government would regard with horror the possibility of another comprehensive reorganisation such as that which took place between 1973 and 1975.

There are therefore a series of reasons why the territorial dimension of government is likely to return to the agenda before too long and it raises important issues for the public administrator. For example, such bodies as Regional Health Authorities and Regional Tourist Boards might be transferred to the control of regional councils but in the former case this is likely to provoke resistance from the medical profession with its long-standing resistance to local authority control of the NHS (Willcocks, 1967). We may also need to consider whether parts or all of the regional offices of Whitehall departments could or should be transferred to the new councils. Responsibility for strategic land-use planning would probably be transferred from the county councils to the new regional authorities. Staff will have to be recruited or transferred, committee structures established and the legal relationships among the new authorities defined. Hence, an important consequence of preparing a new territorial settlement is to bring into question the unwritten Constitution itself.

A Written Constitution?

The future of the unwritten Constitution has already been rendered uncertain by several developments during the Thatcher years. One is the challenge that has been mounted to local government, in particular the Government's repeated attempts to restrict the scope of local choice through financial restrictions including rate-capping, the abolition of some councils and the compulsion to put services out to competitive tenders. The Government could argue that local choice has been increased by other means such as granting increased powers to school governors and developing the local management of schools. None the less, the choices available to councillors have been constrained, leading George Jones and John Stewart to argue that a Charter for Local Government ought to be prepared which will define the powers, rights and responsibilities of local authorities and protect them from undue and unpredictable central intervention (Jones and Stewart, 1984). If devolution occurs, that Charter would also have to define the relationships that would exist between the new regional authorities and central government on the one hand and local authorities on the other. Such a Charter would also increase the role of the courts in arbitrating in disputes between the different tiers of government regarding their respective spheres of competence. Hence, the Court of Appeal and the House of Lords might come to play an arbitral role between the central government, the devolved councils and local authorities which might become somewhat analogous to that of the United States Supreme Court in regulating the relationships between the Federal Government and the 50 States of the Union.

Another development which has rendered the case for drawing up a written Constitution more pressing is the erosion of the 'buffer principle', under which the broadcasting agencies, the universities and the Press were protected from unwarranted restrictions on their freedoms (see Document 4). The Thatcher governments have shown scant respect for this principle and in several cases have replaced the institutions which were supposed to protect it with others which are more amenable to Government pressure. Concern has also been expressed that the Government's considerable expenditure on publicity has at times been used to promote the interests of the Conservative Party rather than the public interest. At present, there are constitutional conventions which require that public resources are not used for partisan purposes but there is no definition of that dividing line which can be employed to hold to account Ministers who cross it.

Lastly, attacks on citizens' rights, such as the sudden and arbitrary decision to ban trade union membership at GCHQ in 1984, have increased demands for a written guarantee of such basic rights as freedom of speech and assembly. Furthermore, such a definition has been rendered more necessary by the decisions of the European Court of Human Rights in Strasbourg. Under Article 25 of the European Convention on Human Rights, an individual or a group can petition the Court for redress if their civil rights have, so they believe, been invaded by their government. Since Britain granted its citizens the right of individual petition to the Court in 1965, there have been over a dozen complaints against the British government heard in Court, most of which the government lost, causing Michael Zander (1986) to remark that 'the level of success in actions brought against the UK in Strasbourg suggests that all is in fact not well with our system.' (pp. 33–4) This has led to repeated demands that the Convention should be incorporated into Britain's domestic law. If this were done, redress could be obtained more quickly than at present, when aggrieved citizens must exhaust the remedies domestically available before beginning the long process of seeking redress from the European Court. However, if this were done, Britain would have moved a long way towards acquiring a written Constitution. In any case, as a result of legislation in many fields, including local government, industrial relations, race and gender discrimination, the Constitution is becoming increasingly codified. If legislation is required to regulate the relations between local, regional and national governments and the European Convention is incorporated into domestic law, a written Constitution will have been created by default.

The Environment

The emergence of Green parties as significant political forces in many European countries, together with increasing scientific anxiety about global warming and the long-term effects of pollution, have combined to push the environment to the top of political agendas. It was regarded as important in the early 1970s (Solesbury, 1976) after the publication of the Club of Rome report and the energy shortage which resulted from the Arab-Israeli war of 1972. It receded somewhat as the energy shortage eased but its importance has increased again in the late 1980s.

This is not the place to debate the seriousness of the dangers facing the planet from over-population, deforestation, carbon dioxide emissions, pollution and so on. However, we can suggest a number of implications arising from these issues for the future of public administration, both as an activity and as a subject of academic study. These are:

- The perceived need to control emissions which contribute to global warming, cause acid rain or otherwise pollute the Earth, will entail government intervention on a national and international scale to regulate the activities of polluters. The need to ban CFCs, protect rain forests and reduce hot gas emissions from power stations and motor vehicles, all entails the development of new regulations and enforcement agencies. These are, of course, long-standing pre-occupations of public administrators, who will therefore have important roles to play at all levels, from the local authority to the United Nations, in developing realistic, enforceable regulations and then in enforcing them.

- The need to control development, protect agricultural land and endangered species must also restore the place of land-use planning systems even where, as in Britain, they have been weakened by governments who regard them as undesirable restraints on free markets. Strategic land-use planning will come to be regarded as both necessary and desirable, so that the approaches to Structure Planning discussed in earlier chapters will become useful in developing new planning systems or reviving old ones.

- The 'age explosion' also requires spatial, economic and social planning. Locations for old people's residences must be found, the services they need must be provided and provision must be made to enable them to live out the remainder of their lives in dignity and comfort. However, this provision will be expensive and generating the income needed to support the increasing number of retired people will be the task of a shrinking labour force.

- The reduction in the available work force will entail making better use of the workers available. The resources devoted to education and training must be increased, employment practices must be changed, for example to make it easier for women to continue working while they are bringing up children or to return to work once their children are attending school. Patterns of work must become more varied, with more job-sharing and part-time working becoming available.

CONCLUSION: THE WATCHWORDS FOR THE FUTURE

It seems, therefore, that although Mrs Thatcher may leave behind her a public sector which has gained in efficiency and consumer responsiveness, the issues facing Britain and other developed nations will result in both the regulatory role of the State and spending by governments increasing – indeed, it is one of the paradoxes of the Thatcher years that public spending has rarely decreased during the last decade, although it has fallen as a proportion of the Gross National Product. If the issues are to be coped with effectively, there will have to be developments in all the three public administration issue areas discussed in Chapter 2. These were:

1. *Creativity.* New solutions will be required to developing problems such as the 'age explosion', the declining workforce and development planning in an overcrowded island. There will therefore be an increasing role for public and private 'Think Tanks', research institutes and policy analysts because, as Dror (1973) argued, incrementalism will no longer suffice to deal with new and ever-pressing problems; nor will it enable governments to take full advantage of the rapidly expanding opportunities made available by, for example, information and communications technology.

2. *Government Intervention* will have to increase if the environment is to be protected and central to this need is the reduction of uncertainty. We have seen that planning not only gives clear policy guidance to the planning organisation itself; it also provides a framework within which other individuals and organisations can make decisions and be reasonably sure that they will be acceptable. Reducing uncertainty also entails improving co-ordination, both within organisations and between them. Hence, the roles of the planner and the reticulist will remain vital.

3. *Legitimation.* Lastly, the radical changes that will be required to meet local, national and global threats or problems will require giving much attention to legitimation. Policies will be implemented only if those responsible for them or affected by them accept their wisdom and necessity. Hence, processes of social learning in which consultation and negotiation play a central role will form an essential part of the processes whereby policies are developed to deal with the problems which face us in the 1990s.

In sum, many long-standing, even traditional preoccupations of public administration are likely to be reasserted in the years to come and the current rather narrow managerial focus will become part of a wider discipline. Exactly how this process takes place will depend on circumstances but the reassertion of the discipline's traditional scope is inevitable. Hence, all of us who are involved in public administration – whether as practitioners or academics – must not become so preoccupied with public management that we lose sight of the wider issues that distinguish public from business administration.

Documentary Appendix

This section presents a series of extracts from Statutes, official publications, Hansard and academic writings which relate to some of the principal points made in this book. Many of the excerpts printed here can only be obtained with some difficulty from their original sources. They are presented under a series of headings.

ASPECTS OF ACCOUNTABILITY

Ministerial Responsibility

When Ministers should resign. i. Statement by the Home Secretary defining the scope of Individual Ministerial Responsibility for Departmental Faults, House of Commons Debates, 5th Series, 20 July, 1954, c. 1284 ff.

The Secretary of State for the Home Department (Sir David Maxwell Fyfe): ...There has been considerable anxiety...as to how far the principle of Ministerial responsibility goes. We all recognise that we must have the principle in existence and that Ministers must be responsible for the acts of civil servants. Without it, it would be impossible to have a civil service which would be able to serve Ministers and Governments of different political faiths and persuasions with the same zeal and honesty which we have always found....

There has been criticism that the principle operates so as to oblige Ministers to extend total protection to their officials and to endorse their acts, and to cause their position that civil servants cannot be called to account and are responsible to no one. That is a position which I believe is quite wrong, and I think it is the cardinal error that has crept into the appreciation of this situation. It is quite untrue that well-justified public criticism of actions of civil servants cannot be made on a suitable occasion. The position of the civil servant is that he is wholly and directly responsible to his Minister. It is worth stating again that he holds his office 'at pleasure' and can be dismissed at any time by the Minister; and the power is none the less real because it is seldom used. The only exception relates to a small number of senior posts, like permanent secretary, deputy secretary, and principle financial officer, where, since 1920, it has been necessary for the Minister to consult the Prime Minister, as he does on appointment.

I would like to put the different categories where different considerations apply. I am in agreement…that in a case where there is an explicit order by a Minister, the Minister must protect the civil servant who has carried out his order. Equally, where the civil servant acts properly in accordance with the policy laid down by the Minister, the Minister must protect and defend him.

I come to the third category, which is different…Where an official makes a mistake, or causes some delay, but not on an important issue of policy and not where a claim to individual rights is seriously involved, the Minister acknowledges the mistake and he accepts the responsibility, although he is not personally involved. He states that he will take corrective action in the Department…(He) would not, in those circumstances, expose the official to public criticism….

But when one comes to the fourth category, where action has been taken by a civil servant of which the Minister disapproves and has no prior knowledge, and the conduct of the official is reprehensible, then there is no obligation on the part of the Minister to endorse what he believes to be wrong, or to defend what are clearly shown to be errors of his officers. The Minister is not bound to defend action of which he disapproves. But, of course, he remains constitutionally responsible to Parliament for the fact that something has gone wrong, and he alone can tell Parliament what has occurred and render an account of his stewardship.

The fact that a Minister has to do that does not affect his power to control and discipline his staff. One could sum it up by saying that it is part of the Minister's responsibility to Parliament to take necessary action to ensure efficiency and the proper discharge of the duties of his Department. On that, only the Minister can decide what it is right and just to do, and he alone can hear all sides, including the defence.

It has been suggested…that there is another aspect which adds to our difficulties, and that is that today the work and the tasks of Government permeate so many spheres of our national life that it is impossible for the Minister to keep track of all these matters.

I believe that that is a matter which can be dealt with by the instructions which the Minister gives in his Department. He can lay down standing instructions to see that his policy is carried out. He can lay down rules by which is ensured that matters of importance, of difficulty or of political danger are brought to his attention. Thirdly, there is the control of this House...

When Ministers Do Resign. ii. S. E. Finer,'The Individual Responsibility of Ministers', in *Public Administration*, Volume 34, 1956, pp. 377–96. Excerpt from pp. 383–90.

The Effectiveness of the Convention. Resignations 1855–1955. In what follows I have tried to particularise resignations which are not only 'forced' but, moreover, forced by overt criticism from the House of Commons. It is a somewhat subjective category of cases. To begin with, it excludes the very frequent cases where Ministers have voluntarily resigned – Mr Duff Cooper over the Munich affair, or (more recently) the resignations of Mr Bevan and Mr Wilson from the Attlee Government in 1951. It also excludes the considerably rarer cases where the whole Cabinet has chosen to go out rather than the individual under attack. Such was the case when Mr Chamberlain and his Cabinet resigned after the Narvik Vote in 1940. Mr Chamberlain was the Minister under attack. Since, however, he was Premier, his resignation entailed, by convention, the resignation of the whole Cabinet. Thirdly, I have had to omit Ministers who quit or were 'dropped' from the Cabinet, sometimes upon the reconstruction of the Ministry, sometimes (apparently) in mid-career. Very often we do not know why they were dropped. In some cases – e.g., Salisbury's dismissal of Iddesleigh in 1886 – we do know the reasons. But where such cases are, as it were, internal to politics of the Cabinet, and not (overtly at any rate) initiated by the censure of the House of Commons, I have omitted them; for they palpably cannot be cited in support of the convention that Ministers are individually answerable *to the House* for the misconduct of their Departments.

Bearing these qualifications in mind, it would seem that in the last century very few Ministers have resigned their offices in deference to the convention. The following list only includes senior Ministers. If not complete, it must be nearly so.

Lord John Russell	..	..	1855
Lord Ellenborough	..	..	1858
Robert Lowe	..	..	..	1864
Lord Westbury	..	..	..	1865
S. H. Walpole	..	..	..	1867

A. J. Mundella	..	..	..	1894
G. Wyndham	..	..	..	1905
Col. J. E. B. Seeley		..	..	1914
A. Birrell		..	..	1916
A. Chamberlain	..	..	..	1917
N. Chamberlain	..		..	1917
Lord Rothermere	..	..	..	1918
E. S. Montagu	..	..	..	1922
Sir S. Hoare	..	..	..	1935
J. H. Thomas	..	..	..	1936
Viscount Swinton	..	...	..	1938
Earl Winterton	..	..	..	1938
Sir Ben Smith	..	..	..	1946
H. Dalton	..	..	..	1947
Sir T. Dugdale	..	..	..	1954

The list does in fact contain two technically junior Ministers: viz., Lowe and Earl Winterton. Lowe was technically the junior to Lord Granville, the Lord President of the Council. Earl Winterton was, from 1937, Chancellor of the Duchy. In March, 1938, he was given a seat in the Cabinet, and, with the style of 'Deputy Secretary of State for Air,' became the junior colleague of Lord Swinton.

There are some important cases involving junior Ministers as well as senior. Among them may be mentioned Stansfeld (resigned 1864), Sir Robert Boothby (resigned 1941) and Belcher (resigned 1949).

These resignations fall into three not too well defined categories relating to (a) the man, (b) the personal act or policy, and (c) the vicarious act or policy – departmental mismanagement proper.

(a) *The Man*

Three of the cases turned upon a personal misadventure of the Minister which raised such doubt about his personal prudence or integrity as to cause him to resign. These are the cases of Mundella, Thomas and Dalton. Mundella, in 1894, was deeply implicated in the suspicious affairs of a trading company which had crashed at the very moment when it lay on him, as President of the Board of Trade, to decide what proceeding should be taken against the company. Accordingly he resigned. J.H. Thomas, as Colonial Secretary and a Cabinet Minister, was in 1936 suspected of having disclosed the Budget proposals to unauthorised persons as a result of which insurances took place at Lloyds. An official tribunal found that there had been such disclosure by Mr Thomas. He accordingly resigned (albeit with some reluctance). In 1947, while in the Lobby, Mr Hugh Dalton, the then Chancellor of the Exchequer, inadvertently disclosed to a journalist facts about the Budget he was to open in the House later that afternoon, with the consequence that a London evening paper printed the news before the House received it. Mr Dalton openly admitted his fault and instantly resigned.

(b) *Personal Acts or Policies*
In 1855, Lord John Russell returned from his Vienna negotiations with a drafty treaty. The terms of this leaked out and were disapproved by the House. In face of a motion 'that the conduct of our Minister in the recent negotiations at Vienna has in the opinion of this House shaken the confidence of this country in those to whom its affairs are entrusted,' Lord John resigned and the Prime Minister thereupon promptly stated that the projected treaty had been abandoned. In 1858, Lord Ellenborough published a despatch to Lord Canning, the Governor General of India, without consulting his colleagues: after some prevarication they disowned him, and he himself resigned. Westbury, the Lord Chancellor, was forced to retire by motions of censure in the House of Commons in 1865 consequent on charges of gross nepotism and (possibly) bribery being made against him. In 1914, Colonel Seeley resigned after making a personal addendum to the agreed Memorandum which the Cabinet had approved for transmission to General Gough; the addendum made a vital difference to the Memorandum, and Asquith and his colleagues took the strongest exception to it. In 1922, Montagu, Secretary of State for India, published a telegram from the Viceroy urging a pro-Turkish settlement in the Middle East: his action was taken without the knowledge of his colleagues and on their repudiating it he resigned. Sir Samuel Hoare's peace plan for Abyssinia, when it leaked into the press, was repudiated by his colleagues and he resigned.

(c) *Vicarious Act and Policy*
We have already describe two of these cases, viz., those of Lowe and Wyndham in the earlier part of this article.

S. H. Walpole resigned the Home Secretaryship in 1867, after the Hyde Park Riots and the fear of renewed disturbances had broken his nerve. He had been subjected to severe attack in press and Parliament. It is doubtful whether his case ought not to be put into the 'personal actions' category. It would seem that he acted throughout as the increasingly unwilling tool of his Cabinet colleagues and resigned when their policy became too much for him to carry through. Lord Derby, the Prime Minister, in explaining Walpole's resignation, was at pains to insist that the 'weakness and vacillation' shown must fairly be attributed to the Cabinet as a whole and not to the fallen Minister. Birrell resigned in 1916, blamed by all except Asquith perhaps, for failing to foresee and forestall the Sinn Fein movement and its culmination in the Easter Rising. Austen Chamberlain resigned in 1917, not because the Mesopotamia Commission had imputed to him some of the blame for the disastrous Baghdad-Kut campaign of 1916, but because the Government had decided to set up a further Commission of Enquiry to hear charges against the persons so named. Neville Chamberlain's case is a little queer; as Lloyd George's Director of National Service, he was not an M.P. He fell foul of Lloyd George and then, when a Select Committee of the House condemned his Ministry as wasteful and inefficient, he resigned. Lord Rothermere, Lloyd George's Air Minister, affected by two tragic bereavements and by ill-health, soon resigned under sharp criticisms of his administration and especially of his dismissal of General Trenchard. Viscount Swinton, another Secretary of State for Air, similarly resigned under adverse criticism in the Commons, criticism which his Deputy (Earl Winterton) was unable to repel and which he himself, as a Peer, could not grapple with; and Earl Winterton resigned also. Sir Thomas Dugdale's case is too recent to need restatement.

The list shows twenty resignations in a century: a tiny number compared with the known instances of mismanagement and blunderings. It is clear then that certain factors operate so as to prevent the full operation of the convention: and of these there appear to be four.

The first factor prevents the convention from coming into play at all. This is the counter-convention of the collective responsibility of the Cabinet, backed up by an appeal to party solidarity. Practically all cases of incompetence tend to be treated thus, and so the House is not called on to adjudicate on the merits of a Minister but is challenged to overthrow the Government.

Next in order of importance, and used where the House is singling out individual Ministers for attack, comes the Cabinet re-shuffle. The delinquent Minister is not deprived of office as according to the 'punitive' theory of the convention he ought to be, but is placed in some other office of profit.

However, between the bouts of re-shuffling, the House does sometimes make a 'fair cop': i.e., responsibility for some patent mismanagement is placed squarely on a particular Minister. But what happens then depends very much on personal factors – on the relationship between the delinquent, his colleagues and the Prime Minister.

Finally, as in 'Oranges and Lemons,' it does sometimes happen that the chopper comes down fairly and squarely on somebody's head, and no amount of personal protest fails to shake the basic convention of the game: the Minister must resign. Yet the resources of civility are not quite exhausted. *Soles occidere et redire possunt*. After a decent interval the delinquent is reinstated, usually in a different office – but, at any rate, in office.

For reasons of exposition it will be convenient to take these factors in inverse order to that stated here: and so we begin with Removal and Reappointment.

(a) *Removal and Re-appointment*

In some cases, viz. where the resignation took place because of a constitutional punctilio, there is clearly every good reason why the fallen Minister should be appointed to another office as soon as is decent. Such were the cases of Austen Chamberlain, of Hugh Dalton and of Robert Lowe (1864). Similarly the return of Russell after his débâcle in 1855 is fully justifiable, since the cause of the offence ceased with the Crimean settlement. On the other hand, where the offending Minister is reinstated to a position where he can continue the very offence for which he had to resign, the practice reduces the convention to a mere formality. Only one case in twenty seems to fall into this category, viz. the reappointment of Sir Samuel Hoare six months after his fall. It is true that the office was the Admiralty, not the Foreign Office, and that within a year he moved again, this time to the Home Office: but on his own admission he was, by 1938, one of the quadrumvirate that made the Cabinet's foreign policy. Clearly, the resignation of 1935 had been a formality. Indeed, it is fully explicable as such if one makes the justifiable assumption that, like Russell's resignation of 1855, it was designed to permit the Cabinet to divest itself of collective responsibility for a policy which the House clearly disapproved.

(b) *The Personal Factors*

It is not always easy for a Prime Minister to induce a Minister to resign. The Prime Minister may not wish to give offence, as Gladstone did not wish to give offence to Lord Carlingford in 1884. The Minister may have powerful friends in the Ministry as did Chamberlain in the Salisbury and Balfour Ministries, or Lloyd George in Asquith's Coalition; he may have a following whom he can lead out of the party, as Carson had, or (in a different context) as Sir J. Simon had when he left the Coalition in 1915 on the conscription issue. He may – despite his unsuitability – be wildly popular in the country as Lord Kitchener was between 1914 and 1916.

Consequently, even where a Minister is censured by the House, the outcome – whether he resigns or not – is often influenced by the personal character of the Minister, his colleagues and the Prime Minister; and in the delinquent Minister the matter may be said to turn on the nicety of his conscience *versus* his tenacity of office.

Observe, first of all, the case of Lowe and Monsell and of Ayrton in 1873. All three had been clearly proved guilty yet not one offered to resign, nor did Gladstone insist: instead he arranged a re-shuffle (as described below). Gladstone's letter to the Queen explained the reasons:

> There probably have been times when the three gentlemen who in their several positions have been chiefly to blame would have been summarily dismissed from Your Majesty's service. But on none of them could any ill-intent be charged. Two of them had, among whatever errors of judgement, done much and marked good service to the State: and two of them were past 60 years of age. Mr Gladstone could not under the circumstances resort to so severe a course without injustice and harshness, which Your Majesty would be the last to approve. The last embarrassment has been this: that all three have shown a tenacity and attachment to office certainly greater than is usual. And unfortunately the willingness of each person to quit or retain office, and still more their active desire, form a very great element in cases of this kind apart from the question how far the retention of it, or its abandonment, may on other grounds be desirable.

Next, we may compare the cases of Dalton and Thomas with Ll George's failure to resign over the Marconi case. The first Minister resigned instantly and unhesitatingly. Thomas denied the charges, protested his innocence to the end, and had to be restrained by his Prime Minister from making 'a fighting farewell speech.' Lloyd George did not resign, and we still have no real knowledge of what went on in Asquith's mind. According to Tom Jones, 'Margot Asquith says that Asquith was determined to retain Reading and therefore had to hold on to Lloyd George also', but this is perhaps Lady Oxford's reading back into 1913 the Asquith-Lloyd George feud of post-1916 days. In the early days of the scandal, when it was suddenly revealed that Lloyd George and Isaacs had invested in American Marconis (albeit not in the British), Lloyd George did in fact offer to resign and Asquith, at this stage,'ridiculed the idea.' Later, however, after the Committee of Enquiry had reported, Asquith suggested that the word 'indiscretion' should be introduced into the Government's (whitewashing) amendment to the Opposition's vote of censure. 'Lloyd George resolutely refused to accept [it]. He told Churchill, who thereupon went to Asquith and told him that Lloyd George's mind on the matter was utterly made up and that if he did not have his way he meant to go; this would bring down the Government.' It would seem as though the very venom of his malignant foes stiffened Lloyd George's attitude, and indeed, that of his colleagues and, above all, the back-benchers: and that Asquith was not prepared thereupon to risk the collapse of his Government or even the admission of scandal. Yet, inherently. Dalton's step was no worse than Lloyd George's: indeed perhaps less so.

Another contrast lies in the Austen Chamberlain case in 1917 and the groundnuts debate of 1949, in which Mr John Strachey was the target. Chamberlain was not deeply implicated in the Mesopotamia muddle; but if a Minister were to have to resign, then he as Secretary of State for India was that Minister. Mr Strachey may not have been any more deeply implicated in Kenya than Chamberlain in the Garden of Eden, but certain it is that *if* any Minister were to have to resign, he was that Minister. In the first case, Chamberlain not only resigned, but in a dashing and convincing speech, exonerated himself from moral blame, won over the entire House and contemptuously threw his resignation in its face. To Mr Strachey's support rallied the whole Parliamentary Labour Party.

(c) *Reshuffle*

A prodigious number of Ministers are saved from even the form of resignation by timely removal into another office. This painlessly extracts the punitive sting of 'deprivation of office' on which Macaulay set much store, and it also may give the Ministry collectively a new lease of life, for the new incumbent cannot morally be blamed for the faults of his predecessor. Observe, for instance, Mr Dalton's comment on the Chamberlain Government's decision to resist an inquiry into the Air Ministry, after Swinton and Winterton had resigned and Kingsley Wood had become the new Secretary of State:

> An inquiry need not embarrass the Rt. Hon. Gentleman (Mr Kingsley Wood). I can well understand that it may have embarrassed Lord Swinton, but he is gone. He had three years of personal responsibility to answer for before such an enquiry. The new Minister is not in that position. He is coming fresh to his job. Inquiry need not embarrass him or diminish his prestige or dignity.
>
> (H.C. Deb.,25th May, 1938, col. 1234.)

We have seen that Gladstone feared to make Lowe, Monsell and Ayrton resign. Instead he gave himself no end of trouble in finding them new places. Lowe was pushed into the Home Office. Ayrton, after protracted diplomacy, was persuaded to become Judge-Advocate-General. As for Monsell, he was to be permitted to retire, and was then to receive a peerage, but only after a successor could be found: the negotiations for a new Postmaster-General went on for months, being hawked around from one candidate to another, until in the end Lyon Playfair was induced to take it.

In 1887, Salisbury got the 'inadequate' Hicks Beach to retire from the Irish Secretaryship in place of Balfour, and in the following year was able to move Stanley to the Governor-Generalship of Canada and put Hicks Beach in his place at the Board of Trade. In 1900 he moved Lansdowne from the War Office, where his administration had been criticised, to the Foreign Office; and dropped Ridley and Chaplin from the reconstructed Cabinet in favour of Ritchie and Walter Long. The First World War brought a crop of such changes. Carson was moved from the Admiralty to the War Cabinet in place of Geddes; Derby was induced to become the ambassador to France to make way for Milner at the War Office; and Cowdray was to have been reshuffled out of the Air Ministry in favour of Northcliffe (however, he learned of the move before the alternative office had been offered to him, and resigned in a rage). Snowden recounts how J. H. Thomas insisted on MacDonald's moving him out of the Duchy of Lancaster, where he was responsible for unemployment, to another office not so exposed to criticism. He went to the Dominions Office and was replaced by Hartshorn. In the Labour Governments of 1945–51, notable reshuffles were those of Shinwell, who was moved from Fuel and Power a decent interval after the fuel crisis and became Secretary for War; and John Strachey who, after being discredited at the Food Ministry over the groundnuts affair, was moved, in the Second Attlee Cabinet of 1950, into Shinwell's place at the War Office, Shinwell himself becoming Minister of Defence.

Brief passages of memoirs every now and again bring to life the compulsions behind and the mechanisms of these re-shuffles. 'There'll have to be [a reshuffle] within a year,' says Baldwin. 'To do so now would mean a peck of trouble, then. Of course, the Whips are always wanting jobs for our fellows. Margesson wants to move Ormsby-Gore to the Colonies and put Philip Sassoon at the Office of Works because he's not strong enough for the Air Ministry. But we can't do that now. He'll have to hold on.' The most vivid account is that given by Sir John Reith of Sir Winston Churchill's major reshuffles of 1942 – the unusual summons of the junior Ministers to a meeting, the unexpected presence of Whips staring hard at certain individuals, furiously scribbling down notes; the sudden summons to Reith to resign; and finally the publication of the reconstructed Ministry.

(d) *Collective Solidarity*

The most effective of all the factors in thwarting the convention is, of course, the tendency on nearly every occasion, for the Ministry to regard an attack on one of its members as an attack on itself and to throw itself as a buckler over the delinquent. It shielded Mr Shinwell from the attacks made on his handling of the fuel crisis in 1947; it shielded Mr Bevin and Mr Henderson (the unfortunate Secretary of State for Air) in the affair of the loss of the British Spitfires over Israel in January, 1949; it shielded Mr Strachey in the groundnuts debate in the same year. In such cases, however restive, the majority party have but two alternatives – to pursue their vendetta and turn out their own Government (and, incidentally, themselves); or to drop the matter. They choose the latter.

> The ritual of each party is rehearsed
> Dislodging not one vote of prejudice;
> The Ministers their Ministries retain
> And Ins as Ins, and Outs as Outs remain.

Low (1904) and Lowell (1908) both commented on the phenomenon. 'The party machine,' wrote the first, 'always does intervene if the occasion is sufficiently serious to protect the departmental chief; so that the theoretical power residing in Parliament to bring about the dismissal of a Minister if he offends is not a very effectual check upon the conduct of any member of the Supreme Executive.' 'Joint responsibility,' wrote the second, 'has in fact become greater, and the several responsibility less.' It is this fact that has induced Sir Ivor Jennings to regard individual responsibility as, in practice, an aberration from the common rule of collective responsibility; and to say of this: 'Ministers do get attacked. They are, however, defended by other Ministers, and the attack is really aimed not at the Ministers but at the Government. It may be convenient for a Prime Minister to promote a difficult Minister to a different office; but it is not the Opposition's intention; their principal anxiety is to cause the Government to lose votes at the next election.'

Nevertheless, ministerial resignations do take place; they are the exception, not the rule, but there are clearly occasions where the collective weight of the Ministry is *not* thrown into the scale. What special conditions have to operate for the convention of individual responsibility to end in resignation? They must be summarised as (i) where no party has an absolute majority in the House, and (ii) where the Minister's act has not so much offended the Opposition as alienated his own party, or a substantial element of it. The first needs no long explanation – it is enough to remark that the first five of our twenty precedents are governed by it. The second does, however, need explanation. It is still assumed that because parties tend to follow a rigid voting discipline on the floor of the House, they are therefore 'monolithic.' In fact, the tighter the floor discipline, imposed as it is by the need to remain in the office and to win elections, the fiercer and more factious is the struggle for the party leadership. The parliamentary parties are full, always, of factions, of cabals, of Caves of Adullam.

The 'Buffer Principle'
'*Directions of a General Character*' iii. The Coal Industry Nationalisation Act, 1946, Section 3.

3   (1) The Minister may, after consultation with the Board, give to the Board directions of a general character as to the exercise and performance by the Board of their functions in relation to the matters appearing to the Minister to affect the national interest, and the Board shall give effect to any such directions.

      (2) In framing programmes of reorganisation or development involving substantial outlay on capital account, the Board shall act on lines settled from time to time with the approval of the Minister.

      (3) In the exercise and performance of their functions as to training, education and research, the Board shall act on lines settled as aforesaid.

      (4) The Board shall afford to the Minister facilities for obtaining information with respect to the property and activities of the Board, and shall furnish him with returns, accounts and other information with respect thereto and afford to him facilities for the verification of information furnished, in such manner and at such times as he may require.

Academic Freedom iv. Report of the Committee on Higher Education (Robbins Report), Cmnd. 2154, paras 725–30.

Safeguards for Academic Freedom: The Grants Committee Principle

725. We believe that responsible academic opinion recognises the inevitability of these limitations. There may be some who still believe that it is an outrage if the role of the State or its organs is anything but completely passive; but they are not many. Nevertheless, the whole question of control is understandably the subject of widespread apprehension. It is recognised that subvention involves allocation and that allocation may involve co-ordination and certain controls; and it is not felt that such measures need be an improper encroachment on legitimate academic freedoms. But it is felt that, without proper safeguards, the necessity of such co-ordination may easily come to be considered in the context of political considerations and pressures and that the orderly development of academic institutions may be liable to interruption by forces quite foreign either to education or to the advancement of knowledge.

726. We think that there is substance in these apprehensions. No one acquainted with the history of academic institutions in those countries where education is directly controlled by the State can deny that from time to time irruptions of this sort take place. Nor

can it be denied that on occasions they have been very damaging and grievous. Unless we hold that British traditions and habits are so immensely superior to those of the rest of the human race that this sort of thing can never happen here, it is certainly not unreasonable to fear that, given the same setting, the same evils might occur.

727. Fortunately, this country seems to have hit upon an administrative invention that, although not precluding all such dangers, has the effect of making them much less probable – the device of interposing between the Government and institutions a committee of persons selected for their knowledge and standing and not for their political affiliation. In this way it is possible to ensure that the measures of co-ordination and allocation that are necessary are insulated from inappropriate political influences. This device is exemplified in the present arrangements for the famous University Grants Committee, and the principles it embodies are best explained by a description of its constitution and mode of operation.

728. The majority of the Committee consists of persons actively engaged in university teaching or research; the rest are drawn at present from other forms of education, from industry and from research establishments. It is presided over by a full-time chairman, himself, by tradition, of academic experience, and served by an independent staff. The Committee has the twofold function of advising the Chancellor of the Exchequer about the magnitude of the total grant which it is appropriate to give to the universities as a whole and of distributing this grant between the different possible recipients once it is made available. The Government is thus advised by a body which, though appointed by the Government, is independent of ministerial and departmental control and is composed chiefly of persons with intimate knowledge of university life and its conventions. This immunity from direct ministerial intervention is further strengthened by immunity from the normal obligation of public accountability. The Public Accounts Committee and its servant, the Comptroller and the Auditor General , have available to them the published accounts of the universities and the information given in the annual estimates; but they have no access to the books of the universities or of the University Grants Committee. The Treasury receives from the Committee information about the distribution of grants for major building works and proposals for any major variations in the distribution of grants among the main heads of capital expenditure; and this information is also accessible to the Comptroller and Auditor General, who may, if he wishes, seek supplementary information from the Treasury.

729. Thus individual universities are very largely insulated from direct intervention by the Government or Parliament in the detailed ordering of their affairs; and their freedom of action is further safeguarded by the practice of the University Grants Committee in making its main subventions to recurrent expenditure as block grants, with no specification of detailed uses to which they may be put. Supplementary grants earmarked for special purposes have indeed been made from time to time when it was thought that reasons of national policy demanded special developments. But these are exceptions; the money thus given is absorbed into the block grant as soon as may be.

730. Nevertheless, the University Grants Committee is not passive in regard to the policy of particular universities. Its terms of reference direct it to make allocations in the light of national needs. While the block grant is given without special limitations, it is only given after an examination against such a background of the programmes proposed. Moreover, if, in retrospect, the grant given for any quinquennium is regarded as having been spent in a way contrary to public needs as the Committee conceives them, this may easily influence the size of the grant for the next quinquennium. Even more important is the fact that, beyond the grants for recurrent expenditure, there are capital grants for sites and buildings. These are necessarily specific to particular projects, and in the nature of things every application is examined on its merits. Here there is no question of passivity in matters of policy. While universities draw up their building programmes, these are evolved and discussed in detail in the light of views expressed by the Committee. It has been argued by several witnesses that, especially in a period of expansion, the general policy of universities is more dependent on capital grants than on any others; and we have little doubt that this is correct.

CIVIL SERVICE MANAGEMENT

The Attack on the Dilettante

v. Report of the Committee on the Civil Service (Fulton Report), Cmnd 3638, Chapter 1, pp 9–14.

The Civil Service Today

1. The Home Civil Service today is still fundamentally the product of the nineteenth-century philosophy of the Northcote–Trevelyan Report. The tasks it faces are those of the second half of the twentieth century. This is what we have found; it is what we seek to remedy.

2. The foundations were laid by Northcote and Trevelyan in their report of 1854. Northcote and Trevelyan were much influenced by Macaulay whose Committee reported in the same year on the reform of the India Service. The two reports, so remarkable for their bluntness and brevity (together they run to about twenty pages in the original printing), have such a far-reaching influence that we reproduce them in full.

3. These reports condemned the nepotism, the incompetence and other defects of the system inherited from the eighteenth century. Both proposed the introduction of competitive entry examinations. The Macaulay Report extolled the merits of the young men from Oxford and Cambridge who had read nothing but subjects unrelated to their future careers. The Northcote-Trevelyan Report pointed to the possible advantages of reading newer, more relevant subjects, such as geography or political economy, rather than the classics. But as the two services grew, this difference between the two reports seems to have been lost. There emerged the tradition of the "all-rounder" as he has been called by his champions, or "amateur" as he has been called by his critics.

4. Both reports concentrated on the graduates who thereafter came to form the top of each service. They took much less notice of the rest. In India, the supporting echelons were native, and the technical services, such as railways and engineering, were the business of specialists who stood lower than the ruling administrators. At home, the all-round administrators were to be supported by non-graduates to do executive and clerical work and by specialists (e.g. Inspectors of Schools) in those departments where they were needed. A man had to enter the Service on completing his education; once in, he was in for life. The outcome was a career service, immune from nepotism and political jobbery and, by the same token, attractive for its total security as well as for the intellectual achievement and social status that success in the entry examination implied.

5. Carrying out the Northcote-Trevelyan Report took time; there was long debate. Over the years other committees and commissions have considered various aspects of the Civil Service. Many new specialist

classes have been added to the system, notably the scientists, engineers and their supporting classes. There is now an impressive amount of detailed training. Many other modifications have been made. The reports of the main committees and commissions are summarised and discussed in a note published in Volume 3.

6. Nevertheless, the basic principles and philosophy of the Northcote-Trevelyan Report have prevailed: the essential features of their structure have remained.

7. Meanwhile, the role of government has greatly changed. Its traditional regulatory functions have multiplied in size and greatly broadened in scope. It has taken on vast new responsibilities. It is expected to achieve such general economic aims as full employment, a satisfactory rate of growth, stable prices and a healthy balance of payments. Through these and other policies (e.g. public purchasing, investment grants, financial regulators) it profoundly influences the output, costs and profitability of industry generally in both the home and overseas markets. Through nationalisation it more directly controls a number of basic industries. It has responsibilities for the location of industry and for town and country planning. It engages in research and development both for civil and military purposes. It provides comprehensive social services and is now expected to promote the fullest possible development of individual human potential. All these changes have made for a massive growth in public expenditure. Public spending means public control. A century ago the tasks of government were mainly passive and regulatory. Now they amount to a much more active and positive engagement in our affairs.

8. Technological progress and the vast amount of new knowledge have made a major impact on these tasks and on the process of taking decisions; the change goes on. Siting a new airport, buying military supplies, striking the right balance between coal, gas, oil and nuclear-powered electricity in a new energy policy – all these problems compel civil servants to use new techniques of analysis, management and co-ordination which are beyond those not specially trained in them.

9. The increase in the positive activities of government has not been solely an extension of the powers and functions of the State in an era of technological change. There has also been a complex intermingling of the public and private sectors. This has led to a proliferation of para-state organisations: public corporations, nationalised industries, negotiating bodies with varying degrees of public and private participation, public participation in private enterprises, voluntary bodies financed from public funds. Between the operations of the public and private sector, there is often no clear boundary. Central

and local government stand in a similarly intricate relationship; central government is generally held responsible for services that it partly or mainly finances but local authorities actually provide. As the tasks of government have grown and become more complex, so the need to consult and co-ordinate has grown as well.

10. The time it takes to reach a decision and carry it out has often lengthened. This is partly because of technological advances and the resulting complexity e.g. of defence equipment. Another reason is that the public and Parliament demand greater foresight and order in, for example, the development of land, the transport system and other resources, than they did in the past.

11. Governments also work more and more in an international setting. The improvement in communications and the greater inter-dependence of nations enlarges the difficulties as well as the opportunities of government.

12. To meet these new tasks of government the modern Civil Service must be able to handle the social, economic, scientific and technical problems of our time, in an international setting. Because the solutions to complex problems need long preparation, the Service must be far-sighted; from its accumulated knowledge and experience, it must show initiative in working out what are the needs of the future and how they might be met. A special responsibility now rests upon the Civil Service because one Parliament or even one Government often cannot see the process through.

13. At the same time, the Civil Service works under political direction and under the obligation of political accountability. This is the setting in which the daily work of many civil servants is carried out; thus they need to have a lively awareness of the political implications of what they are doing or advising. The Civil Service has also to be flexible enough to serve governments of any political complexion – whether they are committed to extend or in certain respects to reduce the role of the State. Throughout, it has to remember that it exists to serve the whole community, and that imaginative humanity sometimes matters more than tidy efficiency and administrative uniformity.

14. In our view the structure and practices of the Service have not kept up with the changing tasks. The defects we have found can nearly all be attributed to this. We have found no instance where reform has run ahead too rapidly. So, today, the Service is in need of fundamental change. It is inadequate in six main respects for the most efficient discharge of the present and prospective responsibilities of government.

15. First, the Service is still essentially based on the philosophy of the amateur (or 'generalist' or 'all-rounder'). This is most evident in the

Administrative Class which holds the dominant position in the Service. The ideal administrator is still too often seen as the gifted lay-man who, moving frequently from job to job within the Service, can take a practical view of any problem, irrespective of its subject-matter, in the light of his knowledge and experience of the government machine. Today, as the report of our Management Consultancy Group illustrates, this concept has most damaging consequences. It cannot make for the efficient despatch of public business when key men rarely stay in one job longer than two or three years before being moved to some other post, often in a very different area of government activity. A similar cult of the generalist is found in that part of the Executive Class that works in support of the Administrative Class and also even in some of the specialist classes. The cult is obsolete at all levels and in all parts of the Service.

16. Secondly, the present system of classes in the Service seriously impedes its work. The Service is divided into classes both horizontally (between higher and lower in the same broad area of work) and vertically (between different skills, professions or disciplines). There are 47 general classes whose members work in most government departments and over 1,400 departmental classes. Each civil servant is recruited to a particular class; his membership of that class determines his prospects (most classes have their own career structures) and the range of jobs on which he may be employed. It is true that there is some subsequent movement between classes; but such rigid and prolific compartmentalism in the Service leads to the setting up of cumbersome organisational forms, seriously hampers the Service in adapting itself to new tasks, prevents the best use of individual talent, contributes to the inequality of promotion prospects, causes frustration and resentment, and impedes the entry into wider management of those well fitted for it.

17. Thirdly, many scientists, engineers and members of other specialist classes get neither the full responsibilities and corresponding authority, nor the opportunities they ought to have. Too often they are organised in a separate hierarchy, while the policy and financial aspects of the work are reserved to a parallel group of 'generalist' administrators; and their access to higher management and policy-making is restricted. Partly this is because many of them are equipped only to practise their own specialism; a body of men with the qualities of the French *polytechnicien* – skilled in his craft, but skilled, too, as an administrator – has so far not been developed in Britain. In the new Civil Service a wider and more important role must be opened up for specialists trained and equipped for it.

18. Fourthly, too few civil servants are skilled managers. Since the major managerial role in the Service is specifically allocated to members of the Administrative Class it follows that this criticism applies particularly to them. Few members of the class actually see themselves as managers, i.e. as responsible for organisation, directing staff, planning the progress of work, setting standards of attainment and measuring results, reviewing procedures and quantifying different courses of action. One reason for this is that they are not adequately trained in management. Another is that much of their work is not managerial in this sense; so they tend to think of themselves as advisers on policy to people above them, rather than as managers of the administrative machine below them. Scientists and other specialists are also open to criticism here: not enough have been trained in management, particularly in personnel management, project management, accounting and control.

19. Fifthly, there is not enough contact between the Service and the rest of the community. There is not enough awareness of how the world outside Whitehall works, how government policies will affect it, and the new ideas and methods which are developing in the universities, in business and in other walks of life. Partly this is a consequence of a career service. Since we expect most civil servants to spend their entire working lives in the Service, we can hardly wonder if they have little direct and systematic experience of the daily life and thought of other people. Another element in this is the social and educational composition of the Civil Service; the Social Survey of the Service which we commissioned suggests that direct recruitment to the Administrative Class since the war has not produced the widening of its social and educational base that might have been expected. The public interest must suffer from any exclusiveness or isolation which hinders a full understanding of contemporary problems or unduly restricts the free flow of men, knowledge and ideas between the Service and the outside world.

20. Finally, we have serious criticisms of personnel management. Career-planning covers too small a section of the Service – mainly the Administrative Class – and is not sufficiently purposive or properly conceived; civil servants are moved too frequently between unrelated jobs, often with scant regard to personal preference or aptitude. Nor is there enough encouragement and reward for individual initiative and objectively measured performance; for many civil servants, especially in the lower grades, promotion depends too much on seniority.

21. For these and other defects the central management of the Service, the Treasury must accept its share of responsibility. It is unfortunate that there was not a major reform in the post-war years when the government took on so many new tasks and the Service had been loosened by war-time temporary recruitment and improvisation. There was then a great opportunity to preserve and adapt to peace-time conditions the flexibility which war had imposed. For a number of reasons, not all of them internal to the Service, this opportunity was not taken. In the 1950's the old ways reasserted themselves. The nature of the task was changing and the Service was left behind. Only recently has any attempt been made to introduce significant reforms. Despite the recent improvement in its management services the Treasury has failed to keep the Service up to date.

22. To some extent the urgent need for fundamental reform has been obscured by the Service's very considerable strengths, notably its capacity for improvisation – aptly demonstrated by the speed with which new departments have been set up in the last four years. There are exceptionally able men and women at all levels. There is a strong sense of public service. Its integrity and impartiality are unquestioned. We believe that the country does not recognise enough how impressively conscientious many civil servants are in the personal service they give to the public. It is of high importance that these and other qualities should be preserved.

23. In making our proposals for reform we have been influenced by what we have seen of foreign civil services – the emphasis on training and professionalism in France, the way young men of thrust and vigour in France and Sweden quickly reach posts of high responsibility where they are directly advising ministers, the contributions the "in-and-outers" make to government in the United States and the role played by specialists in both the United States and France.

24. One basic guiding principle should in our view govern the future development of the Civil Service. It applies to any organisation and is simple to the point of banality, but the root of much of our criticism is that it has not been observed. The principle is: look at the job first. The Civil Service must continuously review the tasks it is called upon to perform and the possible ways in which it might perform them; it should then think out what new skills and kinds of men are needed, and how these man can be found, trained and deployed. The Service must avoid a static view of a new ideal man and structure which in its turn could become as much of an obstacle to change as the present inheritance.

25. We have sought to devise a form of management for the Civil Service that will ensure that it is better run and able to generate its own self–criticism and forward drive. One of the main troubles of the Service has been that, in achieving immunity from political intervention, a system was evolved which until recently was virtually immune from outside pressures for change. Since it was not immune from inside resistance to change, inertia was perhaps predictable.

The Attack on Inefficiency

vi. The principles of the Financial Management Initiative, from *Efficiency and Effectiveness in the Civil Service*, Cmnd. 8616, HMSO, 1982, paras 13–16.

Financial Management

13. The aim of the Financial Management Initiative is to promote in each department an organisation and system in which managers at all levels have:
   a. a clear view of their objectives and means to assess and, wherever possible, measure outputs or performance in relation to those objectives;
   b. well-defined responsibility for making the best use of their resources, including a critical scrutiny of output and value for money; and
   c. the information (particularly about costs), the training and the access to expert advice that they need to exercise their responsibilities effectively.

14. The working document with which the Initiative was launched on 17 May 1982 is at Appendix 3. Departments are called upon to examine the way they manage all aspects of their programmes and to work out the best pattern of managerial responsibility, financial accounting and control. Keeping in touch throughout with the Treasury and the MPO, each department is to develop and define a plan which on completion will be sent to the Treasury and the MPO (before the end of January 1983); those departments will publish a central report by July 1983.

15. It is expected that every department's plan will include the following points:
   a. there will be an outline development plan which will cover the whole of the department's activities. The assembly of each plan may proceed in stages, including pilot projects;
   b. there will be an information system that not only provides higher management with aggregated information needed for estimating

and control, but managers at successive levels down the line with the information they need to do their job properly;

c.   the responsibilities of managers for the control of the resources they consume and, wherever feasible, the results they achieve will be specified systematically;

d.   the plan will include a system for the budgeting and control of administrative costs;

e.   where practicable, performance indicators and output measures will be developed which can be used to assess success in achievement of objectives. This is no less important than the accurate attribution and the monitoring of costs; the question departments will address is 'where is the money going *and* what are we getting for it?'.

The full achievement of the aims of the initiative will require a heavy commitment of resources, including the efforts of senior management, and departments will need time. However, some departments were already well ahead. The MOD, for example, has had for some time cost and management accounts covering expenditure approaching £4^1/2 billion and widespread staff and travel budgets. It had already conducted a major study of financial accountability in the Department and is now considering proposals for a system of responsibility budgets for line managers.

16.   A small MPO/Treasury unit comprising civil servants and management consultants has been set up to help departments in the preparation and review of their plans. It will work mainly in departments, advising senior management in the light of its experience gained from other departments and from the private sector. It will also help to identify Service–wide issues and to point to useful changes in existing practices and rules.

'Hiving Off'

vii. Excerpts from the Prime Minister's Efficiency Unit, *Management in Government: The Next Steps*, HMSO, 1988: paras 2–12 and 17–24.

2.   As part of this scrutiny we have spent three months in discussions with people in the Civil Service throughout the country. We have also reviewed the evidence from other scrutinies in the central programme since 1979 and looked at earlier reports on the management of the Civil Service. The themes which have emerged during the scrutiny have followed a broadly consistent pattern, whether in discussions in a small local benefit office or in a Minister's room. Some are also

common themes in earlier scrutinies and in reports on the Civil Service. There are seven main findings.

3. First, the management and staff concerned with the delivery of government services (some 95 per cent of the Civil Service) are generally convinced that the developments towards more clearly defined and budgeted management are positive and helpful. The manager of a small local office in the north east said that for the first time in 20 years he felt that he could have an effect on the conditions under which his staff worked and therefore on the results they produced. But this kind of enthusiasm is tempered by frustration at constraints. Although there is a general acceptance of the importance of delegating meaningful authority down to the most effective level, diffused responsibility still flourishes, especially in offices away from the sharp end of delivery of services to the public. Middle managers in particular feel that their authority is seriously circumscribed both by unnecessary controls and by the intervention of Ministers and senior officials in relatively minor issues. People who had recently resigned from the Civil Service told us that frustration at the lack of genuine responsibility for achieving results was a significant factor in encouraging them to move to jobs outside.

4. Second, most civil servants are very conscious that senior management is dominated by people whose skills are in policy formulation and who have relatively little experience of managing or working where services are actually being delivered. In any large organisation senior appointments are watched with close attention. For the Civil Service the present signals are, as one senior Grade 2 told us, that 'the golden route to the top is through policy not through management'. This is reflected in the early experience and training of fast-stream recruits. This kind of signal affects the unwritten priorities of a whole organisation, whatever the formal policy may be.

5. Managing large organisations involves skills which depend a great deal on experience; without experience senior managers lack confidence in their own ability to manage. Although, at the most senior levels, civil servants are responsible for both policy and service delivery, they give greater priority to policy, not only because it demands immediate attention but because that is the area in which they are on familiar ground and where their skills lie, and where ministerial attention is focused. A proper balance between policy and delivery is hard to achieve within the present framework, even though taxpayers are becoming increasingly conscious of what they should expect from the public expenditure on health, education and other services and hold Ministers to blame for their deficiencies.

6.   Third, senior civil servants inevitably and rightly respond to the priorities set by their Ministers which tend to be dominated by the demands of Parliament and communicating government policies. In this situation it is easy for the task of improving performance to get overlooked, especially where there is, as we observed, confusion between Ministers and Permanent Secretaries over their responsibilities for the management of service delivery. This confusion is made worse when short-term pressure becomes acute. Nevertheless the ability of Ministers supported by their senior officials to handle politics and political sensitivities effectively is a crucial part of any government's credibility. Changes in the management process should therefore aim to increase rather than diminish this crucial skill.

7.   Fourth, the greater diversity and complexity of work in many departments, together with demands from Parliament, the media and the public for more information, has added to ministerial overload. Because of other pressures on Ministers, and because for most of them management is not their forte and they don't see it as their function, better management and the achievement of improved performance is something that the Civil Service has to work out largely for itself. It is unrealistic to expect Ministers to do more than give a broad lead. Most Ministers who are worried about overload are of the view that while changes in management that reduced the ministerial load would be welcomed, provided they entailed no major political risks, 'Ministers themselves do not have time or the experience needed to develop such changes.

8.   Fifth, the pressures on departments are mainly on expenditure and activities; there is still too little attention paid to the results to be achieved with the resources. The public expenditure system is the most powerful central influence on departmental management. It is still overwhelmingly dominated by the need to keep within the levels of money available rather than by the effectiveness with which that money is used.

9.   Sixth, there are relatively few external pressures demanding improvement in performance. The Prime Minister has given a valuable lead and holds seminars to discuss value for money in individual departments. Her Adviser on Efficiency and Effectiveness has annual discussions with Ministers about their priorities for getting better value for money. These are useful but occasional rather than continuous pressures. Pressure from Parliament, the Public Accounts Committee and the media tends to concentrate on alleged impropriety or incompetence, and making political points, rather than on demanding evidence of steadily improving efficiency and effectiveness. This

encourages a cautious and defensive response which feeds through into management. On the positive side, the Treasury and the National Audit Office (NAO) are developing work on value for money. But the process of searching for improvement is still neither rigorous nor sustained; it is not yet part of the basic institution of government.

10. Seventh, the Civil Service is too big and too diverse to manage as a single entity. With 600,000 employees it is an enormous organisation compared with any private sector company and most public sector organisations. A single organisation of this size which attempts to provide a detailed structure within which to carry out functions as diverse as driver licensing, fisheries protection, the catching of drug smugglers and the processing of Parliamentary Questions is bound to develop in a way which fits no single operation effectively.

11. At present the freedom of an individual manager to manage effectively and responsibly in the Civil Service is severely circumscribed. There are controls not only on resources and objectives, as there should be in any effective system, but also on the way in which resources can be managed. Recruitment, dismissal, choice of staff, promotion, pay, hours of work, accommodation, grading, organisation of work, the use of IT equipment, are all outside the control of most Civil Service managers at any level. The main decisions on rules and regulations are taken by the centre of the Civil Service. This tends to mean that they are structured to fit everything in general and nothing in particular. The rules are therefore seen primarily as a constraint rather than as a support; and in no sense as a pressure on managers to manage effectively. Moreover, the task of changing the rules is often seen as too great for one unit or one manager or indeed one department and is therefore assumed to be impossible.

12. In our discussions it was clear that the advantages which a unified Civil Service are intended to bring are seen as outweighed by the practical disadvantages, particularly beyond Whitehall itself. We were told that the advantages of an all-embracing pay structure are breaking down, that the uniformity of grading frequently inhibits effective management and that the concept of a career in a unified Civil Service has little relevance for most civil servants, whose horizons are bounded by their local office or, at most, by their department.

19. We recommend that 'agencies' should be established to carry out the executive functions of government within a policy and resources framework set by a department. An 'agency' of this kind may be part of government and the public service, or it may be more effective outside government. We use the term 'agency' not in its technical sense but to describe any executive unit that delivers a service for

government. The choice and definition of suitable agencies is primarily for Ministers and senior management in departments to decide. In some instances very large blocks of work comprising virtually a whole department will be suitable to be managed in this way. In other instances, where the scale of activity is too small for an entirely separate organisation, it may be better to have one or even several smaller agencies within departments.

20. These units, large or small, need to be given a well defined framework in which to operate, which sets out the policy, the budget, specific targets and the results to be achieved. It must also specify how politically sensitive issues are to be dealt with and the extent of the delegated authority of management. The management of the agency must be held rigorously to account by their department for the results they achieve.

21. The framework will need to be set and updated as part of a formal annual review with the responsible Minister, based on a long-term plan and an annual report. The main strategic control must lie with the Minister and Permanent Secretary. But once the policy objectives and budgets within the framework are set, the management of the agency should then have as much independence as possible in deciding how those objectives are met. A crucial element in the relationship would be a formal understanding with Ministers about the handling of sensitive issues and the lines of accountability in a crisis. The presumption must be that, provided management is operating within the strategic direction set by Ministers, it must be left as free as possible to manage within that framework. To strengthen operational effectiveness, there must be freedom to recruit, pay, grade and structure in the most effective way as the framework becomes sufficiently robust and there is confidence in the capacity of management to handle the task.

22. Once the framework had been set the head of the agency would be given personal responsibility to achieve the best possible results within it. He or she must be seen to be accountable for doing so. In due course formal accountability, before the Public Accounts Committee for example, might develop so that for significant agencies the Permanent Secretary would normally be accompanied by the head of the agency. The Permanent Secretary's role would be to justify and defend the framework; the manager would have to answer for his or her performance within that framework.

23. Placing responsibility for performance squarely on the shoulders of the manager of an agency also has implications for the way in which Ministers answer to Parliament on operational issues. Clearly Ministers

have to be wholly responsible for policy, but it is unrealistic to suppose that they can actually have knowledge in depth about every operational question. The convention that they do is in part the cause of the overload we observed. We believe it is possible for Parliament, through Ministers, to regard managers as directly responsible for operational matters and that there are precedents for this and precisely defined ways in which it can be handled. If management in the Civil Service is truly to be improved this aspect cannot be ignored. In view of its importance it is considered in more detail in Annex A, where it is suggested that to achieve changes in the arrangements for formal accountability would generally require legislation and that in suitable instances this should be considered.

24. The detailed nature of the relationship between a department and an agency will vary with the job to be done or the service to be delivered. The agency structure could be used to cover a substantial proportion of the activities of the Civil Service. It is clear from our discussions with Permanent Secretaries that some departments are already moving towards this concept. What is needed is a substantial acceleration and broadening of this trend through a major initiative. Ultimately some agencies could be in a position where they are no longer inside the Civil Service in the sense they are today. Any decision of this kind should be taken pragmatically – the test must always be adopting the structure which best fits the job to be done.

MANAGEMENT IN LOCAL GOVERNMENT

The Management Board Model

viii. Report of the Committee on the Management of Local Government (Maud Report), HMSO, 1967, paras. 143–58.

143. *Policy and administration.* We refer in paragraph 109 to the often expressed view that the function of members is to decide 'policy' and of officers to 'execute' or 'administer' it. We argue that 'policy' cannot be defined and indeed that it should not be defined. Some issues are, to reasonable men, so important that they can safely be termed 'policy issues'. But what may seem to be a routine matter may be charged with political significance to the extent that it becomes a matter of policy. Other routine matters may lead by practice and experience to the creation of a principle or a policy; an isolated case may itself be a precedent for a line of similar cases. In

advising on major issues officers are clearly contributing to the formulation of policy, but in shaping administrative decisions officers may also, even if less obviously, be formulating a policy. 'Policy' and 'administration' will not serve to distinguish between the responsibilities of members and of officers. How they can be distinguished is set out in the following paragraphs.

144. *Managing the affairs of a local authority.* A local authority, in addition to providing a wide range of public services on a scale and to standards prescribed by Parliament or a minister, must necessarily study the present physical and social environment of the area it serves, and assess its future needs and developments. In the light of this it must come to conclusions on what its objectives are to be and the means to be adopted to attain them. The problems cannot be taken in isolation; the objectives have to be reconciled with one another. Key decisions have to be taken on the means and plans to attain these objectives. It is necessary to ensure that resources are available to do what is wanted when it is wanted and to do it effectively and efficiently. Action needs to be co-ordinated, performance watched and timing and costs reviewed, so that corrective action can be taken when necessary.

145. It is the members who should take and be responsible for the key decisions on objectives, and on the means and plans to attain them. It is they who must periodically review the position as part of their function of directing and controlling. It is the officers who should provide the necessary staff work and advice which will enable the members to identify the problems, set the objectives and select the means and plans to attain them. It is the officers who should direct and co-ordinate the necessary action, and see that material is presented to enable members to review progress and check performance.

146. The previous paragraphs have been written in terms of the major enterprises of a local authority. Much of the work of a local authority, however, lies not in the planning and execution of major projects but:

    (a) In the provision of day-to-day services e.g. the domiciliary health services carried out by the mid-wife and the health visitor, the running of children's homes and homes for old people, of schools and libraries; the maintenance of parks and of roads, the collection and disposal of refuse.

    (b) In work for individuals e.g. taking a child into care; the allocation of a council house; finding a place for a particular child in a particular school; a decision on a scholarship.

(c) In routine inspections and controls e.g. of the conditions of shop premises, of the cleanliness of milk, in the administration of smokeless zones, in handling planning applications, in inspection of weights and measures.

Most of these examples, and they can be multiplied, affect individuals intimately or the public immediately and directly: many result in coercion and restrictive action liable to provoke resentment and harsh publicity. It is quite as necessary to define the relative functions of members and of officers in these spheres of activity as it is for the major issues we have already discussed. While it is clear that the overall development and control of services should be the responsibility of members, in our view the day-to-day administration of services, the decisions in case work, the routine process of inspection and control should normally be the functions of the paid officers and not of the members.

147. *Responsiveness to the public.* The members can only assume the responsibilities of ultimate direction and control of the affairs of the authority if they have an understanding of the present and future problems of the public that they serve. They must act as guardians of the public interest and must individually serve as channels of communication between the public and the authority and vice versa.

148. Although routine day-to-day work and decisions should rest with the officers, such is the nature of much of it that there should in appropriate circumstances be clear channels of appeal to the members. This is consistent with our view that ultimate direction and control should rest with the members.

149. If the officers are responsible for day-to-day administration and the many sensitive decisions involved, they must be alive to the difficult case, the instance which is likely to cause an outcry, the hard cases for which no precedent exists, and they must be prompt in bringing any such cases to the notice of the members for decision. This does not imply any interference with the right of the public to make direct approaches to members on such matters.

150. We recommend that local authorities conduct a radical review of the respective functions and responsibilities of members and officers.

151. We recommend that local authorities consider a division of functions and responsibilities between members and officers as follows:
   (a) Ultimate direction and control of the affairs of the authority to lie with the members.
   (b) The members to take the key decisions on the objectives of the authority and on the plans to attain them.
   (c) The members to review, periodically, progress and the

performance of the services.

(d) The officers to provide the necessary staff work and advice so that members may set the objectives and take decisions on the means of attaining them.

(e) The officers to be responsible for the day-to-day administration of services,

(f) The officers to be responsible for identifying and isolating the particular problem or case which in their view, and from their understanding of the minds of the members, has such implications that the members must consider and decide on it.

152. Reference is made in Chapter 2 to the unfortunate effects that a rather narrow interpretation sometimes placed on the word 'democracy' has had in local government in this country. It is thought that unless members determine how the smallest things are to be done, they are failing in their duties, and that to allow any but the most trivial discretion to an officer is undemocratic. The effect of this is to force issues however trivial upwards to the top for consideration in the committees. This in turn involves principal officers and their immediate subordinates in dealing with matters on their way to the committees which would otherwise be disposed of at a lower level. It is perhaps symptomatic of this tendency for issues to be dealt with at the highest level that letters are signed by heads of departments or by their subordinates writing the head of department's name. We recommend that local authorities adopt the guiding principle that issues are dealt with at the lowest level consistent with the nature of the problem.

A scheme of internal organisation

153. The form of organisation we propose should not be regarded as applicable in every detail to every local authority. Our first aim is that local authorities should look at their organisation anew and that they should be freed from the checks and controls which inhibit experiment with new forms. But we believe that form of organisation we suggest is the best way of implementing the principles we stated in the preceding paragraphs.

154. *The council.* In local authorities in those countries whose practice we have examined, the supremacy of the council is unchallenged and everywhere the functions of the council are remarkably similar. The existence of executive or managing bodies does not affect this ultimate supremacy. In Eire the council has its 'reserved' functions; under the strong mayor system in the United States the council has the ultimate power and retains the right to approve policy, pass the

budget and to legislate; under the Manager system the council makes orders and regulations, decides the extent and pattern of activities and passes the budget. In the later paragraphs we make recommendation on the setting up of a management board and delegation to officers. We think it is important to emphasise that whatever recommendations we make in this respect we adhere firmly to the principle that it is the members in council of a local authority who are ultimately supreme in the direction and control of its affairs.

155. It is the council which should consider the major objectives of the authority and take the major decisions involved. It should approve the estimates of expenditure and fix, or precept, the rate. The council should be the final place of inquisition and the focal point of the authority's activities; it should be the place where the public and the authority are brought together. It should serve as a forum for debate where views, complaints and grievances of the public can be expressed by members and answered. It should provide the arena where the acts of the management board and of the authority's officers can be challenged. The council should prescribe the standing orders of the authority and approve the organisation of the committees and of the departments. It should provide in standing orders for the rights of members to raise matters at question time and to propose motions of their choosing.

156. *The managing body.* In Chapter 5, paragraph 332, we recommend that the size of a council should not exceed 75 members in the largest authorities. A council of this size will still remain a relatively large body. It will meet only periodically; by its nature, its procedures will be those of debate and not of management. In earlier paragraphs we make two points:

   (a) local authorities in England and Wales are alone (in countries we have examined) in not providing for a managing body in some form or other;

   (b) the absence of a managing body leads to confusion in the functions and responsibilities of members and officers.

157. Dr Marshall's report on local government abroad shows the wide variation in the types of managing body (or executive). We ascribe great importance to the local authority being responsive to people's needs and views and therefore the managing body should be composed of members. This leads us to reject an arrangement whereby control and direction are entrusted to a paid officer, similar to the Manager in Eire or the City Manager in the United States, as this would reduce the participation of members to an extent which we consider undesirable. The manager system would not necessarily

be any more efficient than an elected managing body if the organisation of the officers to provide the staff work and to execute the decisions of the authority is efficient. .... We do not favour any move towards direction and control being in the hands of a single elected person on the pattern of the 'strong mayor' in the United States and in Bavaria and Baden-Wurttemberg, nor do we favour the appointment of a managing body by superior authority as in the case of the Burgomaster in the Netherlands. We see no merit in a separately elected management committee on the analogy of the Ontario Board of Control, nor do we favour a management body composed of both members and officers. There are, in our view, advantages in maintaining the practice of the central government (which is generally understood) by which the controlling and directing organ, although distinct in its functions, is part of the elected council, answerable to it and ultimately dependent on it for support for its actions.

158. We recommend that local authorities establish a managing body, to be called 'the management board' composed of from five to nine members of the council.

The Bains Model

ix. Excepts from *The New Local Authorities: Management and Structure*, (Bains Report), HMSO, 1972, paras 4: 1–4: 15, pp. 18–24

Fulfilling the member's role-organisational implications
The Council

4.1 The Council is the ultimate decision-making body within any local authority and by the very nature of the democratic institution which local government is, that role is one which must remain with the Council.

4.2 The way in which that role is exercised differs widely from authority to authority. At one extreme the full Council receives and considers copies of the minutes and reports of every committee meeting and the members in Council are at liberty to reserve any individual item for debate by the Council. In the centre are those authorities where the Council receives and considers reports of every committee. As in the first example, members can then raise individual matters for debate but unlike the earlier example they are limited to the major matters which are included in the reports. At the other extreme we have received evidence from an authority where virtually nothing comes before the full Council unless members specifically so require. In fact the difference between the two extremes is basically one of procedure, because in each case members receive all necessary information and select which issues they wish to be debated in Council. The difference lies in the process by which that selection is made.

4.3 Despite these variations, we have found that in many authorities the full Council is increasingly being regarded as a body whose major function, in terms of agenda content if not in importance, is to rubber-stamp decisions which have effectively been taken elsewhere, whether by officer, committee or party group. The result is that the proceedings of the full Council become more and more formal and ritualistic and its role is downgraded in the eyes of members, officers and, most important perhaps, the public.

4.4 The Council will usually wish to reserve to itself in the terms of delegation to committees the more important policy matters. In that case it will receive reports and recommendations from the committees on these reserved matters, with concurrent reports from the policy and resources committee where the latter considers it necessary. We believe that the Council should also have a role as a debating and policy-formulating forum. Debates on the broad policy options, perhaps on the basis of papers from committees of the sort issued from time to time by central government to stimulate discussion of particular issues, would enable the arguments on each side to be heard before effective decisions are taken. The press and public too would be better informed and, we believe, encouraged to play their part if they felt that important matters were to be debated before the effective decisions were taken.

The committee system

4.5 In our interim report (Appendix A) we urged the removal of all statutory requirements upon local authorities to appoint particular committees and although the Government did not wholly accept our recommendations, there will in future be more freedom for each local authority to set up the organisation which it feels will meet the needs of its own particular situation. We remain of the opinion that from a management point of view it is undesirable to require a local authority to appoint particular committees; doing so not only restricts the freedom of the authority to select an organisational structure for itself, but by creating 'statutory' and therefore 'special' committees for particular services it encourages both members and officers for those and other services to adopt a departmental rather than a corporate approach.

4.6 The achievement of this corporate approach is perhaps the major task facing the new local authorities and although the opportunity for change presented by the reorganisation of local government will help, there will inevitably be substantial problems to be faced. Not the least of these will be the difficulty of welding into a team members from different authorities, each with his own traditions, practices and loyalties. It is at the level of the individual member that the seeds of corporate planning and management must be sown, for it is there that it must flourish. Corporate management is not something which is done behind closed doors in a policy committee meeting; it is a process involving every member and many officers.

4.7 Because the traditional committee system has been retained by the Government's decision in relation to certain services, we have not sought to find radical alternative systems of organisation at member level. What we have attempted to do is to bring more flexibility to the traditional system, without jeopardizing its strengths.

4.8 Perhaps the first point to establish is that a change in structure does not necessarily result in a change. To illustrate the point, we have received evidence from a number of authorities who have established a central policy committee, though it may be called a management committee or some other title. We have also had the opportunity of discussing the work of such committees with members and officers in the authorities which we have visited. In a number of authorities we have found that the so-called policy committee is in fact not concerned with the central policy and strategic decisions at all. In some cases it has become what one member called 'the waste paper basket of the Council', operating as a low-key general purpose committee; in others it is responsible for any matter which comes up between meetings of other committees. What has happened in these authorities is that the structure has changed, but the management process has not.

4.9 We have chosen to illustrate our point by reference to the policy committee; it is, therefore, logical that we should commence our discussion of structure from this central point.

4.10 In their evidence to us, the then Society of Clerks of the Peace of Counties and of Clerks of County Councils said:

> ...the authority tends to have a number of separate plans with separate programmes, and while there is normally some co-ordination of each of these programmes between the departments concerned, the authority does not have adequate opportunities of examining the programmes as a whole to decide whether they provide the best overall strategy.

4.11 This is a view which has also been supported by the findings of management consultants who have reported on the management and organisation of local authorities. For example, McKinsey and Co Inc concluded that one authority which they had studied:

> ...in common with many other authorities, finds itself with an organisation and a system of making decisions that has changed little since the present structure of authorities was created out of the tangled web of local boards and functional administrations in the latter half of the 19th century. The democratic forms of Council and committee and the rigid hierarchical structure of the service have some great strengths but in many ways are not geared to the modern task of managing thousands of people and hundreds of millions of pounds of assets, nor to making complex often technical decisions on the development of those assets. The city has neither the organisation structure nor the planning system nor the management methods commensurate with the job.

4.12 We believe that these words apply with some force to all levels of local authority.

4.13 The two statements which we quoted clearly imply the need for some form of overall plan towards which the authority will work and against which it can measure its achievements. There can be no improvement in the quality of the critical decisions regarding resource allocation unless there is in existence some yardstick against which priorities can be evaluated and competing claims can be resolved.

The Policy and Resource Committee

4.14 As we have already said, the Council is the ultimate decision-making body of authority, and the broad policy decisions which themselves determine the overall plan for the community should be taken by the Council. In order to take those decisions the Council needs comprehensive and co-ordinated advice on the implications for the community and we believe that this function requires the creation of a central policy committee. Such a committee will aid the Council in setting its objectives and priorities and, once the major policy decisions have been taken, will be instrumental in co-ordinating and controlling the implementation of those decisions. It would have a particular role to play in the formulation of the structure plan for the area, either directly in a county or by way of consultation in a district.

4.15 This 'Policy and Resources Committee' as we have chosen to call it, would, as its name implies, have ultimate responsibility under the Council for the major resources of the authority, finance, manpower and land (with which we include buildings). The central control of finance has long been accepted and we believe that dual role of the policy and resources committee in advising the Council on future plans, necessitates overall control of the major resources. It may be that in certain special circumstances, for example where a large central area redevelopment scheme is in progress, control over land and buildings should be delegated to the committee which has responsibility for the redevelopment programme, but we suggest that those occasions should be exceptional.

The Local Authority's Role

x. Three views of the Role of a Local Authority, from R. Greenwood and J. D. Stewart (eds), *Corporate Planning in English Local Government,* Institute of Local Government Studies and Charles Knight, 1974, pp. 1–2.

This book has two aims. The first is to meet one of the needs of management education by making material available which, although important, is either little known or difficult to secure. The second is to select and order that material to illustrate the main patterns of change that occurred during 1967–72. In particular, it is intended to illustrate the development of corporate planning. The conceptual framework of the readings is set out in the remaining sections of this introduction.

The initial assumption of our analysis is that many of the changes that are being introduced in local government are manifestations of a changing conception of the role of the local authority in relation to its environment. It may be posited that the traditional conception emphasises the provision of limited, statutorily defined services each of which has a distinct and separate influence upon the environment of the local authority, and which therefore require a minimum of co-ordination. Such a conception is consistent with the history of local government in England and Wales which has seen services and functions added or taken away more for administrative and political convenience than for anything they might have in common. An alternative conception, which received emphasis during the 1960s, also assumes that the primary function of a local authority is the provision of services prepared and provided in isolation, but recognises that a common organisational framework provides opportunities for economies of scale in the use of resources, and for the recognition of departmental interdependencies that arise in the implementation of policies. This conception – referred to elsewhere as *'federal'* – led a number of local authorities to develop management services units based upon 'organisation and methods' and work study because of their contribution to administrative efficiency. The movement underlying the growth of federal systems can be described as the movement to administrative efficiency.

During the 1960s this conception of the local authority's role was prevalent in local government. It led to the introduction of organisational changes that were designed to secure administrative co-ordination and greater efficiency. The changes included the merging of departments and the streamlining of committees. They involved greater delegation to officers, and the appointment of a principal officer recognised as head of the authority's paid service with authority over other chief officers as far as necessary for the efficient management and execution of the authority's activities.

A third conception emerged during the same period and is central to our analysis. It is a conception which emphasises the *governmental* function of the local authority based on a responsibility for the well-being of the local area, rather than for the mere provision of the defined and statutorily conceived services. Thus, the Royal Commission on Local Government in England 1966–69 stated that the substance of local government is

> an all-round responsibility for the safety, health and well-being, both material and cultural, of people in different localities, in so far as these objectives can be achieved by local action and local initiative, within a framework of national policies.

Similar views are expressed in reports on the management arrangements of particular local authorities. McKinsey and Company, Inc., in their report for Liverpool argued that

> the job of any city government is to create an environment in which the citizens can live and work comfortably and conveniently in health and safety. It carries out this task by planning, directing and performing a wide range of services – building roads and sewers, ensuring adequate water supplies, providing schools, and constructing housing, for example – that largely determine the shape of the environment.

More recently, perhaps more explicitly, the Study Group on the new local authorities confirmed that

> Local government is not, in our view, limited to the narrow provision of a series of services to the local community, though we do not intend in any way to suggest that these services are not important. It has, within its purview the overall economic, cultural and physical well-being of that community, and for this reason, its decisions impinge with increasing frequency upon the individual lives of its citizens.

Reinterpretation of the local authority's role, with greater emphasis upon the local authority as the primary arm of government in a particular area, has underlain much of the movement towards corporate planning.

That movement has perhaps two elements, which, although united within the framework of corporate planning, may for conceptual purposes be considered separately. One element, which corresponds to the word 'corporate', represents an attempt to secure unity of purpose in the affairs of the local authority. The second element, which corresponds to the word 'planning', emphasises the adjustment of activities to changing needs and problems.

PLANNING AND CREATIVITY

Planning as Arrogance

xi. Aaron Wildavsky,'If Planning is Everything, Maybe it's Nothing', *Policy Sciences*, volume 4, 1973, pp. 127-53. Excerpt, pp.141–6.

Planning as Rationality. Certain key terms appear over and over again: planning is good because it is *systematic* rather than random, *efficient* rather than wasteful, *co-ordinated* rather than helter-skelter, consistent rather than contradictory, and above all, *rational* rather than unreasonable. In the interest of achieving a deeper understanding of why planning is preferred, it will be helpful to consider these norms as instructions to decisionmakers. What would they do if they followed them?

Be systematic! What does it mean to say that decisions should be made in a systematic manner? A word like 'careful' will not do because planners cannot be presumed to be more careful than other people. Perhaps 'orderly' is better; it implies a checklist of items to be taken into account, but anyone can make a list. Being systematic implies further that one knows the right variables in the correct order to put into the list, can specify the relationship among them. The essential meaning of systematic, therefore, is having qualities of a system, that is a series of variables whose interactions are known and whose outputs can be predicted from knowledge of their inputs. System, therefore, is another word for theory or model explaining and predicting events in the real world in a parsimonious way that permits manipulation. To say that one is being systematic, consequently implies that one has causal knowledge.

Here we have part of the answer we have been seeking. Planning is good because inherent in the concept is the possession of knowledge that can be used to control the world. Knowledge is hard to obtain; the mind of man is small and simple while the world is large and complex. Hence the temptation to imply by a cover word possession of the very thing, causal knowledge, that is missing.

Be efficient! There is in modern man a deeply-rooted belief that objectives should be obtained at the least cost. Who can quarrel with that?

But technical efficiency should never be considered by itself. It does not tell you where to go but only that you should arrive there (or part way) by the least effort.

The great questions are: efficiency for whom and for what? There are some goals (destroying other nations in nuclear war, decreasing the living standards of the poverty-stricken in order to benefit the wealthy) that one does not wish achieved at all, let alone efficiently. Efficiency, therefore, raises once more the prior question of objectives.

One of the most notable characteristics of national objectives is that they tend to be vague, multiple and contradictory. Increasing national income is rarely the only social objective. It has to be traded off against more immediate consumption objectives, such as raising the living standards of rural people. Cultural objectives such as encouraging the spread of native languages and crafts, may have to be undertaken at a sacrifice of income. Political objectives, such as the desire to improve racial harmony or assert national independence, may lead to distribution of investment funds for economically unprofitable regions and to rejection of certain kinds of foreign aid. A great deal depends on which objectives enter into national priorities first, because there is seldom room for emphasis on more than a few.

Stress on efficiency assumes that objectives are agreed upon. Conflict is banished. The very national unity to which the plan is supposed to contribute turns out to be one of its major assumptions.

Co-ordinate! Co-ordination is one of the golden words of our time. I cannot off -hand think of any way in which the word is used that implies disapproval. Policies should be co-ordinated; they should not run every which-way. No one wishes their children to be described as unco-ordinated. Many of the world's ills are attributed to lack of co-ordination in the government. Yet, so far as we know, there has never been a serious effort to analyse the term. It requires and deserves full discussion. All that can be done here, however, is barely to open up the subject.

Policies should be mutually supportive rather than contradictory. People should not work at cross purposes. The participants in any particular activity should contribute to a common purpose at the right time and in the right amount to achieve co-ordination. A should facilitate B in order to achieve C. From this intuitive sense of co-ordination four important (and possibly contradictory) meanings can be derived.

If there is a common objective, then efficiency requires that it be achieved with the least input of resources. When these resources are supplied by a number of different actors, hence the need for co-ordination, they must all contribute their proper share at the correct time. If their actors are efficient, that means they contributed just what they should and no more or less.

Co-ordination, then, equals efficiency, which is highly prized because achieving it means avoiding bad things: duplication, overlapping and redundancy. These are bad because they result in unnecessary effort, thereby spending resources that might be used more effectively for other purposes. But now we shall complicate matters by introducing another criterion that is (for good reasons) much less heard in discussion of planning. I refer to reliability, the probability that a particular function will be performed. Heretofore we have assumed that reliability was taken care of in the definition of efficiency. It has been discussed as if the policy in mind had only to work once. Yet we all know that major problems of designing policies can center on the need to have them work at a certain level of reliability. For this reason, as Martin Landau has so brilliantly demonstrated, redundancy is built-in to most humble enterprises. We ensure against failure by having adequate reserves and by creating several mechanisms to perform a single task in case one should fail.

Co-ordination of complex activities require redundancy. Telling us to avoid duplication gives us no useful instruction at all; it is just a recipe for failure. What you need to know is how much and what kind of redundancy to build-in to our programme. The larger the number of participants in an enterprise, the more difficult the problem of co-ordination, the greater the need for redundancy.

Participants in a common enterprise may act in a contradictory fashion because of ignorance: when informed of their place in the scheme of things, they may obediently to be expected to behave properly. If we relax the assumption that a common purpose is involved, however, and admit the possibility (indeed the likelihood) of conflict over goals, then co-ordination becomes another term for coercion. Since actors A and B disagree with goal C, they can be co-ordinated by being told what to do and doing it. The German word, *Gleichschaltung,* used by the Nazis in the sense of enforcing a rigid conformity, can give us some insights into this particular usage of co-ordination. To co-ordinate one must be able to get others to do things they do not want to do. Co-ordination thus becomes a form of coercive power.

When one bureaucrat tells another to co-ordinate a policy, he means that it should be cleared with other official participants who have some stake in the matter. This is a way of sharing the blame in case things go wrong (each initial on the documents being another hostage against retribution). Since they cannot be coerced, their consent must be obtained. Bargaining must take place to reconcile the differences with the result that the policy may be modified, even at the cost of compromising its original purpose. Co-ordination in this sense is another word for consent.

Co-ordinating means achieving efficiency and reliability, consent and coercion. Telling another person to achieve co-ordination, therefore, does not tell him what to do. He does not know whether to coerce or bargain or what mixture of efficiency and reliability to attempt. Here we have another example of an apparently desirable trait of planning that covers up the central problems – conflicts versus co-operation, coercion versus consent – that its invocation is supposed to resolve. Planning suffers from the same disability that Herbert Simon illustrated for proverbial wisdom in administration: each apparently desirable trait may be countered by its opposite – look before you leap, but he who hesitates is lost. An apt illustration is the use of 'consistency'.

Be consistent! Do not run in all directions at once. Consistency may be conceived as horizontal (at a moment in time) or vertical (over a series of time periods extending into the future). Vertical consistency requires that the same policy be pursued, horizontal consistency that it mesh with others existing at the same time. The former requires continuity of a powerful regime able to enforce its preferences, the latter tremendous knowledge of how policies affect one another. These are demanding prerequisites. One requires extraordinary rigidity to ensure continuity, the other unusual flexibility to achieve accommodation with other policies. Be firm, be pliant, are hard directions to follow at one and the same time.

The divergent directions implied in the term suggest that the virtues of consistency should not be taken for granted. It may well be desirable to pursue a single tack with energy and devotion but it may also prove valuable to hedge one's bets. Consistency secures a higher payoff for success but also imposes a steeper penalty for failure. If several divergent policies are being pursued in the same area they may interfere with each other but there also may be a greater chance that one will succeed. The admonition 'Be consistent' may be opposed by the proverb, 'Don't put all your eggs in the same basket.'

Consistency is not wholly compatible with adaptation. While it may be desirable to pursue a steady course, it is also commonsensical to adapt to changing circumstances. There is the model of the unchanging pursued by numerous detours and tactical retreats but never abandoned and ultimately achieved. There is also the model of learning in which experience leads men to alter their objectives as well as the means of obtaining them. They may come to believe the cost is too high or they may learn that they prefer a different objective. Apparent inconsistency may turn out to be a change in objectives. If both means and ends, policies and objectives, are changing simultaneously, consistency may turn out to be a will of the wisp that eludes one's grasp whenever one tries to capture it. The resulting inconsistency may not matter so much, however, as long as alternative courses of action are thoroughly examined at each point of decision. Consider alternatives! Which ones? How many? Answers to these questions depend on the inventiveness of the planners; the acknowledged constraints: (such as limited funds, social values), and the cost in terms of time, talent, and money that can be spent on each. While it used to be popular to say that all alternatives should be systematically compared, it has been evident that this won't work; knowledge is lacking and the cost is too high. The number of alternatives considered could easily be infinite if the dimensions of the problem (such as time, money, skill and size) are continuous.

Let us suppose that only a small number of alternatives will be considered. Which of the many conceivable ones should receive attention? Presumably those will be selected that are believed most compatible with existing values and to work more efficiently. But this presupposes that the planner knows at the beginning how the analysis will turn out; otherwise he must reject some alternatives to come out with the preferred set. At the same time there are other matters up for decision and choices must be made about whether they are to be given analytical time and attention. The planner needs rules telling him when to intervene in regard to which possible decisions and how much time to devote to each one. His estimate of the ultimate importance of the decision undoubtedly matters, but also it requires predictive ability he may not have. He is likely to resort to simple rules such as the amount of money involved in the decision and an estimate of his opportunities for influencing it.

We have gone a long way from the simple advice to consider alternatives. How to know that this command does not tell anyone which decisions should concern him, how many alternatives he should consider, how much time and attention to devote to them or whether he knows enough to make the enterprise worthwhile. To say that alternatives should be considered is to suggest that something better must exist without being able to say what it is.

Be rational! If rationality means achieving one's goals in the optimal way, it refers here to technical efficiency, the principle of least effort. As Paul Diesing argues, however, one can conceive of several levels of rationality for different aspects of society. There is the rationality of legal norms and of social structures as well as political rationality, which speaks to the maintenance of structures for decision, and economic rationality which is devoted to increasing national wealth.

What is good for the political system may not be good for the economy and *vice versa*. The overweening emphasis upon economic growth in Pakistan may have contributed to the relative neglect of the question of governmental legitimacy in the eastern regions. Any analysis of public policy that does not consider incompatibility among the different realms of rationality is bound to be partial and misleading.

Strict economic rationality means getting the most national income out of a given investment. The end is to increase real GNP, no matter who receives it, and the means is an investment expenditure, no matter who pays for it. To be economically rational is to increase growth to its maximum. Speaking of economic rationality is a way of smuggling in identification with the goal of economic development without saying so.

Rationality is also used in the broader sense of reason. The rational man has goals that he tries to achieve by being systematic, efficient, consistent and so on. Since rationality in the sense of reason has no independent meaning of its own it can only have such validity as is imparted by the norms that tell us about what reasonable action is.

The injunction to plan (!!) is empty. The key terms associated with it are proverbs or platitudes. Pursue goals! Consider alternatives! Obtain knowledge! Exercise power! Obtain consent! Or be flexible but do not alter your course. Planning stands for unresolved conflicts.

Yet planning has acquired a reputation for success in some rich countries. Perhaps a certain level of affluence is required before planning becomes effective. Instead of stacking the deck against planning by asking whether it works in poor nations, let us play its best cards by looking at the record under the most propitious circumstances.

Planning as Policy

xii. P. Self, 'Is Comprehensive Planning Possible and Rational?, *Policy and Politics*, Volume 2, No. 3, pp. 193–203.

Academic discussion of planning veers easily into the dead ends of sophisticated scepticism or pragmatic optimism. The sceptics usually have the advantage of a more coherent intellectual framework, but the pragmatists seem closer to reality in the sense that governments still go on trying to plan, and many politicians, officials, professionals, and even (perhaps especially) 'plain citizens' have a degree of faith in planning. Doubtless the latter group often suppose or pretend that they are planning when they are merely 'muddling through'. Still it is my contention that forms of *comprehensive* planning are possible and desirable, and can be described as rational, in some, not infrequent circumstances.

Nobody denies the usefulness of planning in simple contexts, such as a plan for a holiday or a (contingent) plan for coping with fires. Hardly anyone doubts that there is some utility in the plans made by business firms or individual public agencies. The controversy primarily concerns forms of *comprehensive* public planning, which seek to guide and co-ordinate a considerable number of independently-based public and or private decision-makers. Examples are national economic planning, local community planing, environmental planning (national, regional, or local), and broad-based welfare planning. There is a fuzzy line between the useful but limited planning of a unitary agency and the level of comprehensive planning because (a) the definition of a unitary agency turns out to be obscure (government is in many respects an organisational continuum); (b) there are many possible and actual 'planning levels' between the unitary agency (insofar as it can be distinguished) and the totality of government; and (c) the range and scope of planning may vary very considerably – and reasonably so – at different organisational levels.

Thus clear-cut alternatives concerning the organisation of planning arise only in specific and unique contexts, and cannot be generalised. Instead in theoretical terms we can inquire only into the circumstances in which 'higher level' forms of planning might be more desirable than any alternative arrangements. How far up the ladder of comprehensive planning can governments reasonably go?: what modes and levels of such planning are the most necessary and defensible?: what range, scope, and authority must such planning possess or achieve to be worthwhile? The concept of comprehensive planning is as we have seen a composite one, entailing different mixes of range of subject-matter and range of power or authority. Some 'mixes' may be much more necessary or desirable than others, but how are we to know which?

Unfortunately most discussions of planning dodge these gritty and difficult middle-range issues. Either they are pitched at an abstract level where organisational issues are ignored, save in an illustrative or very general way; or they are concerned with the problems of particular policy sub-systems or with questions of methods and techniques.

This short paper makes only a minor claim to remedy these defects. Its first aim is to try to clarify the relationship between *intellectual* and *organisational* limitations upon the feasibility of comprehensive planning, since confusion on this point often leads to an unwarranted scepticism or pessimism about the desirable scope of planning. Secondly and more positively it is intended to sketch some of the conditions under which a considerable measure of comprehensive planning will be preferable to a more fragmented pattern of decision-making.

Intellectual and organisational limits on planning

Models of rational decision-making are contemporary intellectual toys. The requirements of a conventional model of a Herbert Simon type are too well-known to need much description. They usually include the specification of a policy problem; the conduct of the broadest possible search procedure subject to any immutable constraints; the fullest possible forecasting of the outcomes of each policy option; the evaluation of these outcomes on some schematic comparative basis, utilising cost-benefit analysis, a goals matrix, a mix of the two, or some other system; and the selection of the highest-ranking option.

The difficulties of this 'synoptic' review of policy-making have often been pointed out. In practice, it is said, neither individuals nor organisations come within sight of complying with these requirements of rationality, nor could they do so.

So far the argument is clear and the criticisms of the Simon model broadly true – indeed they have been made by Simon himself. However a sort of seachange comes over the analysis when and if these *criticisms* of *intellectual* capacity are transmitted into those of organisational capacity. It is now claimed that, because a comprehensive, synoptic approach to making decisions or policies is so very difficult, therefore organisational centralisation of decision making is erroneous because the central actor or actors must manipulate such a large number of relevant factors. By contrast centralised or fragmented forms of decision-making enable responsibilities to be factorised – thus fitting tasks more adequately to the cognitive and learning capacities of individuals or organisations. For these and other reasons, a spontaneous form of partisan mutual adjustment (PMA) among the various decision actors and centres is much to be preferred to the vain (but perhaps vainglorious) intellectual labours of central planners.

So run in summary form the now familiar arguments of the 'incrementalists'. However their transition from conclusions about intellectual to organisational phenomena is unwarranted, and occurs through a mixture of arguments which require a separate examination.

(a) It is easy to see that the Simon model of decision-making could never be closely approached as a working method because it logically entails collecting virtually an infinity of relevant data, and ordering the whole system of human values into some system of goals and constraints, or (if idealised welfare economics is preferred) of hypothesised monetary benefits and costs. Long before this point is reached, information costs become prohibitive and the elucidation and harmonisation of values becomes enormously slippery and intractable.

But this is really only to acknowledge the very limited utility of *any* model of rationality. Policies are made within an enormous context of values and constraints that can never be systematically traced, and are concerned with outcomes which can only usually be guessed at. The decision-maker must perforce confine his analysis to a limited field of phenomena whose size and shape is largely settled by extraneous and uncontrollable considerations, although the field may be extended through reflection or under pressure. 'Rationality' consists in no more than a belief in systematic treatment of the relevant data, together perhaps with a bias (which arises naturally from a systematic approach) towards widening the frontiers of analysis. The general models of rationality that can be suggested are very limited aids to the decision-maker, whose basic difficulties derive from value conflicts, the confused relations between values and facts, and the great uncertainty of outcomes.

(b) Has the comprehensive planner a more intractable or impossible *intellectual* task than someone planning on a much more modest scale? Not necessarily, if we consider the above analysis. At both levels, a Simon or similar model is an equally impossible counsel of perfection if taken literally, and an equally limited working tool if used pragmatically. It may be said that the comprehensive planner must consider a larger range of possible outcomes and criteria of evaluation, but this is not logically necessary. The number of factors considered is a matter of judgement or opinion, and the modest planner (or an individual making a minor decision) will often attend to a lot of factors, may wish that he had thought of more, and could extend his list to infinity. At both the modest and comprehensive levels of operation, the critical factors affecting the feasibility of planning do not appear primarily to be of an intellectual kind, and it is curious that the incrementalists who criticise the intellectual arrogance of the 'synoptic' approach should also exaggerate the importance for planning of rational methods.

(c) What then are the critical factors that govern the feasibility of planning at any level? One factor would seem to be the practicality or feasibility of reconciling conflicting goals, values, and interests, and in some circumstances such reconciliation becomes easier at a more comprehensive than a more limited level of operation. The realisation of this opportunity (where it exists) has nothing to do with the planner's intellectual capacity, and is a great deal more significant for the outcome of planning than his choice of intellectual models. This factor is linked with others, such as the possibility of structuring the subject-matter of planning in an effective way, and of applying to it appropriate techniques. These tasks do call for intellectual contributions from planners (or rather from professional teams), but these intellectual contributions have also be supported and legitimised by the more general perception and beliefs (Vickers' 'appreciative judgements') of politicians and of informed opinion.

(d) How much factorisation of responsibilities is necessary or desirable? One can argue for such 'factorisation' with some force on both intellectual and moral grounds. It can be said that pure intellectual ability is less important in policy-making than the old-fashioned 'quality of judgement', which is shorthand for an ability to reconcile values and to connect values with facts in relevant and effective ways that are sensitive to the public opinion though perhaps non-conformist on occasion. It is not clear that qualities of judgement in this loose sense are any more evenly distributed than intellectual capacities, but it may be that they are. Moreover, as compared with intelligence, judgement is closely linked with practical experience, and the fact that the total range of such experience is limited and must be confined to one role at a time constitutes an argument for factorising responsibility rather than unifying it. Finally it might seem that in moral sense and on democratic grounds the maximum possible factorisation and diffusion of responsibilities is desirable, because whatever the range of individual intelligence and ability it is better to stretch the capacities of average men to the utmost than to foster elitism; and this is particularly so if we accept that the solution of many policy problems requires 'judgement' (in a practical, valuational sense) more than it does intelligence.

(e) It is possible to have every sympathy and agreement with these ethical and democratic arguments (which have been of course much better expressed by Lindblom and others than I can manage here) and still to resist the conclusion that they militate against comprehensive forms of planning. The crucial question here is their practical application. There must be some limitation to the desirable dispersion and fragmentation of decision-making, but it is not clear where these limits lie. At the same time a bias in favour of the dispersion of duties and decisions runs up against the requirements of collective decision-making that derive from societal scale and social interaction. It is familiar ground that modern societies utilise sophisticated, large-scale types of technology; perform in broad and still widening economic and political arenas; are administered through complex and interlinked pyramidal systems of public agencies; and must cope somehow with a large and growing volume of socially perceived problems that include both those of simpler societies (like poverty, insecurity, injustice) and those that derive from the economic and social uses of modern technology (like pollution, traffic chaos, structural unemployment). While 'big government' and big bureaucracy have well-known defects and dysfunctions that call for amendment, societies still need the organisational tools and the forms of planning that can enable them to cope with these problems as well as is possible. Thus organisational structure cannot be adjusted to the sort of prescriptive requirement about diffusion of responsibilities which might reasonably be applied, for example, in an old-fashioned New England town meeting. Instead ethical and democratic values have to be introduced into a more relevant organisation and planning framework.

(f) Need these values therefore be lost or badly diluted? The answer is no, because the values in question depend much more upon organisational and sociological *methods* of policy-making than upon the scale or comprehensiveness of the action being undertaken. Consider a simple situation where the officials and experts who previously worked for three separate agencies are transferred to an integrated agency entrusted with a more comprehensive type of planning. Participatory, democratic, and 'organic' procedures for planning are just as practical in the new situation as the old. The likelihood of such procedures working well, or even occurring at all, will also be affected by the intrinsic feasibility of the tasks that the agency has been set. If these can in fact be better stated and realised at the higher than the lower level, organisational morale will improve and organic methods of team work which stress the 'authority of knowledge' will have a greater likelihood of success. If not the reverse will occur.

(g) Finally there is the place of partisan mutual adjustment (PMA). Common opinion would hold, and rightly, that partisanship may be a virtue (or anyhow a useful vice) in certain situations but becomes undesirable in other contexts and when pushed to extremes. In the same way PMA can have merits for the resolution of issues both within an organisation and also through the mutual reactions and accommodations of different organisations, but PMA can be excessive or inappropriate. Of course PMA, particularly in democratic societies, always exists and displays plenty of vigour, but in certain circumstances its operations can be transmitted and modified.

Typical stages of this process are: (1) separate agencies within a general policy field react and adjust to each others' acts exclusively according to their own goals and priorities; (2) the agencies are advised by a central agency while retaining their independence of action; (3) the agencies are controlled in a limited way by the guidelines established by the central agency; (4) the agencies are formally integrated within a single new organisation but retain substantial independence as sub-units; (5) a central co-ordinating and planning unit is established containing representatives (partisans) of the sub-units; (6) measures are taken to reduce or abolish the independence of the sub-units and to establish a non-aligned central planning staff.

Through all these stages PMA continues to function in some form, but its focus shifts gradually from an inter-organisation to an intra-organisational dimension. At the same time *organisational* partisanship tends to give away (to some extent) to *professional* or *intellectual* partisanship. Admittedly the development may be a confused one, since organisational and professional loyalties are blended in subtle ways. Moreover the development posited may not occur at all; for example, the independently-based actions and rivalries of a few separate organisations may merely be replaced by more intimate and petty frictions between the multiple cells (and combinations of cells) of a formally integrated organisation. In that event one suspects that the integration was mistaken, and the conditions for its successful achievement did not exist as is made clear in the next section.

Another correct common opinion is that organisational partisanship and independence, whatever its merits for concentrating responsibility and achieving specific goals, can have a myopic and frustrating influence upon the capacity of a society to recognise or to tackle higher-level types of problems. If the ground conditions do exist or can be created for some kind of comprehensive planning, then the reduction and transformation of PMA can have a liberating and innovative effect upon the exercise of skills and may enable problems to be perceived and tackled in terms which over-come some of the social frustrations and resource wastes which could be seen to occur under the previous systems. Of course again this may *not* happen – it all depends upon the nature of the situation and the organisational changes that are in fact adopted.

To summarise this section: comprehensive planning is here defined as organisational attempts to handle societal problems of a broad kind by means of investigation, analysis, and suggested solutions followed by co-ordinative measures of advice, guidance, and control applied to a broad range of actors. The two processes of problem-solving and administration unite, but they need synchronisation if planning is to be operational.

It has been urged that the feasibility of such planning does not depend in any way upon the capacity of planners to comply with formal models of rational analysis, and that the intellectual problems of comprehensive planning need be no harder or more intractable than exercises on a much more modest scale. The difficulty of resolving a given set of issues will turn upon the degree of fit between the societal characteristics of the problem on the one hand and organisational structure and capacity on the other. In some circumstances an upward organisational movement will permit intellectual formulations and resolutions of a set of issues which could previously not be attempted, save perhaps notionally and imaginatively. In other cases of course the results may merely be intellectually puzzling and organisationally frustrating.

At the same time the modification of PMA will release intellectual skills (if the conditions are right) for innovatory exercises in planning and problem-solving. Whether or not these exercises present increased intellectual difficulties, a more detached attitude itself possesses intellectual worth in certain circumstances. Most forms of comprehensive planning suffer from the difficulty that they must tackle relationships between various subjects each of which can be much more expertly handled (as a rule) by some appropriate agency and group of experts. But the more detached position of a planning agency enables it to observe the unwanted side effects and mutual frustration arising from the acts of specialised agencies, and the possession of this eyrie can be worth a lot of intellectual capital. To utilise the advantage, the planning agency needs a back-up of generalised abilities or skills in each main specialised field – a set of generalised specialists, so to speak. Thus equipped it can in some circumstances go a little way towards implementing Victor Thompson's prescription that the 'authority of hierarchy' should yield to the 'authority of knowledge'.

The conditions of comprehensive planning

Can we then formulate the conditions under which comprehensive planning is possible and desirable? To some extent I think we can.

Consider a situation where the processes of marginal incrementalism and PMA appear to be working badly. Socially perceived problems exist which fall through the net of existing organisational responsibilities, while at the same time a number of separate organisations are frustrating each other's aims and all or some of them are producing socially unwanted by-products. A comprehensive planning approach will now be possible if:

(a) The problems are structured and viewed by sufficient people in a way that permits and facilitates a comprehensive solution.
(b) The interests of concerned groups can be more effectively reconciled by comprehensive planning than under existing arrangements.
(c) Appropriate professional techniques exist or can be developed to support the technical requirements of comprehensive planning.

An example would be urban transportation planning. For a long time, public transport operators, highway authorities, and traffic management authorities (not to mention car manufacturers) pursued separate goals and worked under quite disparate financial conditions. The highway authorities could not build enough roads to satisfy the unconstrained demand for motoring, but the car boom plus the road conditions frustrated and sometimes bankrupted the transport operators. Traffic chaos and environmental blight were the unwanted results. Comprehensive planning of urban transportation is now becoming possible because:

(a) The fragmented 'pictures' of the situation held by participants and opinion leaders are being superseded by more comprehensive views or visions.

(b) The clash of interests between motorists and public transport users has been modified by a learning process, and the scope for comprehensive solutions is increasingly accepted though doubtless these solutions are differently understood and interpreted.

(c) A general profession of transportation planning is emerging that integrates (up to a point) older techniques and pulls in new disciplines.

We are here describing a learning process and in that sense the whole change is 'incrementalist'. But in another sense it is not because at some point PMA between the various agencies has to be much modified or transformed and an effective measure of comprehensive planning introduced.

Moreover the rationalist and leadership elements of the process need to be stressed. The three elements in the acceptability of comprehensive planning are respectively intellectual (new appreciative judgements); political (a new harmonisation of interests); and professional (new techniques). Putting the intellectual element first is a logical device, not a casual explanation, and the relation between ideas and interest (whether sectional or professional) need not be debated here in detail. Undoubtedly though there is a subtle two-way interrelationship going on. Interests themselves are not objectively certain and demonstrable facts, but interpretations by leaders and commentators of the alleged needs of some groups of people. In any 'interest group' there is always conflict between those taking a narrower and a broader view of the interest in question, with the latter seeking some kind of harmonisation with other related interests. In these discussions, an important part is played by appreciative judgements about the interaction of interest and the nature of the 'general interest' which is loosely conceived as a highest common factor (where positive action is sought) or as a lowest common denominator (for purposes of minimal regulation).

The intellectual basis for comprehensive planning is conveyed both in popular and political terms (through public debate and the media) and also in professional and academic terms (through for instance, learned journals). The two versions interact with each other, as well as providing the intellectual framework for (b) the reconciliation of interests and (c) the integration of professions and techniques. Thus in the urban transportation cases, popular statements about the need for integrated are now two a penny, while academic statements exist in the form of models developed by engineers, systems analysts, economist, and others. Each kind of statement has its own species of bias (undue simplification in the first case,'smuggled' value judgement in the second), and one should not assume that the academic theorising contains the greater degree of objective wisdom, although this is another subject. The point here is to note the importance for comprehensive planning of intellectual leadership in respect of how problems are viewed and structured.

If the necessary conditions do not exist comprehensive planning will not succeed although it may be attempted. An example from Britain which neatly follows the previous one is the attempt, following the Buchanan Report *Traffic in Towns*, to integrate transportation planning with physical (town and country) planning. Much administrative effort has been put into this attempt, including Departmental requirements that local authorities prepare integrated land use and transportation plans, and in the case of the Greater London Council the creation of a single integrated department and co-ordinating committee for both purposes. But the three basic conditions are inadequately met:

(a) *Traffic in Towns* provides some useful leading ideas, but nothing like an adequate intellectual blueprint for effecting such a complex integration.

(b) The reconciliation of the relevant interests is possibly harder to effect than in the case of urban transportation. It is true that in both cases a large part of the problem is to integrate the interests of the same individuals acting in different capacities.

(c) The integration of relevant professions and techniques is weak or non-existent. Town planners still speak quite a different language from transport experts. The former are theoretically a much broader profession but in practice their influence depends upon a very localised recognition of interests ('the environment' is generally a localised concern, whereas it has often been noted that transportation is one of the few issues – some claim the only issue – providing political support for metropolitan authorities). The town planners also have more diffuse goals and use 'softer' techniques than the transport experts.

Possibly I have exaggerated the differences between the feasibility of transportation planning and what may be called total environmental planning; I would not wish to be too pessimistic about the latter. But anyhow these are illustrations and two further points have to be added. Just as many motorists (or members of their families) are also public transport users, so even more obviously virtually all travellers are also interested in the enjoyment of a quiet and attractive environment. But the reciprocity of interest is less direct and less apparent in the latter case. Motorists directly frustrate each other as well as themselves or their families when using public transport; but the environments that they injure are not well correlated with the environments that they inhabit, nor do they necessarily see themselves as committing such injuries – a limitation on their appreciative judgements.

The relation between policy integration and administrative integration is a subtle one. The latter may be attempted either because the former is feasible (for instance, through comprehensive planning) or paradoxically, because it is not feasible but frequent policy conflicts are occurring which require arbitration. Thus the British Department of the Environment is not, or anyhow not yet, an instrument for comprehensive environmental planning so much as a device for the more continuous and prompt arbitration of conflicts between transportation claims and environmental claims. (The Department also has other tasks which do not concern us here.) Of course an arbitral function can shade by degrees into a planning function, and this may occur, but the roles are in principle different: an arbitrator delivers *ad hoc* judgements on the basis of the evidence (political and professional) placed before him, whereas a planner lays down the basic policy framework within which particular decisions are to be taken.

Where comprehensive planning is impractical, other remedial types of actions can still be taken. In the case of environmental-transportation conflicts, for example, it may be desirable to have a strong 'umpire' policing these conflicts, and also to broaden the education of the relevant experts – particularly in this context the transportation ones. An internalisation of more balanced professional and political attitudes, and recognition of the inevitability of policy conflicts, will be more effective than over-ambitious and necessarily superficial attempts at comprehensive planning before the time is ripe.

Conclusion
The paper has dealt with planning essentially in its old-fashioned sense of comprehensive policy-making. It has not gone into questions about the

techniques and methods of planning and their many difficulties. Great as these difficulties are, one has to remember that even badly-done planning may still sometimes be preferable to a non-planning situation. In particular, I have tried to suggest that the difficulties of planning (both intellectual and political) do not necessarily increase as planning becomes more comprehensive in its range. Organisational levels of planning have to be related to the points at which societal problems can be most effectively stated and solved, and some principles have been suggested to help the plotting of these relationships.

At the same time there is no intention here of pressing for organisational centralisation for its own sake, or of denying the advantages of polycentricity of decision-making in appropriate circumstances. It would be naive indeed to take up either position. What need more attention are the problems and feasibility of planning on different scales and at different levels, and the relation between planning and organisation. We need both descriptive and normative models of planning, and more attention to its organisational dimensions.

xiii. Humberside County Council: *Structure Plan*, volume 2, *Policies*, paras. 1. 1–1. 10.

Introduction

1.1 The Humberside Structure Plan will be set out in three volumes. 'Background Studies' contains the report to the survey of the County which has been undertaken and describes the 'social, economic and physical systems' or structure of the area. 'Participation', to be prepared after the draft policies have been discussed this summer, will describe the series of exercises in public participation which the County Council has initiated. It will record the first attempts to involve people and organisations in the decision-making process which could affect their future quite significantly. Thirdly this volume, 'Policies', is a statement of the County Council's aims and objectives which are designed to make Humberside a better place in which to live, work, move around and spend one's leisure time. It is this document that is formally submitted to the Secretary of State for the Environment for his approval although he must obviously take into account the other two complementary volumes.

1.2 The Structure Plan has been prepared quickly and in accordance with a philosophy worked out in the early days of Humberside's existence. As a new County with new boundaries and made up of parts of five previous planning authorities, there was mixed inheritance of plans and policies. Clearly, there was a need for a fresh look at many of the policies which had become outdated, an urgency about achieving some consistency and coherence throughout the new administrative area and, of course, a necessity to consider some aspects of Humberside which were subject to strong pressures for change. In particular, the Estuary, in a sense one of the reasons for the existence of Humberside, was apparently ripe for development and yet contained unique ecological features. The Humber Bridge, which was already beginning to dominate the nearby areas, was stimulating many applications for development. These situations and others called for plans to diminish the uncertainty and to lay down a purpose and sense of direction.

1.3 There was considerable dissatisfaction, however, with traditional plans with their precisely drawn blue-prints for a period of time perhaps twenty years in the future. These sorts of plans had many admirable features and yet had been inadequate policy instruments in the past with their inherent inflexibility, their tendency to be out of date before the end of the long preparation period and their inability to deal with the complexities of uncertainty about the future. Above all, there seemed to be a basic difficulty in offering a comprehensive programme of development over twenty years because this implied that we should still be dealing with today's problems in the future and not the ones which would be exciting then. In a rapidly changing world, this sort of planning is obviously no longer effective.

1.4 But it is necessary to look ahead, to have a set of aims and objectives which act as a framework for decision-making and for the allocation of scarce resources. Also, it seems reasonable in a time of low budgets and few staff to tackle the more urgent problems first. Most importantly, it is necessary to produce something of practical value to those people faced with all the difficulties of making choices in a strategic sense. It is not just the County Council which is making strategic decisions. The central government, water authorities, British Rail, British Transport Docks Board, industrialists, any number of bodies and organisations are also influential in changing the structure of the sub-region. All these people, together with individuals who live and work in the area, must therefore be involved in the process of planning since their decisions will govern and be governed by the development process. Their actions must be co-ordinated and harnessed together. Success depends upon them abiding by and helping to implement the policies they have been involved in formulating. So far over 2,000 groups have been contacted and many have contributed to the decision-making process.

1.5 Work has concentrated on those areas where change is likely and where decisions can most influence the future of Humberside. Six key issues have been identified with the help of a programme of public participation and consultation. These are 'Transport', 'Industrial Development and the Humber Estuary','Development near the Humber Bridge', 'Housing', 'Rural Settlement' and 'Shopping'. They are dealt with in turn and the same format has been adopted in each case, following, as nearly as possible, the way in which work has evolved over the past two years. Typically this involves identifying and defining the issue and looking at the existing policies to see how far they are still relevant. The facts and assumption from 'Background Studies' are summarised and the County Council's broad aims stated. Some alternative choices are considered and the favoured policy is worked up into a series of policy statements. The resources implications of the policy are explained and the important features for monitoring and review identified. Finally a schedule of short term action and medium term objectives sets out some tactical steps against which progress can be measured.

1.6 The process adopted was to draft a paper on these lines and after approval as a basis for consultation by elected members of the County Council it was sent out to the District Councils and any bodies who had an interest. A further report would be drafted on the basis of the replies received and options preferred. A policy would then be put forward for adoption and incorporation in this 'policies' volume. Everyone who had been part of the process would then be informed.

1.7 Perhaps an unusual feature of the first Humberside Structure Plant is the treatment of alternatives. Traditional methods construct an elaborate edifice of alternative strategies which are tested using various complicated techniques. Only then are policies for the particular problems or issues written into the preferred strategy. This comprehensive Master Strategy approach can ensure that inconsistencies are avoided but is perhaps unnecessarily detailed and time consuming when there is an urgent need for up to date policies and when changes quickly can render an over-elaborate strategy irrelevant. To avoid these problems, the Humberside approach concentrates on the alternative choices for each key issue rather than on those for an overall strategy. By preparing a set of policies for each of the six key issues and checking constantly that there are no obvious inconsistencies, an overall strategy has been arrived at step by step. The theme underlying the strategy is one of caution. Population is not growing substantially, the jobs outlook is uncertain and there is little money for new growth, but the experience over the past twenty years has shown how trends can change and how rapidly a seemingly insignificant innovation can radically affect our lives. So the Humberside strategy is to make the best of what we have. As long as the national recession continues this is the only real choice, but when things pick up, this strategy makes sure that Humberside is ready to play a leading part in a national economic recovery.

1.8 In Humberside the structure planning process is seen as a way of learning about the problems of the area and how they can be tackled. The main question being asked is, 'How can we develop effective ways of democratically guiding the course of the County's affairs?' The problems focus on the management of local and sub-regional change and how it can be influenced and planned, bearing in mind the vast numbers of bodies and individuals who make decisions affecting our future. Many arrangements have been made during the last two years to facilitate the flow of information between everyone involved and to synchronise the large number of different programmes of development. It is this continuous process of structure planning which has now been established with its infinitely complex network of contacts and influences, matching the equally complex systems we are attempting to control, that is perhaps the most important aspect of the work so far.

1.9 The preparation of this first Structure Plan is not an end itself; it is merely one step in the process of implementing development. More detailed proposals for specific areas will be set out in local plans which will be prepared mainly by District Planning Authorities. The Development Plan Scheme was agreed and published in 1975 and contains the full programme of local plans which will elaborate the Structure Plan policies at District level in the same way that the Structure Plan itself spells out for Humberside the regional policies worked out in association with central government. Other plans are contained, for example, in the Transport Policies and Programme (reviewed and submitted annually to the Secretary of State for the Environment) and a wide range of County Council objectives is to be found in Education and Social Services plans. The public policy-making process which has been developed in Humberside will not stop with the submission of the Structure Plan. There are always new problems to be tackled, new decisions to be taken and new views to take into account. This statement, however, reports on what has been agreed since April 1974 and lays down a foundation which can be built on in the future. The intention is to review and expand it at regular intervals.

1.10 The rest of this document comprises the background to the Structure Plan summarising the main features of the County, government policies, the positions regarding people, jobs and resources (Chapter 2–6) and the policies. Chapters 7–12 set out the main policies and proposals for the key issues together with the reasoning behind them; Chapter 13 looks at other non-key issues and describes what is being done; and Chapter 14 outlines how the County Council will seek to influence the implementation of the Plan and how the Plan will be monitored to check the success or otherwise of the policies and the validity of the basic assumptions.

Creativity in Government

xiv. Role of the Central Policy Review Staff, from *The Reorganisation of Central Government*, Cmnd. 4506, HMSO, November 1970, paras 45-8.

45. In recent years, however, it has become clear that the structure of inter-departmental committees, each concerned with a separate area of policy, needs to be reinforced by a clear and comprehensive definition of government strategy which can be systematically developed to take account of changing circumstances and can provide a framework within which the Government's policies as a whole may be more effectively formulated. For lack of such a clear definition of strategic purpose and under the pressures of the day to day problems immediately before them, governments are always at some risk of losing sight of the need to consider the totality of their current policies in relation to their longer term objectives; and they may pay too little attention to the difficult, but critical, task of evaluating as objectively as possible the alternative policy options and priorities open to them.

46. The Government recognise that the task of producing a strategic definition of objectives, in the sense describe above, is a new and formidable one and can only be approached gradually. They therefore propose to begin by establishing a small multi-disciplinary central policy review staff in the Cabinet Office.

47. This staff will form an integral element of the Cabinet Office and, like the Secretariat and other staffs in the Cabinet Office, will be at the disposal of the Government as a whole. Under the supervision of the Prime Minister, it will work for Ministers collectively; and its task will be to enable them to take better policy decisions by assisting them to work out the implications of their basic strategy in terms of policies in specific areas, to establish the relative priorities to be given to the different sectors of their programme as a whole, to identify those areas of policy in which new choices can be exercised and to ensure that

the underlying implications of alternative courses of action are fully analysed and considered.

48. The new staff will not duplicate or replace the analytical work done by departments in their own areas of responsibility. But it will seek to enlist their co-operation in its task of relating individual departmental policies to the Government's strategy as a whole. It will therefore play an important part in the extended public expenditure survey process described below, and it will also be available to promote studies in depth of interdepartmental issues which are of particular importance in relation to the control and development of the Government's strategic objectives.

POWER

The Hidden Faces of Power

xv. P. Bachrach and M.S. Baratz, 'Two Faces of Power', *American Political Science Review*, Volume 56, 1962, pp. 947–52.

The concept of power remains elusive despite the recent and prolific outpourings of case studies on community power. Its elusiveness is dramatically demonstrated by the regularity of disagreement as to the locus of community power between the sociologists and the political scientists. Sociologically oriented researchers have consistently found that power is highly centralised, while scholars trained in political science have just as regularly concluded that in 'their' communities power is widely diffused. Presumably, this explains why the latter group styles itself 'pluralist', its counterpart 'elitist'.

There seems no room for doubt that the sharply divergent findings of the two groups are the product, not of sheer coincidence, but of fundamental differences in both their underlying assumptions and research methodology. The political scientists have contended that these differences in findings can be explained by the faulty approach and presuppositions of the sociologists. We contend in this paper that the pluralists themselves have not grasped the whole truth of the matter; that while their criticisms of the elitists are sound, they, like the elitists, utilise an approach and assumptions which predetermine their conclusions. Our argument is cast within the frame of our central thesis: that there are two faces of power, neither of which the sociologists see and only one of which the political scientists see.

Against the elitist approach to power several criticisms may be, and have been, levelled. One has to do with its basic premise that in every human institution there is an ordered system of power, a 'power structure' which is an integral part and the mirror image of the organisation's stratification. This postulate the pluralists emphatically – and, to our mind, correctly – reject, on the ground that

> ...nothing categorised can be assumed about power in any community...If anything, there seems to be an unspoken notion among pluralist researchers that at bottom nobody dominates in a town, so that their first question is not likely to be, 'Who runs this community?', but rather, 'Does anyone at all run this community?' The first query is somewhat like, 'Have you stopped beating your wife?', in that virtually any response short of total unwillingness to answer will supply the researchers with a 'power elite' along the lines presupposed by the stratification theory.

Equally objectionable to the pluralists – and to us – is the sociologists' hypothesis that the power structure tends to be stable over time.

> Pluralists hold that power may be tied to issues, and issues can be fleeting or persistent, provoking coalitions among interested groups and citizens, ranging in their duration from momentary to semi-permanent...To presume that the set of coalitions which exists in the community at any given time is a timelessly stable aspect of social structure is to introduce systematic inaccuracies into one's description of social reality.

A third criticism of the elitist model is that it wrongly equates reputed with actual power:

> If a man's major life work is banking, the pluralist presumes he will spend his time at the bank, and not in manipulating community decisions. This presumption holds until the banker's activities and participations indicate otherwise...If we presume that the banker is 'really' engaged in running the community, there is practically no way of disconfirming this notion, even if it is erroneous. On the other hand, it is easy to spot the banker who really does run community affairs when we presume he does not, because his activities will make this act apparent.

This is not an exhaustive bill of particulars; there are flaws other than these in the sociological model and methodology – including some which the pluralists themselves have not noticed. But to go into this would not materially serve our current purposes. Suffice it simply to observe that whatever the merits of their own approach to power, the pluralists have effectively exposed the main weaknesses of the elitist model.

As the foregoing quotations make clear, the pluralists concentrate their attention, not upon the sources of power, but its exercise. Power to them means 'participation in decision-making' and can be analysed only after 'careful examination of a series of concrete decisions' (Dahl, 1958). As a result, the pluralist researcher is uninterested in the reputedly powerful. His concerns instead are to

1. Select for study a number of 'key' as opposed to 'routine' political decisions.
2. Identify the people who took an active part in the decision-making process.
3. Obtain a full account of their actual behaviour while the policy conflict was being resolved.
4. Determine and analyse the specific outcome of the conflict.

The advantages of this approach, relative to the elitist alternative, need no further exposition. The same may not be said, however, about its defects – two of which seem to us to be of fundamental importance. One is that the model takes no account of the fact that power may be, and often is, exercised by confining the scope of decision-making to relatively 'safe' issues. The other is that the model provides no objective criteria for distinguishing between 'important' and 'unimportant' issues arising in the political arena.

There is no gainsaying that an analysis grounded entirely upon what is specific and visible to the outside observer is more 'scientific' than one based upon pure speculation. To put it another way:

> If we can get our social life stated in terms of activity, and of nothing else, we
> have not indeed succeeded in measuring it, but we have at least reached a
> foundation upon which a coherent system of measurements can be built
> up...We shall cease to be blocked by the intervention of unmeasurable
> elements, which claim to be themselves the real causes of all that is happening,
> and which by their spook-like arbitrariness make impossible any progress
> toward dependable knowledge.   (Bentley, 1908)

The question is, however, how can one be certain in any given situation that the 'unmeasurable elements' are inconsequential, are not of decisive importance? Cast in slightly different terms, can a sound concept of power be predicated on the assumption that power is totally embodied and fully reflected in 'concrete decisions' or in activity bearing directly upon their making?

We think not. Of course power is exercised when A participates in the making of decisions that affect B. But power is also exercised when A devotes his energies to creating or reinforcing social and political values and institutional practices that limit the scope of the political process to public consideration of only those issues which are comparatively innocuous to A. To the extent that A succeeds in doing this, B is prevented, for all practical purposes, from bringing to the fore any issues that might in their resolution be seriously detrimental to A's set of preferences.

Situations of this kind are common. Consider, for example, the case – surely not unfamiliar to this audience – of the discontented faculty member in an academic institution headed by a tradition-bound executive. Aggrieved about a long-standing policy around which a strong vested interest has developed, the professor resolves in the privacy of his office to launch an attack upon the policy at the next faculty meeting. But, when the moment of truth is at hand, he sits frozen in silence. Why? Among the many possible reasons, one or more of these could have been of crucial importance:

1. The professor was fearful that his intended action would be interpreted as an expression of his disloyalty to the institution.
2. He decided that, given the beliefs and attitudes of his colleagues on the faculty, he would almost certainly constitute on this issue a minority of one.
3. He concluded that, given the nature of the law-making process in the institution, his proposed remedies would be pigeon-holed permanently. 'But whatever the case, the central point to be made is the same: to the extent that a person or group – consciously or unconsciously – creates or reinforces barriers to the public airing of policy conflicts, that person or group has power.' Or, as Schattschneider (1960, p. 71) has so admirably put it: 'All forms of political organisation have a bias in favour of the exploitation of some kinds of conflict and the suppression of others because *organisation is the mobilisation of bias*. Some issues are organised into politics while others are organised out.'

Is such bias not relevant to the study of power? Should not the student be continuously alert to its possible existence in the human institution that he studies, and be over prepared to examine the forces which brought it into being and sustain it? Can he safely ignore the possibility, for instance, that an individual or group in a community participates more vigorously in supporting the *nondecision-making* process than in participating in actual decisions within the process? Stated differently, can the researcher overlook the chance that some person or association could limit decision-making to relatively non-controversial matters, by influencing community values and political procedures and rituals, notwithstanding that there are in the community serious but latent power conflicts? To do so is, in our judgement, to overlook the less apparent, but none the less extremely important, face of power.

In his critique of the 'ruling-elite model', Dahl argues that

the hypothesis of the existence of a ruling elite can be strictly tested only if…(t)here is a fair sample of cases involving key political decisions in which the preferences of the hypothetical ruling elite run counter to those of any other likely group that might be suggested.

With this assertion we have two complaints. One we have already discussed, that is, in erroneously assuming that power is solely reflected in concrete decisions, Dahl thereby excludes the possibility that in the community in question there is a group capable of preventing contests from arising on issues of importance to it. Beyond that, however, by ignoring the less apparent face of power Dahl and those who accept his pluralist approach are unable adequately to differentiate between a 'key' and a 'routine' political decision.

Polsby, for example, proposes that 'by pre-selecting as issues for study those which are generally agreed to be significant, pluralist researchers can test stratification theory' (Polsby, 1960). He is silent, however, on how the researcher is to determine what issues are 'generally agreed to be significant', and on how the researcher is to appraise the reliability of the agreement. In fact, Polsby is guilty here of the same fault he himself has found with elitist methodology: by presupposing that in any community there are significant issues in the political arena, he takes for granted the very question which is in doubt. He accepts as issues what are reputed to be issues. As a result, his findings are fore-ordained. For even if there is no 'truly' significant issue in the community under study, there is every likelihood that Polsby (or any like-minded researcher) will find one or some and, after careful study, reach the appropriate pluralistic conclusions.

Dahl's definition of 'key political issues' in his essay on the ruling-elite model is open to the same criticism. He states that it is 'a necessary although possibly not a sufficient condition that the (key) issue should involve actual disagreement in preferences among two or more groups' (1961, p. 467). In our view, this is an inadequate characterisation of a 'key political issue', simply because groups can have disagreements in preferences on unimportant as well as on important issues. Elite preferences which border on the indifferent are certainly not significant in determining whether a monolithic or polylithic distribution of power prevails in a given community. Using Dahl's definition of 'key political issues', the researcher would have little difficulty in finding such in practically any community; and it would not be surprising then if he ultimately concluded that power in the community was widely diffused.

The distinction between important and unimportant issues, we believe, cannot be made intelligently in the absence of an analysis of the 'mobilisation of bias' in the community; of the dominant values and the political myths, rituals, and institutions which tend to favour the vested interest of one or more groups, relative to others. Armed with this knowledge, one could conclude that any challenge to the predominant values or to the established 'rules of the game' would constitute an 'important' issue; all else, unimportant. To be sure, judgements of this kind cannot be entirely objective. But to avoid making them in a study of power is both to neglect a highly significant aspect of power and thereby to undermine the only sound basis for discriminating between 'key' and 'routine' decisions. In effect, we contend, the pluralists have made each of these mistakes; that is to say, they have done just that for which Kaufman and Jones (1954) so severely taxed Floyd Hunter: they have begun 'their structure at the mezzanine without showing us a lobby or foundation', i.e., they have begun by studying the issues rather than the values and biases that are built into the political system and that, for the student of power, give real meaning to those issues which do enter the political arena.

There is no better fulcrum for our critique of the pluralist model than Dahl's recent study of power in New Haven (1961).

At the outset it may be observed that Dahl does not attempt in his work to define his concept, 'key political decision'. In asking whether the 'notables' of New Haven are 'influential overtly or covertly in the making of government decisions', he simply states that he will examine 'three different "issue-areas" in which important public decisions are made: nominations by the two political parties, urban redevelopment, and public education'. These choices are justified on the grounds that 'nominations determine which persons will hold public office. The New Haven redevelopment program measured by its cost – present and potential – is the largest in the country. Public education, aside from its intrinsic importance, is the costliest item in the city's budget.' Therefore, Dahl concludes, 'It is reasonable to expect...that the relative influence over public officials wielded by the...Notables would be revealed by an examination of their participation in these areas of activity' (p. 64).

The difficulty with this latter statement is that it is evident from Dahl's own account that the 'notables' are in fact uninterested in two of the three 'key' decisions he has chosen. In regard to the public school issue, for example, Dahl points out that many of the notables live in the suburbs and that those who do live in New Haven choose in the main to send their children to private schools. 'As a consequence,' he writes, 'their interest in the public schools is ordinarily rather slight' (p. 70). Nomination by the two political parties as an important 'issue-area', is somewhat analogous to the public schools, in that the apparent lack of interest among the notables in this issue is partially accounted for by their suburban residence – because of which they are disqualified from holding public office in New Haven. Indeed, Dahl himself concedes that with respect to both these issues the notables are largely indifferent: 'Business leaders might ignore the public schools or the political parties without any sharp awareness that their indifference would hurt their pocketbooks...' He goes on, however, to say that the prospect of profound changes (as a result of the urban-redevelopment program) in ownership, physical layout, and usage of property in the down-town area and the effects of these changes on the commercial and industrial prosperity of New Haven were all related in an obvious way to the daily concerns of businessmen (p. 71).

Thus, if one believes – as Dahl did when he wrote his critique of the ruling-elite model – that an issue, to be considered as important, 'should involve actual disagreement in preferences among two or more groups' (p. 67), then clearly he has now for all practical purposes written off public education and party nomination as key 'issue-areas'. But this point aside, it appears somewhat dubious at best that 'the relative influence over public officials wielded by the social notables' can be revealed by an examination of their nonparticipation in areas in which they were not interested.

Furthermore, we would not rule out the possibility that even on those issues to which they appear indifferent, the notables may have a significant degree of *indirect* influence. We would suggest, for example, that although they send their children to private schools, the notables do recognise that public school expenditures have a direct bearing upon their own tax liabilities. This being so, and given their strong representation on the New Haven Board of Finance, the expectation must be that it is in their direct interest to play an active role in fiscal policy-making, in the establishment of the educational budget in particular. But on this, Dahl is silent: he inquires not at all into either the decisions made by the Board of Finance with respect to education nor into their impact upon the public schools. Let it be understood clearly that in making these points we are not attempting to refute Dahl's contention that the notables lack power in New Haven. What we **are** saying, however, is that this conclusion is not adequately supported by his analysis of the 'issue-areas' of public education and party nominations.

The same may not be said of redevelopment. This issue is by any reasonable standard important for purposes of determining whether New Haven is ruled by 'the hidden hand of an economic elite' (Dahl, 1961, p. 124). For the economic notables have taken an active interest in the program and, beyond that, the socio-economic implications of it are not necessarily in harmony with the basic interests and values of businesses and businessmen.

In effort to ensure that the redevelopment program would be

In effort to ensure that the redevelopment program would be acceptable to what he dubbed 'the biggest muscles' in New Haven, Mayor Lee created the Citizens Action Commission (CAC) and appointed to it primarily representatives of the economic elite. It was given the function of overseeing the work of the mayor and other officials involved in redevelopment, and, as well, the responsibility for organising and encouraging citizens' participation in the program through an extensive committee system.

In order to weigh the relative influence of the mayor, other key officials and the members of the CAC, Dahl reconstructs 'all the *important* decisions on redevelopment and renewal between 1950–58 ...[to] determine which individuals most often initiated the proposals that were finally adopted or most often successfully vetoed the proposals of the others'. The results of this test indicate that the mayor and his development administrator were by far the most influential, and that the 'muscles' on the Commission, excepting in a few trivial instances, 'never directly initiated, opposed, vetoed or altered any proposal brought before them' (p. 131).

This finding is, in our view, unreliable, not so much because Dahl was compelled to make a subjective selection of what constituted *important* decisions within what he felt to be an *important* 'issue-area', as because the finding was based upon an excessively narrow test of influence. To measure relative influence solely in terms of the ability to initiate and veto proposals is to ignore the possible exercise of influence or power in limiting the scope of initiation. How, that is to say, can a judgement be made as to the relative influence of Mayor Lee and the CAC without knowing (through prior study of the political and social views of all concerned) the proposals that Lee did not make because he anticipated that they would provoke strenuous opposition and, perhaps, sanctions on the part of the CAC?

In sum, since he does not recognise both faces of power, Dahl is in no position to evaluate the relative influence or power of initiator and decision maker, on the one hand, and of those persons, on the other, who may have been indirectly instrumental in preventing potentially dangerous issues from being raised. As a result he unduly emphasises the importance of initiating, deciding, and vetoing, and in the process casts the pluralist conclusions of his study into serious doubt.

We have contended in this paper that a fresh approach to the study of power is called for, an approach based upon recognition of the two faces of power. Under this approach the researcher would begin – not, as does the sociologist who asks, 'Who rules?' – but by investigating the particular 'mobilisation of bias' in the institution under scrutiny. Then having analysed the dominant values, the myths and the established political procedures and rules of the game, he would make a careful inquiry into which persons or groups, if any, gain from the existing bias and which, if any, are handicapped by it. Next, he would investigate the dynamics of nondecision-making; that is, he would examine the extent to which and the manner in which the status quo oriented persons and groups influence those community values and those political institutions – as, e.g., the unanimity 'rule' of New York City's Board of Estimates (see Sayre and Kaufman, 1960, p. 640) – which tend to limit the scope of actual decision making to 'safe' issues. Finally, using his knowledge of the restrictive face of power as a foundation for analysis and as a standard for distinguishing between 'key' and 'routine' political decisions, the researcher would, after the manner of the pluralists, analyse participation in decision making of concrete issues.

We reject in advance as unimpressive the possible criticism that this approach to the study of power is likely to prove fruitless because it goes beyond an investigation of what is objectively measurable. In reacting against the subjective aspects of the sociological model of power, the pluralists have, we believe, made the mistake of discarding 'unmeasurable elements' as unreal. It is ironical that, by so doing, they have exposed themselves to the same fundamental criticism they have so forcefully levelled against the elitists: their approach to and assumptions about power predetermine their findings and conclusions.

xvi. Excerpts from S. Lukes, *Power: A Radical Analysis*, pp. 25 and 34–35.

One-dimensional view of power
Focus on (a) behaviour (b) decision–making (c) (key) issues (d) observable (overt) conflict (e) (subjective) interests, seen as policy preferences revealed by political participation

Two-dimensional view of power
(Qualified) critique of behavioural focus. Focus on (a) decision–making and nondecision–making (b) issues and potential issues (c) observable (overt or covert) conflict (d) (subjective) interests, seen as policy preferences or grievances

Three-dimensional view power
Critique of behavioural focus. Focus on (a) decision-making and control over political agenda (not necessarily through decisions) (b) issues and potential issues (c) observable (overt or covert) and latent conflict (d) subjective and real interests

Power and Interests

I have defined the concept of power by saying that A exercises power over B when A affects B in a manner contrary to B's interests. Now the notion of 'interests' is an irreducibly evaluative notion (see [8] and [5]): if I say that something is in your interests, I imply that you have a prima facie claim to it, and if I say that 'policy x is in A's interest' this constitutes a prima facie justification for that policy. In general, talk of interests provides a licence for the making of normative judgements of a moral and political character. So it is not surprising that different conceptions of what interests are associated with the different moral and political positions. Extremely crudely, one might say that the liberal takes men as they are and applies want–regarding principles to them, relating their interests to what they actually want or prefer, to their policy preferences as manifested by their political participation. The reformist, seeing and deploring that not all men's wants are given equal weight by the political system, also relates their interests to what they want or prefer, but allows that this may be revealed in more indirect and sub-political ways – in the form of deflected, submerged or concealed wants and preferences. The radical, however, maintains that men's wants may themselves be a product of a system which works against their interests, and, in such cases, relates the latter to what they would want and prefer, were they able to make the choice. Each of these three picks out a certain range of the entire class of actual and potential wants as the relevant object of his moral appraisal. In brief, my suggestion is that the one-dimensional view of power presupposes a liberal conception of interests, the two-dimensional view a reformist conception, and the three-dimensional view a radical conception. (And I would maintain that any view of power rests on some normatively specific conception of interests.)

THE ABSENCE OF CIVIL RIGHTS

xvii. Official Secrets Act, 1911, Sections 1 and 2.
An Act to re–enact the Official Secrets Act, 1889, with Amendments. [22nd August 1911.]

1. (1) If any person for any purpose prejudicial to the safety or interests of the State:
  (a) approaches or is in the neighbourhood of, or enters any prohibited place within the meaning of this Act; or
  (b) makes any sketch, plan, model, or note which is calculated to be or might be or is intended to be directly or indirectly useful to an enemy; or

(c) obtains or communicates to any other person any sketch, plan, model, article, or note, or other document or information which is calculated to be or might be or is intended to be directly or indirectly useful to an enemy;
he shall be guilty of felony, and shall be liable to penal servitude for any term not less than three years and not exceeding seven years.

(2) On a prosecution under this section, it shall not be necessary to show that the accused person was guilty of any particular act tending to show a purpose prejudicial to the safety or interests of the State, and, notwithstanding that no such act is proved against him, he may be convicted if, from the circumstances of the case, or his conduct, or his known character as proved, it appears that his purpose was a purpose prejudicial to the safety or interests of the State; and if any sketch, plan, model, article, note, document, or information relating to or used in any prohibited place within the meaning of this Act, or anything in such a place, is made, obtained, or communicated by any person other than a person acting under lawful authority, it shall be deemed to have been made, obtained, or communicated for a purpose prejudicial to the safety or interests of the State unless the contrary is proved.

2.   (1) If any person having in his possession or control any sketch, plan, model, article, note, document, or information which relates to or is used in a prohibited place or anything in such a place, or which has been made or obtained in contravention of this Act, or which has been entrusted in confidence to him by any person holding office under His Majesty or which he has obtained owing to his position as a person who holds or has held office under His Majesty, or as a person who holds or has held a contract made on behalf of His Majesty, or as a person who is or has been employed under a person who holds or has held such an office or contract,

(a) Communicates the sketch, plan, model, article, note, document, or information to any person to whom he is not authorised to communicate it, or a person to whom it is in the interest of the State his duty to communicate it, or

(b) retains the sketch, plan, model article, note, or document in his possession or control when he has no right to retain it or when it is contrary to his duty to retain it:
that person shall be guilty of misdemeanour.

(2) If any person receives any sketch, plan, model, article, note, document, or information, knowing, or having reasonable ground to believe, at the time when he receives it, that the sketch, plan, model, article, note, document, or information is communicated to him in contravention of this Act, he shall be guilty of misdemeanour, unless he proves that the communication to him of the sketch, plan, model, article, note, document, or information was contrary to his desire.

(3) A person guilty of a misdemeanour under this section shall be liable to imprisonment with or without hard labour for a term not exceeding two years, or to a fine, or to both imprisonment and a fine.

xviii. Public Order Act, 1936, Section 3, subsections 1 and 2.

3. (1) If the chief officer of police, having regard to the time or place at which and the circumstances in which any public procession is taking place or is intended to take place and to the route taken or proposed to be taken by the procession, has reasonable ground for apprehending that the procession may occasion serious public disorder, he may give directions imposing upon the persons organising or taking part in the procession such conditions as appear to him necessary for the preservation of public order, including the conditions prescribing the route to be taken by the procession and conditions prohibiting the procession from entering any public place specified in the directions:
Provided that no conditions restricting the display of flags, banners, or emblems shall be imposed under this subsection except such as are reasonably necessary to prevent risk of a breach of the peace.

(2) If at any time the chief officer of police is of opinion that by reason of particular circumstances existing in any borough or urban district or in any part thereof the powers conferred on him by the last foregoing subsection will not be sufficient to enable him to prevent serious public disorder being occasioned by the holding of public processions in that borough, district or part, he shall apply to the council of the borough or district for an order prohibiting for such period not exceeding three months as may be specified in the application the holding of all public processions or of any class of public procession so specified either in the borough or urban district or in that part thereof, as the case

may be, and upon receipt of the application the council may, with the consent of a Secretary of State, make an order either in terms of the application or such modifications as may be approved by the Secretary of State.

JUSTICE AND ADMINISTRATION

Justice and Administration are separate

xix. Excerpts from House of Lords judgement in *Local Government Board v. Arlidge, Appeal Cases*, 1915.

My Lords, it is obvious that the Act of 1909 introduced a change of policy. The jurisdiction, both as regards original applications and as regards appeals, was in England transferred from Courts of Justice to the local authority and the Local Government Board, both of them administrative bodies, and it is necessary to consider what consequences this change of policy imported.

My Lords, when the duty of deciding an appeal is imposed, those whose duty it is to decide it must act judicially. They must deal with the question referred to them without bias, and they must give to each of the parties the opportunity of adequately presenting the case made. The decision must be come to in the spirit and with the sense of responsibility of a tribunal whose duty it is to mete out justice. But it does not follow that the procedure of every tribunal must be the same. In the case of a Court of Law, tradition in this country has prescribed certain principles to which in the main procedure must conform. But what that procedure is to be in detail must depend on the nature of the tribunal. In modern times it has been increasingly common for the Parliament to give an appeal in matters which really pertain to administration, rather than to the exercise of the judicial functions of an ordinary Court, to authorities whose functions are administrative and not in the ordinary sense judicial. Such a body as the Local Government Board has the duty of enforcing obligations on the individual which are imposed in the interests of the community. Its character is that of an organisation with executive functions. In this it resembles other great departments of the State. When, therefore, Parliament entrusts it with judicial duties, Parliament must be taken, in the absence of any declaration to the contrary, to have intended it to follow the procedure which is its own, and is necessary if it is to be capable of doing its work efficiently. I agree with the view expressed in an analogous case by...Lord Loreburn. In *Board of Education v. Rice* he laid down that, in disposing of a question which was the subject of an appeal to it, the Board of Education was under a duty to act in good faith, and to listen fairly to both sides, in as much as that was a duty which lay on every one who decided anything. But he went on to say that he did not think it was bound to treat such a question as though it were a trial. The Board had no power to administer an oath, and need not examine witnesses. It could, he thought, obtain information in any way it thought best, always giving a fair opportunity to those who were parties in the controversy to correct or contradict any relevant statement prejudicial to their view. If the Board failed in this duty, its order might be the subject of certiorari and must itself be the subject of mandamus.

My Lords, I concur in this view of the position of an administrative body to which the decision of a question in dispute between parties has been entrusted. The result of its inquiry must, as I have said, be taken, in the absence of directions in the statute to the contrary, to be intended to be reached by its ordinary procedure.

Administrative Procedures ought to be Just

xx. Excerpts from the Report of the Committee on Administrative Tribunals and Public Inquiries (Franks Committee), Cmnd. 218, HMSO 1957, paras 20–34.

20. It is noteworthy that Parliament, having decided that the decisions with which we are concerned should not be remitted to the ordinary courts, should also have decided that they should not be left to be reached in the normal course of administration. Parliament has considered it essential to lay down special procedures for them.

Good administration

21. This must have been to promote good administration. Administration must not only be efficient in the sense that the objectives of policy are securely attained without delay. It must also satisfy the general body of citizens that it is proceeding with reasonable regard to the balance between the public interest which it promotes and the private interest which it disturbs. Parliament has, we infer, intended in relation to the subject-matter of our terms of reference that the further decisions or, as they may rightly be termed in this context, adjudications must be

acceptable as having been properly made.

22. It is natural that Parliament should have taken this view of what constitutes good administration. In this country government rests fundamentally upon the consent of the governed. The general acceptability of these adjudications is one of the vital elements in sustaining that consent.

Openness, fairness and impartiality

23. When we regard our subject in this light, it is clear that there are certain general and closely linked characteristics which should mark these special procedures. We call these characteristics openness, fairness and impartiality.

24. Here we need only give brief examples of their application. Take openness. If these procedures were wholly secret, the basis of confidence and acceptability would be lacking. Next take fairness. If the objector were not allowed to state his case, there would be nothing to stop oppression. Thirdly, there is impartiality. How can the citizen be satisfied unless he feels that those who decide his case come to their decision with open minds?

25. To assert that openness, fairness and impartiality are essential characteristics of our subject-matter is not to say that they must be present in the same way and to the same extent in all parts. Difference in the nature of the issue for adjudication may give good reason for difference in the degree to which the three general characteristics should be developed and applied. Again, the method by which a Minister arrives at a decision after a hearing or enquiry cannot be the same as that by which a tribunal arrives at a decision. This difference is brought out later in the Report. For the moment it is sufficient to point out that when Parliament sets up a tribunal to decide cases, the adjudication is placed outside the Department concerned. The members of the tribunal are neutral and impartial in relation to the policy of the Minister, except in so far as that policy is contained in the rules which the tribunal has been set up to apply. But the Minister, deciding in the cases under the second part of our terms of reference, is committed to a policy which he has been charged by Parliament to carry out. In this sense he is not, and cannot be, impartial.

The allocation of decisions to tribunals and Ministers

26. At this stage another question naturally arises. On what principle has it been decided that some adjudications should be made by tribunals and some by Ministers? If from a study of the history of the subject we

could discover such a principle, we should have a criterion which would be a guide for any future allocation of these decisions between tribunals and Ministers.

27. The search of this principle has usually involved the application of one or both of two notions, each with its antithesis. Both notions are famous and have long histories. They are the notion of what is judicial, its antithesis being what is administrative, and the notion of what is according to the rule of law, its antithesis being what is arbitrary.

28. What is judicial has been worked out and given expression by generations of judges. Its distinction from what is administrative recalls great constitutional victories and marks the essential difference in the nature of the decisions of the judiciary and of the executive.

29. The rule of law stands for the view that decisions should be made by the application of known principles or laws. In general such decisions will be predictable, and the citizen will know where he is. On the other hand there is what is arbitrary. A decision may be made without principle, without any rules. It is therefore unpredictable, the antithesis of a decision taken in accordance with the rule of law.

30. Nothing that we say diminishes the importance of these pairs of antitheses. But it must be confessed that neither pair yields a valid principle on which one can decide whether the duty of making a certain decision should be laid upon a tribunal or upon a Minister or whether the existing allocation of decisions between tribunals and Ministers is appropriate. But even if there is no such principle and we cannot explain the facts, we can at least start with them. An empirical approach may be the most useful.

31. Starting with the facts, we observe that the methods of adjudication by tribunals are in general not the same as those of adjudication by Ministers. All or nearly all tribunals apply rules. No ministerial decision of the kind denoted by the second part of our terms of reference is reached in this way. Many matters remitted to tribunals and Ministers appear to have, as it were, a natural affinity with one or other method of adjudication. Sometimes the policy of the legislation can be embodied in a system of detailed regulations.

Particular decisions cannot, single case by single case, alter the Minister's policy. Where this is so, it is natural to entrust the decisions to a tribunal, if not to the courts. On the other hand it is sometimes desirable to preserve flexibility of decision in the pursuance of public policy. Then a wise expediency is the proper basis of right adjudication, and the decision must be left with a Minister.

32. But in other instances there seems to be no such natural affinity. For

example, there seems to be no natural affinity which makes it clearly appropriate for appeals in goods vehicle licence cases to be decided by the Transport Tribunal when appeals in a number of road passenger cases are decided by the Minister.

33. We shall therefore respect this factual difference between tribunals and Ministers and deal separately with the two parts of the subject. When considering tribunals we shall see how far the three characteristics of openness, fairness and impartiality can be developed and applied in general and how far their development and application must be adapted to the circumstances of particular tribunals. We shall then proceed to the decisions of Ministers after hearing or inquiry and consider how far the difference in method of adjudication requires a different development and application of the three characteristics.

Policy is not our concern

34. Before concluding this Introduction we wish to emphasise that our terms of reference relate to the 'constitution and working' of tribunals and to the 'working' of certain administrative procedures. We have no concern with the policies which have given rise to the various tribunals or administrative procedures, and are not to be understood as approving or disapproving of these policies.

xxi. Excerpt from 'The Ombudsman and Captain Horsley' from Anthony King and Anne Sloman, *Westminster and Beyond*, (Macmillan, 1973), pp. 28–32.

In 'The Case of Flora Ginetio' we described in some detail how an individual Member of Parliament handled a typical constituency case: how it came to him, the government departments he got in touch with, and how eventually he got what was for him and the people who'd come to him a satisfactory outcome. In that particular case the Member of Parliament was always confident he'd get the right answer in the end – and he did.

But what if he hadn't? What if, to his surprise, the departments involved had simply dug in their heels and refused to budge? Ten years ago, even five years ago, that would have been the end of it. The M.P. couldn't really have done anything more, except maybe write an angry letter to the local paper.

Since April 1967, however, there has been something else he could do. He can now, if he wants to, refer the case to the Parliamentary Commissioner for Administration – Britain's version of the Ombudsman.

We are going to look in detail here at the office of the British Ombudsman – and at how he and his staff dealt with a fairly typical case that landed on their desks some months ago. As with Flora Ginetio, the final outcome in this case was a happy one, but, as we'll hear, the story began a very long time ago. Our hero – and hero seems the right word since he is a military man – is Captain R. C. Horsley, holder of the Military Cross and a retired regular army officer. Fully twenty years ago Captain Horsley, who is now seventy-eight and lives with his wife and a very large, friendly dog on the edge of Dartmoor, applied for a war pension. He suffered from a gastric ulcer which he believed to have been caused by his service during the First World War and aggravated during the Second. The Ministry of Pensions, as it then was, rejected Captain Horsley's application. 'Why?' we asked of him.

HORSLEY: Chiefly, I think, because they thought that far too much was probably going to be spent on pensions generally. And they framed the regulations accordingly. So that people who went up to get a pension, with every prospect of getting one, to their amazement found that they were turned down. The very obvious cases – for instance, like losing an arm or a leg or something like that – the very obvious cases they often treated quite generously. But the borderline cases were certainly not treated well. Indeed, they were treated completely ruthlessly.

KING: And the department looked on you as a borderline case?

HORSLEY: Most definitely, in face of all evidence. Not only the evidence in my medical record, but the evidence on me. So naturally I was very indignant about it, but I went on trying and just nothing happened.

KING: At first, there wasn't a great deal Captain Horsley could do, beyond putting his case to the Pensions Appeal Tribunal. This he did, but again his application was turned down. Then a long time later, in 1965, a decision in one of the courts had the effect of making it probable that, if he were to reapply, this time his application would be successful. But, of course, nobody told him about the court's decision. And it wasn't until four years had passed, in 1969, that he finally heard about it, quite by chance from a friend. What happened next?

HORSLEY: Well, I went to the Officers' Association because, when I was nearly dead and given up, my wife nursed me back to health again, but the Officers' Association and the British Legion between them got things moving, you see, on my behalf – thanks to the efforts of these officers. And the War Office handed me what they called compassionate pension for good service, but it wasn't a disability pension, you see. And I was entitled to one and I was jolly well going to get it if I could, and when I got better I went on fighting. And when I eventually got it, you see –

much to my surprise, I may say – when I eventually got it, I said: 'Right, you see, you blighters have done me down for twenty years, I don't see why I shouldn't have my arrears.'

KING: And that was the nub of the matter. Captain Horsley had got his pension all right, but it was to be paid only from the day in 1969 when those acting for him had got in touch with the Department of Health and Social Security. It certainly wasn't backdated to 1951 when he'd first applied. It wasn't even going to be backdated to 1965, the date of the court decision that affected him even though he didn't know about it. Captain Horsley thought this was pretty monstrous. And it was at this point that the Officers' Association suggested he probably ought to get in touch with his M.P. Captain Horsley's M.P. is Peter Mills, the Conservative Member for the Torrington Division, which takes in that part of Dartmoor. I asked Mr Mills how Captain Horsley's predicament had first come to his notice.

MILLS: Well, he wrote to me, as many of my constituents do about their various problems. And I read his letter and immediately I was sympathetic to what he had to say and his problem. Now this isn't always so, but I was in this case.

KING: Being sympathetic, Peter Mills could have done a number of different things. He could have written to the relevant Minister, Sir Keith Joseph; he could have put down a Question in Parliament; he could, as I have said before, have written angry letters to the papers. But in fact he did none of these things and instead referred the case straight away to the Parliamentary Commissioner for Administration, the Ombudsman. And he explained why.

MILLS: By his letter I could see that he'd tried every avenue there was. And, as I say, one almost develops a sort of second sense as to whether a thing is genuine or not, and I felt this ought to go straight to the Ombudsman – for him to decide, of course, whether it was in his range for him to be able to do something about it.

KING: So now the case was on the Ombudsman's desk. More than that, it had arrived on his desk via the only route it could have travelled: not directly from Captain Horsley, but from Captain Horsley through a Member of Parliament. In Britain, unlike a number of other countries, you can't write directly to the Ombudsman with your problem. You have first to approach a Member of Parliament – not necessarily your own M.P., any M.P. Indeed, apart from some people's dislike of foreign words, that's the main reason why the British Ombudsman isn't formally called the Ombudsman but the Parliamentary Commissioner for Administration: the emphasis is on the word 'Parliamentary'. Practically everybody calls him the Ombudsman all the same, as Peter Mills confirms.

MILLS: It's very strange: if you gave him his proper title people wouldn't know him at all. But by this strange – what is it? – Swedish or Danish name, 'Ombudsman', he is known to a very large number of people. And all I can say is that, when people write in when they are dismayed, frustrated, angry at my decision, they say: 'Will you please put this to the Ombudsman?'

KING: The Ombudsman at the moment is Sir Alan Marre, a former senior civil servant, who was appointed to succeed the first holder of the office, Sir Edmund Compton, early in 1970. He and his staff of just under sixty people work on the first and second floors of Church House, a large ecclesiastical-looking office building just round the corner from Westminster Abbey. I put it to Sir Alan that, when a case is referred to him by an M.P., he first has to decide whether it falls within his jurisdiction.

MARRE: This is so. We have what we call a screening test in the office, testing the cases that come to us against various provisions in the Act which exclude things from jurisdiction.

KING: What broadly falls within your jurisdiction? What sort of things can you handle?

MARRE: Broadly what falls within my jurisdiction are complaints against government departments.

KING: But not complaints against, say the nationalised industries and local authorities?

MARRE: No. Nor complaints against hospital authorities either.

KING: So the British Ombudsman – again unlike the Ombudsman in some other countries – isn't permitted under the law to take up every case involving government that is brought to him. Local government is left out, so are the Regional Hospital Boards and so are the big public corporations – the National Coal Board and so on. All he can deal with are cases – and not even all of these – which concern departments of central government – Whitehall, in other words. As regards Whitehall, the Ombudsman's remit is to concern himself with cases of maladministration, or at least suspected maladministration. And what, you may well ask, is maladministration? I asked Sir Alan.

MARRE: The Act itself under which I operate contains no definition of maladministration. And Mr Crossman, who was then Leader of the House, and was piloting the Bill through the House, explained maladministration as best he could by what came to be known as 'the Crossman catalogue'.

KING: And what's in the catalogue?

MARRE: In the catalogue he listed as examples 'bias, neglect, inattention, delay, incompetence, ineptitude, perversity, turpitude, arbitrariness', and so on.

KING: I take it you are not concerned with the question of justice:

provided an unjust decision was reached in a proper way, that's all you need to know about?

MARRE: This is exactly so. The Act itself precludes me from questioning what are called the merits of decisions which are reached without maladministration.

KING: In other words, if Sir Alan Marre is to investigate a case, he must have some reason to think, not just that a particular decision taken somewhere in government is a wrong decision or an unfair decision, he must suspect that the decision was not arrived at properly or is in some way clearly indefensible. In practice it's well up to the Ombudsman to define maladministration as he goes along – by the kinds of cases he takes up and the kinds he leaves alone. Alan Marre described the procedure he follows when a case like Captain Horsley's comes up.

MARRE: When I received a complaint through a Member of Parliament, my first step is to arrange to get advice within the office on jurisdiction. If I'm satisfied that it is within jurisdiction, I then refer the case to the department for their comments. When I receive their comments, I then refer it to the unit in my office which is concerned with the affairs of that department. And what then happens normally is that the unit will get hold of the files – sometimes they are very bulky files – from the department; they will interview officers of the department to supplement information on the file or information which has been received with the complaint; and they will also interview in many cases the complainant himself and other people.

REFERENCES

Acton Society Trust, 1968: Statement of Evidence to the Fulton Committee, by Trevor Smith, December.

Aldous, T, 1972: *Battle for the Environment*, Fontana.

Allison, L, 1975: *Environmental Planning*, G. Allen and Unwin.

Anderson, J, 1975: *Public Policy-Making*, Nelson.

Audit Commission, 1983: *The Impact on Local Authorities' Economy, Efficiency and Effectiveness of the Block Grant Distribution System*.

Bachrach, P and Baratz, M S, 1962: 'Two Faces of Power', *American Political Science Review*, Volume 56, pp. 947-52.

Bains Report, 1972: *The New Local Authorities: Management and Structure*, Department of the Environment.

Balogh, T, 1959: 'The Apotheosis of the Dilettante'. Republished several times; see H Thomas (ed.), 1968, pp. 11-52.

Banfield, E C, 1961: *Political Influence*, Free Press of Glencoe.

Barberis, P and Skelton, A, 1987: 'Oldham Borough Council', in Elcock, H and Jordan A G(eds), 1987, pp 78-87.

Barker, R, 1986: 'Rise of the Great Pretenders', The Times Higher Education Supplement, 4th April.

Barlow, J, 1987: 'Lancashire County Council', in Elcock and Jordan (eds), 1987, pp. 37-49.

Barratt, J, and Downs, J, 1988: *Organising for Local Government: A Local Political Responsibility*, Longman and Local Government Training Board.

Barrett, S and Fudge, C (eds), 1982: *Policy and Action*, Methuen and Co.

Beaverbrook, Lord, 1963: *The Decline and Fall of Lloyd George and Great was the Fall Thereof*, Collins.

Bellamy, C and Franklin, R, 1985: 'BTEC's Educational Policy and Public Administration', *Teaching Politics*, Volume 14, pp. 160-73.

Benewick, R J, Birch, A H, Blumler and A Ewbank, 1969: 'The Floating Voter and the Liberal View of Representation', *Political Studies*, Volume 17, pp. 177-95.

Benn, A W, 1980: 'Manifestoes and Mandarins', in Royal Institute of Public Administration, *Policy and Practice: The Experience of Government*.

Bevins, R, 1965: *The Greasy Pole*, Hodder and Stoughton.

Birch, A H, 1964: *Representative and Responsible Government*, G. Allen and Unwin.

Blackstone, T and Plowden, W, 1988: *Inside the Think Tank: Advising the Cabinet 1971–1983*, Heinemann.

Booth, S and Pitt, D C, 1984: 'Continuity and Discontinuity: IT as a Force for Organisational Change', in Pitt, D and Smith, B C (eds) *The Computer Revolution in Public Administration*, pp. 17-38.

Boyle, E, 1965: 'Who are the Policy-Makers? 1. The Minister', *Public Administration*, Volume 43, pp. 252-9.

Braine, J, 1957: *Room at the Top*, Penguin Books.

Bridges, Lord, 1950: *Portrait of a Profession*, Cambridge University Press.

Brittan, S, 1969, 'The Irregulars', in R Rose (ed.) *Policy-Making in British Government*, Macmillan, pp. 329-39.

Brittan, S, 1988: *A Restatement of Economic Liberalism*, Second edition, Macmillan.

Brown, R G S, 1975: *The Management of Welfare*, Fontana.

Brown, R G S, 1978: *Reorganising the National Health Service*, B Blackwell.

Brown, R G S, 1979: *Reorganising the National Health Service: A Case Study of Administrative Change*, B Blackwell and M Robertson.

Bryson, J, 1988: 'Strategic Planning: Big Wins and Small Wins', *Public Money and Management*, Volume 8, No. 3, Autumn, pp. 11-15.

Buchanan Report, 1963: *Traffic in Towns*, Her Majesty's Stationery Office.

Budd, A, 1978: *The Politics of Economic Planning*, Fontana/Collins.

Bulpitt, J G, 1969: *Party Politics in English Local Government*, Longman, Green and Co.

Butler, D E and Kavanagh, D A, 1971: *The British General Election of 1970*, Macmillan.

Butler, D E and Kavanagh, D A, 1979: *The General Election of 1979*, Macmillan.

Butler-Sloss Report, 1988: *Report of the Inquiry into Child Abuse in Cleveland, 1987*, Cm. 412, Her Majesty's Stationery Office.

Campbell, C and Peters, B Guy (eds) 1989: *Organising Governance, Governing Organisations*, University of Pittsburg Press.

Castle, B, 1980: *The Castle Diaries, 1974-1976*, Weidenfeld and Nicolson

Chandler, J, 1987: *Policy-Making for Local Government,* Croom Helm.

Chapman, L, 1978: *Your Disobedient Servant*, Chatto and Windus.

Chapman, R A, 1973: 'The Vehicle and General Affairs', *Public Administration,* Volume 51, pp. 273-90.

Chapman, R A, 1988a: *Ethics in the British Civil Service*, Routledge.

Chapman, R A, 1988b: 'The Next Steps: A Review', *Public Policy and Administration*, Volume 3, pp. 3-10.

Chapman, R A, 1988c: *The Art of Darkness*, Inaugural Lecture delivered at the University of Durham and published by that University.

Chapman, R A and Hunt, M (eds), 1986: *Open Government*, Croom Helm.

Chapman Pincher, 1988: *Too Secret Too Long*, New English Library.

Charlton, J and Martlew, C: 'Stirling District Council', in Elcock and Jordan (eds), 1987, pp. 181-99.

Chartered Institute of Public Finance and Accountancy: Local Government Statistics, published annually in *Public Finance and Accountancy*.

Chester, D N, 1954: 'The Crichel Down Affair', *Public Administration,* Volume 32, pp. 389-402.

Chinkin, M and Bailey, R J, 1976: 'The Local Ombudsmen', *Public Administration*, Volume 54, pp. 267-82.

Clarke, M and Stewart, J D, 1988: *Managing Tomorrow*, Local Government Training Board.

Clements, R, 1987: 'Avon County Council' in Elcock and Jordan (eds), 1987, pp. 25-36.

Club of Rome, 1970: *Limits to Growth*, Penguin Books.

Cmnd. 4506, 1970: *The Reorganisation of Central Government*, Her Majesty's Stationery Office.

Cmnd. 8616, 1982: *Efficiency and Effectiveness in the Civil Service*, Her Majesty's Stationery Office.

Cockburn, C, 1975: *The Local State*, Pluto Press.

Connolly, M and McChesney, R, 1987: 'Belfast City Council', in Elcock and Jordan (eds), 1987, pp. 227-42.

Coombes, D, 1967: *The MP and the Administration: The Case of the Select Committee on the Nationalised Industries*, G. Allen and Unwin/Hull University Press.

Cousins, P, 1984: 'Local Prime Ministers', *Teaching Public Administration,* Volume 4, No.2, pp. 44-50.

Cox, A, Furlong, P and Page, E, 1985: *Power in Capitalist Society: Themes, Explanations and Cases,* Wheatsheaf Books.

Crick, B, 1962: *The Reform of Parliament,* Weidenfeld and Nicolson.

Crisp, R, 1989: 'Deciding Who Will Die: QALYs and Political Theory', *Politics,* Volume 9, pp. 31-5.

Crossman, R H S, 1975-1977: *The Diaries of a Cabinet Minister,* (3 Volumes) Hamish Hamilton and Jonathan Cape:
Volume 1: *Minister of Housing and Local Government,* 1964-1966.
Volume 2: *Lord President of the Council,* 1966-1968.
Volume 3: *Secretary of State for Social Services,* 1968-1970.

Cullingworth, J B, 1967: *Town and Country Planning,* Second Edition, G. Allen and Unwin.

Dahl, R A, 1962: *Who governs?* University of Yale Press.

Day, J and Klein, R, 1987: *Accountabilities: Five Public Services,* Tavistock Publications.

Dearlove, J, 1979: *The Reorganisation of British Local Government: Old Orthodoxies and a Political Perspective,* Cambridge University Press.

Department of Economic Affairs, 1965: *The National Plan,* Cmnd. 2764, Her Majesty's Stationery Office.

Department of the Environment, 1974: Circular 98/74, *Structure Plans,* Her Majesty's Stationery Office.

Department of the Environment, 1979: *Organic Change in Local Government,* Cmnd. 7457, Her Majesty's Stationery Office.

Department of the Environment, 1983: *Streamlining the Cities,* Cmnd. 9063, Her Majesty's Stationery Office.

Department of the Environment, 1986: *The Future of Development Plans: A Consultation Paper.*

Department of Health and Social Security, 1972: *Management Arrangements in the Reorganised National Health Service* (the 'Grey Book'), Her Majesty's Stationery Office.

Department of Health and Social Security, 1976a: *Priorities in the Health and Personal Social Services in England: A Consultative Document,* Her Majesty's Stationery Office.

Department of Health and Social Security, 1976b: *The National Health Service Planning System* (the 'Blue Book'), Her Majesty's Stationery Office.

Department of Health and Social Security, 1977: *The Way Forward,* Her Majesty's Stationery Office.

Department of Health and Social Security, 1979: *Patients First:* Consultative Paper on the Structure and Management of the National Health Service in England and Wales, Her Majesty's Stationery Office.

Department of Health and Social Security, 1981: *Care In Action,* Her Majesty's Stationery Office.

Deutsch, K, 1966: *The Nerves of Government,* Free Press of Glencoe.

Donnison, D, 1961: *Health, Welfare and Democracy in Greater London,* Greater London Group.

Donoughmore Committee, 1931: Report of the Committee on Ministers' Powers, Cmd. 4060, Her Majesty's Stationery Office.

Downs, A, 1957: *An Economic Theory of Democracy,* Harper and Row.

Drewry, G, 1982: *Law, Justice and Politics*, Longman.

Dror, Y, 1973: *Public Policy-Making Re-Examined*, Leonard Hill.

Dror, Y, 1975: 'Policy Analysis for Local Government', *Local Government Studies*, New Series, Volume 1, pp. 33-46.

Dunsire, A, 1973: *Administration: The Word and the Science*, Martin Robertson.

Dunsire, A *et al.*, 1981: *Bureaumetrics: The Quantitative Analysis of British Central Government Agencies*, Gower Press.

Dunsire, A, 1989: *Holistic Governance*, the Frank Stacey Memorial Lecture, Public Policy and Administration, 1990, (forthcoming)

Easton, D, 1965: *A Systems Analysis of Political Life*, Wiley.

Eckstein, H, 1957: *Pressure Group Politics*, G. Allen and Unwin.

Eddison, T, 1973: *Local Government: Management and Corporate Planning*, L. Hill and INLOGOV.

Efficiency Unit, 1988: *Management in Government: The Next Steps*, Her Majesty's Stationery Office.

Elcock, H J, 1969a: *Administrative Justice*, Longman Green and Co.

Elcock, H J, 1969b: 'Justice and the Political Order', *Political Studies*, Volume 17, pp. 394-412.

Elcock, H J, 1971: 'Opportunity for Ombudsman: The Northern Ireland Commissioner for Complaints', *Public Administration*, Volume 50, pp. 87-93.

Elcock, H J, 1976: *Political Behaviour*, Methuen.

Elcock, H J, 1978: 'Regional Government in Action: The Members of Two Regional Health Authorities', *Public Administration*, Volume 56, pp. 379-98.

Elcock, H J, 1979a: *Strategic Planning Processes in Regional and Local Government*, Hull Papers in Politics No. 5, Department of Politics, University of Hull.

Elcock, H J, 1979b: 'Politicians, Organisations and the Public: The Provision of Gypsy Sites', *Local Government Studies*, May/June, pp. 43-54.

Elcock, H J, 1981: 'Tradition and Change in Labour Politics: The Decline of the City Boss', *Political Studies*, Volume 29, pp. 439-47.

Elcock, H J, (ed) 1982: *What Sort of Society? Economic and Social Policy in Modern Britain*, Martin Robertson.

Elcock, H J, 1983: 'Disabling Professionalism: The Real Threat to Local Democracy', *Public Money*, Volume 3, pp. 23-27.

Elcock, H J, 1984: 'Information Technology: Stopping Big Brother Watching Us, in Pitt and Smith, 1984 pp. 175-190.

Elcock, H J, 1985: Culting Chiefs as well as Indians: The Wardale Review of the Open Structure, *Teaching Public Administration*, Volume 5, No.1, pp. 11-20

Elcock, H J, 1986a: *Local Government: Politicians' Professionals and the Public in Local Authorities*, Second Edition, Methuen and Co.

Elcock, H J, 1986b: 'Going Local in Humberside: Decentralisation as a Tool for Social Services Management', *Local Government Studies*, July/August, pp. 35-49.

Elcock, H J, 1987: *Modelling the Budgetary Process in Local Government*, Local Authority Management Unit Discussion Paper No. 87/2, Newcastle upon Tyne Polytechnic.

Elcock, H J, 1988: 'Alternatives to Representative Government in Britain: Going Local', *Public Policy and Administration*, Volume 3, No. 2, pp. 38-50.

Elcock, H J, Fenwick, J and Harrop, K, 1988: *Partnerships for Public Service*, Local Authority Management Unit Discussion Paper No. 88/2, Newcastle upon Tyne Polytechnic.

Elcock, H J, and Haywood, S C, 1980: *The Buck Stops Where? Accountability and*

Control in the National Health Service, Institute for Health Studies, University of Hull.

Elcock, H J, and Haywood, S, 1981: 'The Centre Cannot Hold... : Accountability and Control in the National Health Service', *Public Administration Bulletin*, No. 36, August, 1981.

Elcock, H J, and Jordan, A G (eds), 1987: *Learning from Local Authority Budgeting*, Avebury Press.

Elcock, H J, Jordan, A G and Midwinter, A F, 1989: *Budgeting in Local Government: Managing the Margins: The Budgetary Process in Local Authorities*, Longman.

Elcock, H J and Stephenson, M, 1985: 'Can We Improve Public Policy?', in Stephenson, M and Elcock, H, *Public Policy and Management: Case Studies in Improvement*, Polytechnic Products, Newcastle upon Tyne.

Etzioni, A, 1968: *The Active Society*, Free Press of Glencoe.

Etzioni, A, 1969: *The Semi-Professions and their Organisation*, Free Press of Glencoe.

Fenwick, J and Harrop, K, 1988: *Consumer Responses to Local Authority Services: Note Towards an Operational Model*, Local Authority Management Unit Discussion Paper No. 88/1, Newcastle upon Tyne Polytechnic.

Fenwick, J, Harrop, K and Elcock, H J, 1989: *The Public Domain in an English Region: Aspects of Adaptation and Change in Public Authorities,* Studies in Public Policy, University of Strathclyde, 1989.

Fiennes, G F, 1967: *I Tried to Run a Railway*, Ian Allen.

Finer, S E, 1956: *Anonymous Empire*, Pall Mall Books.

Franks Report, 1957: *Administrative Tribunals and Public Inquiries*, Cmnd. 218, Her Majesty's Stationery Office.

Friedman, M and Friedman, R, 1980: *Free to Choose,* Penguin Books.

Friend, J K and Jessop, W N, 1969: *Local Government and Strategic Chance,* Tavistock Press.

Friend, J, Power, J M and Yewlett, C J L, 1977: *Public Planning: The Inter-Corporate Dimension*, Tavistock Press.

Fry, G K, Flynn, A, Gray, A, Jenkins, W, and Rutherford, B, 1988: 'Symposion on Improving Management in Government', *Public Administration*, Volume 66, pp. 429-445.

Fulton Committee, 1968: *The Civil Service*, Cmnd. 3638, Her Majesty's Stationery Office.

Volume 1 Report of the Committee
Volume 2 Report of the Management Consultancy Group
Volume 5 Evidence.

Furlong, P, Page, E and Cox A W, 1985: *Power in Capitalist Society: Theory, Explanations and Cases*, Wheatsheaf Books.

Galbraith, J K, 1963: *American Capitalism: The Concept of Countervailing Power*, Penguin Books.

Garlicki, L, 1987: 'Constitutional and Administrative Courts as Custodians of the State Constitutions: The Experience of East European Countries', *Tulane Law Review*, Volume 61, pp.1285-1306.

Garrett, J, 1980; *Managing the Civil Service*, Heinemann.

Glen, J H W, 1948: 'Changes in the Structure of Local Government', *Proceedings of the Institute of Municipal Treasurers and Accountants*, pp. 259-270.

Gower Davies, J, 1972: *The Evangelistic Bureaucrat*, Tavistock Press.

Gray, A and Jenkins, W, 1985: *Administrative Politics in British Government,* Wheatsheaf Books.

Greenleaf, W H, 1966: *Michael Oakshott's Philosophical Politics*, Longman, Green and Co.

Greenwood, R, 1983: 'Changing Patterns of Budgeting in English Local Government,' *Public Administration*, Volume 61, pp. 149-68.

Greenwood, R, 1987: 'Managerial Strategies in Local Government', *Public Administration*, Volume 65, pp. 295-312.

Greenwood, R, Hinings, C R, Ranson, S and Stewart, J D, 1978: *Patterns of Management in Local Government*, Martin Robertson.

Greenwood, R, Hinings, C R, Ranson, S and Stewart J D, 1980: 'The Budgetary Process in English Local Government', *Political Studies*, pp. 25-47.

Greenwood, R, Hinings, C R, Ranson, S and Walsh, K, 1976: *In Pursuit of Corporate Rationality*, Institute of Local Government Studies, University of Birmingham.

Greenwood, R and Stewart, J D (eds), 1974: *Corporate Management in Local Government*, INLOGOV and Charles Knight.

Gregory, R and Hutchesson, P G, 1975: *The Parliamentary Ombudsman*, G. Allen and Unwin.

Griffith, J A G, 1961: 'The Future of Local Government', *Municipal Journal,* pp. 804-806, 809 & 818.

Griffith, J A G, 1966: *Central Departments and Local Authorities*, G. Allen and Unwin.

Griffith, J A G, 1977: *The Politics of the Judiciary*, Fontana Books.

Gunn, L, 1988: 'Public Management: A Third Approach?', *Public Money and Management*, Volume 1, pp. 21-6.

Gyford, J, 1984: *The Politics of Local Socialism*, G. Allen and Unwin.

Hague, D C, 1971: 'The Ditchley Conference: A British View', in BLR Smith and D C Hague (eds), *The Dilemma of Accountability in Modern Government*, Macmillan, pp.70-99.

Ham, C, 1985 : *Health Policy in Britain*, 2nd Edn., Studies in Social Policy, Macmillan.

Ham, C and Hill, M, 1983: *The Policy Process in the Modern Capitalist State*, Wheatsheaf Books.

Harrop, K H, Mason, T, Vielba, C A and Webster, B A, 1978: *The Implementation and Development of Area Management*, Institute of Local Government Studies, University of Birmingham.

Harvey Jones, J, 1988: *Making It Happen*, Collins.

Hayek, F Von, 1944: *The Road to Serfdom*, Routledge and Kegan Paul.

Haynes, R J, 1980: *Organisation Theory and Local Government*, G. Allen and Unwin.

Hayward, J E S, 1975: 'The Politics of Planning in Britain and France', *Comparative Politics*, Volume 7, pp. 285-298.

Haywood, S, 1977: 'Decision-Making in Local Government : The Case of an Independent Council', *Local Government Studies*, Volume 3, pp. 41-55.

Haywood, S and Alaszewski, A, 1980: *Crisis in the NHS: The Politics of Management*, Croom Helm.

Haywood, S and Elcock, H, 1982: 'The Regional Health Authorities' in B Hogwood and M Keating (eds), *Regional Government in England*, Oxford University Press, 1982.

Heclo, H and Wildavsky, A V, 1974: *The Private Government of Public Money*, Macmillan.

Hepworth, N, 1984: *The Finance of Local Government*, G. Allen and Unwin.

Hewart, G, 1929: *The New Despotism*, Benn.

Hewitt, P, 1982: *The Abuse of Power: Civil Liberties in the United Kingdom*, Martin Robertson.

Hill, D, 1970: *Participation in Public Affairs*, Penguin.

Hill, M and Barrett S, 1985: 'Implementation Theory and Research: A New Branch of Policy Studies or a New Name for Old Interests?' Paper read to Political Studies Conference, 1982.

Hoggett, P, and Hambleton, R, 1987: *Decentralisation and Democracy,* School of Advanced Urban Studies, University of Bristol.

Hogwood, B and Gunn, L, 1984: *Policy Analysis for the Real World*, Oxford University Press.

Hood, C C and McKenzie, W J M, 1975: 'The Problem of Classifying Institutions', Appendix 3 of D C Hague, W J M McKenzie and A Barker, *Public Policy and Private Interests: The Institutions of Compromise*, pp. 409-20, Macmillan.

Humberside County Council, 1975: *Transport Policies and Programme.*

Humberside County Council, 1976: *The Humberside Structure Plan*:
  Volume 1: *Background Studies*
  Volume 2: *Policies*
  Volume 3: *Participation.*

Hunter, F, 1953, *Community Power Structure*, University of North Carolina Press.

Illich, I, Zola, I K, McKnight, J, Caplan, J and Shaiken, H, 1977: *Disabling Professions*, M. Boyars.

Isaac-Henry, K, 1980: 'The English Local Authority Associations', *Public Administration Bulletin*, No. 33, pp. 21-41.

Islington Borough Council, 1987: *Going Local: Decentralisation in Practice.*

Jay, P, 1968: 'Whitehall's Brain Drain', Evidence to Fulton Committee, Volume 5, Memorandum No. 32, pp. 929-38.

Jennings, 1977: *Education and Politics: Policy-Making in Local Education Authorities*, Batsford.

Jones, G W, 1964: 'County Borough Expansion: The Local Government Commissioners' View', *Public Administration*, Volume 42, pp. 277-89.

Jones, G W, 1965: 'The Prime Minister's Power', *Parliamentary Affairs*, Volume 18, pp.167-85.

Jones, G W, 1987: 'The United Kingdom', in W Plowden (ed), *Advising the Rulers*, B. Blackwell.

Jones, G W and Norton, A, 1979: *Political Leadership in Local Authorities,* Institute of Local Government Studies, University of Birmingham.

Jones, G W and Stewart, J D, 1984: *The Case for Local Government*, G. Allen and Unwin.

Jordan, A G, 1982: 'Iron Triangles, Woolly Corporatism and Elastic Nets: Images of the Policy Process', *Journal of Public Policy*, Volume 1, pp.95-123.

Jordan, A G, 1987: 'Introduction. Budgeting: Changing Expectations', in H Elcock and A G Jordan 1987, pp. 1-22.

Kalton, G, 1966: *Introduction to Statistical Ideas for Social Scientists*, Chapman and Hall.

Keynes, J M, 1923: *The Collected Writings of John Maynard Keynes*, Volume 8, *A Treatise on Probability*, Royal Economic Society.

Kingdom, J, 1986: 'Public Administration: Defining the Discipline', *Teaching Public Administration*, Volume 6, pp. 1-13.

Kingdom, T D, 1966: 'The Confidential Advisers of Ministers,' *Public Administration*, Volume 44, pp. 267-74.

Klein, R, 1983: *The Politics of the National Health Service*, Longman.

Kogan, M and van der Eycken, W, 1973: *County Hall: The Role of the Chief Education Officer*, Penguin Books.

Kolankiewicz, G and Lewis, P G 1988: *Poland: Politics, Economy and Society*, Pinter Books.

Leach, S, Game, C and Gyford, J, 1989: *The Changing Politics of Local Government*, Unwin Hyman.

Levin, P, 1979: 'Highway Inquiries: A Study of Governmental Responsiveness', *Public Administration*, Volume 57, pp. 21-50.

Lindblom, C E, 1959: 'Incrementalism: The Science of Muddling Through', *Public Administration Review*, Volume 19, pp. 78-88.

Lindblom, C E, 1965: *The Intelligence of Democracy*, Free Press.

Lindblom, C E, 1979: 'Still Muddling, Not Yet Through', *Public Administration Review*, Volume 39, pp. 517-526.

Lipset, S M, 1963: *Political Man*, Mercury Books.

Lipsky, M, 1980: *Street-Level Bureaucracy*, Russell Sage.

Lucas, J R, 1967: *The Principles of Politics*, Oxford University Press.

Lukes, S, 1977: *Power: A Radical Analysis*, Macmillan.

Lynn, J and Jay, A, 1981 and following: *Yes, Minister: The Memoirs of the Rt. Hon. James Hacker*, British Broadcasting Corporation.

Mackintosh, J P, 1968: 'Failure of a Reform', *New Society*, 28 November 1968.

Mallaby Report, 1966: *The Staffing of Local Government*, Her Majesty's Stationery Office.

Marshall, G, 1965: *Police and Government*, Methuen.

Marshall, G, 1970: 'Parliament and the Ombudsman', in Study of Parliament Group, 1970, pp. 114-29.

Marshall, G and Moodie, G, 1959: *Some Problems of the Constitution,* Hutchinson.

Matheson, S, 1984: 'Computerising the Pay as You Earn System', in Pitt and Smith, 1984, pp. 99-104.

Maud Report, 1967: *The Management of Local Government*, Her Majesty's Stationery Office.

McKenzie, R T, 1963, *British Political Parties* (2nd edition), Heinemann.

McKnight, J, 1977: 'Professionalised Service and Disabling Help,' in Illich, *et al.*, 1977, pp.69-92.

Midwinter, A F, 1988: 'Local Budgetary Strategies in a Decade of Retrenchment', *Public Money and Management*, Volume 8, No. 3, pp. 21-8.

Moore, G E, 1939: 'The Existence of an External World', British Academy Lecture, *Proceedings of the British Academy*, Volume 25, pp. 273-300.

Morris, D and Haigh, R, 1987: 'Sheffield City Council', in Elcock and Jordan (eds), 1987, pp. 102-12.

Morrison, H, 1954: *Government and Parliament: A Survey from the Inside*, Oxford University Press.

Moser, K and Kalton, G, 1971: *Survey Methods in Social Investigation* (2nd edition), Heinemann.

Munby, D, 1956: Procedure at Public Inquiries, *Public Administration*,

Newton, K, 1976: *Second City Politics*, Oxford University Press.

Norris, G, 1989: 'The Centre: What Shape for the 1990s?', *Local Government*

Policy-Making, Volume 16, No. 1, pp. 9-14.

Norris, P, 1982: 'Who Should Decide? The Experts or the Public?' in Elcock (ed), 1982, pp. 223-32.

Northcote-Trevelyan Report, 1853: Report on the Organisation of the Permanent Civil Service, Presented to both Houses of Parliament by Command of Her Majesty, 23rd November 1853.

Norton, P, 1981: *The Commons in Perspective*, Martin Robertson.

Norton, P, 1987: *Parliament in Perspective*, Inaugural Lecture delivered at the University of Hull and published by the University of Hull Press.

Oakeshott, M, 1962: *Rationalism in Politics and Other Essays*, Methuen.

Pahl, R, 1970: *Whose City?* Longman, Green and Co.

Pahl, R, 1975: *Whose City?* Longman.

Pannick, D, 1989: *Judges*, Oxford University Press.

Parkinson, M, 1985: *Liverpool on the Brink*, Policy Journals.

Parkinson, M, 1986: 'Creative Accountancy and Financial Ingenuity in Local Government: The Case of Liverpool', *Public Money,* March, 1986, pp. 27-32.

Parkinson, M, 1987a: 'Liverpool City Council', in Elcock and Jordan, (eds), 1987, pp. 68-77.

Parkinson, M, (ed.) 1987b: *Reshaping Local Government*, Policy Journals.

Parry, G, 1969: *Political Elites*, G. Allen and Unwin.

Paterson Committee, 1973: *The New Scottish Local Authorities: Organisation and Management Structures*, Her Majesty's Stationery Office, Edinburgh.

Payne, M, 1978: *Power, Authority and Responsibility in Social Services Departments*, Macmillan.

Perkin, H, 1970: *The Age of the Railway*, Panther Books.

Perry, J L and Kraemer, K L, 1983: *Public Management: Public and Private Perspectives*, Mayfield Publishing.

Peters, T J and Waterman, R H, 1982, *In Search of Excellence: Lessons fron America's Best-run Companies*, Harper and Row.

Peterson J, 1989: 'Eureka and the Symbolic Politics of High Technology', *Politics*, Volume 8, No. 1, pp. 8-13.

Pitt, D and Smith, B C, 1985: *The Computer Revolution in Public Administration*, Wheatsheaf Books.

Plowden Report, 1961: *The Control of Public Expenditure*, Cmnd. 1432, Her Majesty's Stationery Office.

Plowden, W (ed.), 1987: *Advising the Rulers*, B. Blackwell.

Pollard, R S W (ed.), 1954: *Administrative Tribunals at Work*, Stevens.

Pollitt, C, 1974: 'The Central Policy Review Staff 1970-1974,' *Public Administration*, Volume 52, pp. 375-92.

Pollitt, C, 1985: 'Measuring Performance: A New System for the National Health Service', *Policy and Politics*, Volume 13, No. 1, pp. 1-15.

Poole, K, 1978: *The Local Government Service*, G. Allen and Unwin.

Popper, K, 1960: 'On the Sources of Knowledge and Ignorance', *Proceedings of the British Academy* Volume 46, pp.71.

Prentice, R, 1987: 'Managing the Managers', *Labour Party News*, pp. 11-12.

Public Finance Foundation, annual: *Public Expenditure Digest*.

Redcliffe Maud Report, 1969: *Local Government in England*, Cmnd. 4040, Her Majesty's Stationery Office.

Rein, M, 1976: *Social Science and Public Policy*, Penguin Books.

Rethlisberger, P J and Dickinson, W J, 1939: *Management and the Worker*, Harvard

University Press.

Rhodes, G and Ruck, S K, 1970: *The Government of Greater London*, G. Allen and Unwin.

Rhodes, R A W, 1980: *Control and Power in Central-Local Relations*, Gower Press.

Rhodes, R A W, 1987a: *The National World of Local Government*, G. Allen and Unwin.

Rhodes, R A W, 1987b: *Beyond Westminster and Whitehall*, Unwin Hyman.

Richards, P G, 1966: 'Rural Boroughs', *Political Studies*, Volume 14, pp. 87-9.

Richardson, J J and Jordan, A G 1979: *Government under Pressure*, Martin Robertson.

Robinson, D Z, 1969: 'Government Contracting for Academic Research: Accountability in the American Experience', in B L R Smith and D Hague (eds) *The Dilemma of Accountability in Modern Government*, Macmillan.

Robson, W A, 1928: *Justice and Administrative Law*, Macmillan, reprinted 1947.

Rose, C R, 1974: *Do Parties Make a Difference?*, Penguin Books.

Rosenberg, D, 1984: 'The Politics of Role in Local Government: Perspectives on the Role Sets of Treasurers in their Relations with Chief Executives', *Local Government Studies*, Volume 10, No. 1, pp. 47-62.

Rothschild, V, 1977: *Meditations of a Broomstick*, Collins.

Royko, M, 1971: *Boss*, Paladin Books.

Saunders, P, 1979: *Urban Politics*, Penguin Books.

Schon, D, 1975: *Beyond the Stable State*, Penguin Books.

Schulze, C L, 1968: *The Politics and Economics of Public Spending*, The Brookings Institute, Washington DC.

Schumacher, F E, 1973: *Small is Beautiful*, Abacus Books.

Seebohm Report, 1968: *The Local Authority and Allied Social Services*, Her Majesty's Stationery Office.

Self, P, 1974: 'Is Comprehensive Planning Possible and Rational?' *Policy and Politics*, Volume 2, No. 3, pp. 193-203.

Self, P and Storing, H, 1958: *The State and the Farmer*, G. Allen and Unwin.

Simon, H A, 1945: *Administrative Behaviour*, Free Press of Glencoe, second edition 1957, Macmillan and Co., Inc. (New York).

Sisson, C H, 1959: *The Spirit of British Administration*, Faber and Faber.

Smith, T A, 1979: *The Politics of the Corporate Economy*, Martin Robertson.

Snow, C P, 1949: *Time of Hope*, Penguin edn.

Solesbury, W, 1976: 'The Environmental Agenda', *Public Administration*, Volume 54, pp. 379-98.

Stacey, F, 1971: *The British Ombudsman*, Oxford University Press.

Stacey, F, 1975: *British Government 1966-1975: Years of Reform*, Oxford University Press.

Stacey, F, 1978: *Ombudsmen Compared*, Oxford University Press.

Stalker, J, 1988; *Stalker*, Penguin Books.

Stalker, J, 1989: 'The Broken Arm of the Law', *Evening Standard*, 31st July.

Stewart, J D, 1971: *Management in Local Government: A Viewpoint*, Charles Knight.

Stewart, J D, 1983: *Local Government: The Freedom of Local Choice*, G. Allen and Unwin.

Stewart, J D, 1986: *The New Management of Local Government*, G. Allen and Unwin.

Street, H, 1963: *Freedom, the Individual and the Law*, Penguin Books.

Study of Parliament Group:
1970: Hanson, A H and Crick, B (eds), *The Commons in Transition*, Fontana

Books.

1977: Walkland, S and Ryle, M, (eds), *The Commons in the Seventies*, Fontana Books.

1987: Richards, P and Ryle, M (eds), *The Commons under Scrutiny*, Routledge.

Sunter, C, 1986: *South Africa and the World in the 1990s*.

Tarschys, D, 1984: 'Good Cuts, Bad Cuts', *Scandinavian Political Studies*, New Series, Volume 7, pp. 241-59.

Taylor, C, 1967: 'Neutrality in Political Science' in P Laslett and S Runciman (eds), *Philosophy, Politics and Society*, Third Series, Oxford University Press.

Thomas, H (ed.), 1968: *Crisis in the Civil Service*, Anthony Blond.

Thorpe-Tracey, S, 1987: 'The Financial Management Initiative in Practice: Newcastle Central Office', *Public Administration*, Volume 65, pp. 331-8.

Treasury, HM, 1984: 'A Smaller Civil Service', *Economic Progress Report*, No. 168, June 1984.

Treasury, HM, 1985: *Policy Evaluation: A Guide for Managers*, Her Majesty's Stationery Office.

Treasury, HM, 1988: *Policy Evaluation: A Guide for Managers*, Her Majesty's Stationery Office.

Vickers, G, 1965, *The Art of Judgement*, Chapman Hall.

Wardale Committee, 1981: *Chain of Command Review: The Open Structure*, Civil Service Department.

Wasserman, R A, 1961: *The Judicial Decision*, Oxford University Press.

Webb and Wistow, 1982: *Whither State Welfare?* Royal Institute of Public Administration.

Weber, M, 1947: *The Theory of Social and Economic Organisation*, translated by A M Henderson and Talcott Parsons, Free Press of Glencoe.

Weller, P and Jones, G W, 1983: 'Prime Minister's Departments', *Public Administration*, Volume 61, pp. 59-84.

Wells, H G, 1908: *The War in the Air*, Penguin edn.

Whitehead Report, 1987: *The Health Divide: Inequalities in Health in the 1980s*, Health Education Council.

Whyatt Report, 1961: *The Citizen and the Administration*, Justice.

Widdicombe Report, 1986: *The Conduct of Local Authority Business*, Cmnd. 9800, Her Majesty's Stationery Office.

Wildavsky, A V, 1969: 'Rescuing Policy Analysis from PPBS', *Public Administration Review*, Volume 29, pp. 189-202.

Wildavsky, A V, 1973: 'If Planning is Everything, Maybe it's Nothing', *Policy Sciences*, Volume 4, pp. 127-53.

Wildavsky, A V, 1979: *The Politics of the Budgetary Process*, Little Brown.

Wildavsky, A V, 1980: *The Art and Craft of Policy Analysis*, Macmillan.

Willcocks, 1967: *The Creation of the National Health Service*, Routledge and Kegan Paul.

Willetts, D, 1987: 'The Role of the Prime Minister's Policy Unit', *Public Administration*, Volume 65, pp.443-454.

Williams, D, 1985: *Not in the Public Interest*, Hutchinson.

Wilson, H, 1971: *The Labour Government: A Personal Record*, Heinemann and Michael Joseph.

Winch, P, 1967: 'Authority' in A Quinton (ed.), *Political Philosophy*, Oxford University Press.

Wiseman, H V, 1963: 'The Working of Local Government in Leeds,' *Public Administration*, Volume 41, pp. 51-69 and 137-55.

Wistow, G and Brooks, S, 1985: *Joint Planning and Joint Management*, Royal Institute of Public Administration.

Wolman, H, 1984: 'Understanding Local Government Responses to Fiscal Pressure: A Cross-National Analysis', *Journal of Public Policy*, Volume 3, pp. 245-64.

Worswick, G D and Ady, P, 1961: *The British Economy in the 1950s*, Oxford University Press.

Wright, P, 1987: *Spycatcher*, Heinemann.

Young, Hugo, 1989: *One of Us: A Life of Margaret Thatcher*, Macmillan.

Zander, M, 1986: 'A Bill of Rights: The Debate Continues', *Social Studies Review*, January, pp. 32-6.

Index